◆ DEMETRA GEORGE ◆

Mysteries of the Dark Moon

The Healing Power of The Dark Goddess

HarperOne
An Imprint of HarperCollins*Publishers*

HarperOne

Also by Demetra George

Astrology for Yourself (with Douglas Bloch)
Asteroid Goddesses (with Douglas Bloch)

Illustrations in chapters 4, 5, 6, and 8 by Gracie Campbell. Illustrations in chapters 1, 2, 3, and 7 (except figure 1.2) by Clyde H. Breitwieser. Illustration "Moondaughter" on page v by Nancy Bright; on page 1 by JAF; on page 109 by Rohmana D'Arezzo Harris; on page 199 by Terrence Stark. Text design by Irene Imfeld. Composition by TBH/Typecast.

Library of Congress Cataloging-in-Publication Data
George, Demetra.
    Mysteries of the dark moon : the healing power of the dark goddess
Demetra George. — 1st ed.
       p. cm.
    Includes index.
    ISBN: 978–0–06–250370–1
    1. New moon—Mythology.   2. Goddesses.   3. New moon—Religious
aspects.   3. Goddess religion.   I. Title.
BL325.M56G46   1992
291.2'114—dc20   91–55318

22 23 24 25 26 LBC 32 31 30 29 28

Dedication

To She Who Glides the Silver Crescent Moon Boat
Through the Dark Still Waters
of Our Becoming.

✦ CONTENTS ✦

✦

PART I
Revisioning the Dark

✦

PART II
Goddesses of the Dark Moon

✦

PART III
Rites of Rebirth

✦

Acknowledgments

My love and appreciation to Art Fisher, Douglas Bloch, Jim, Michelle, Daniel, and Reina Frankfort, Vicki Noble and the students of Motherpeace Institute, the Monday Night Circle, Natasha Kern, Barbara Moulton, Christiane Carruth, Suzette Bell, Yana Murphy, Jane Mara, Sarah Scholfield, Lynn Jeffries, Phil Russell, Tsering Everest, Fred Heese, Charlie Tabasko, Mary Lou Miller, Rohmana Harris, Spot, Gabby, and my spiritual teacher, Chagdud Tulku Rinpoche.

✦ PART I ✦

Revisioning the Dark

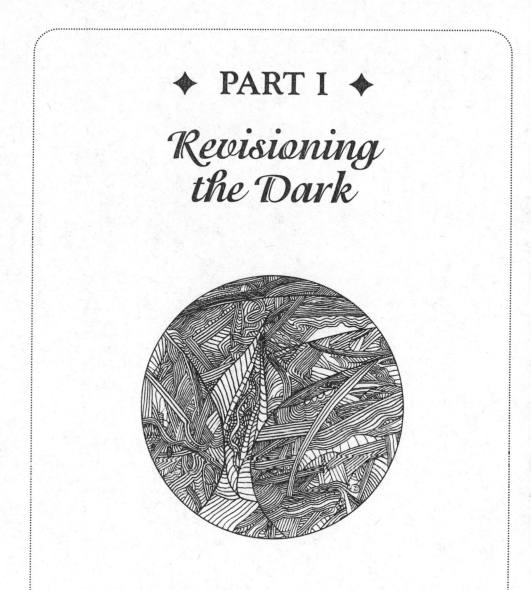

*The story that the moon tells is of birth,
growth, fullness, decay, disappearance,
with rebirth and growth again.*

1

The Dark Moon

✦

O Lady Moon, your horns point toward the east;
Shine, be increased
O Lady Moon, your horns point toward the west:
Wane, be at rest.
—Christina Rossetti[1]

The moon, Queen of the Night in all her silvery splendor, reaches out to us as she glides across the black, moonlit skies. Each night she appears robed in a different garment, which hints at the mysteries surrounding both her luminous and shadowy displays. Who is this lady of the moon, and what gifts does she shine down upon earth creatures? And when, each month, she disappears altogether for several days, what does she conceal behind her dark time, her most secret time?

Mysteries of the Dark Moon will seek to uncover the secret of the moon's mysterious dark phase through exploring the mythical, psychological, and spiritual symbolism of the lunar darkness. If we are fortunate, what we discover can help us to release our fears of the dark.

The title of this book has not been arbitrarily chosen. The word "mystery" comes from the Middle English *misterie* or *mysterie*, from

3

the Latin *mysterium*, and from the Greek *musterion*, or "secret rites";
from *mustes*, one initiated into secret rites. The word "moon" goes
back to the Indo-European root *me-*, and in its extended and suffixed
forms *men-*, *men-en-*, *men-s-*, *men-ot-* has the meaning of month (an
ancient and universal measure of time, with the celestial body that
measures it). "Dark" has the connotation of muddy, clouded, or in
this case, *hidden.*

A literal translation of this book's title could be read, "The secret
rites of the hidden period of the month," which, in fact, is the
essence of what this book is about: a specific aspect of life cycles, the
dark period, which is symbolized here as the dark phase of the moon.

The earliest peoples understood that the power of life lay in the
darkness of the moon. But after thousands of years, humanity forgot
this truth and began to fear the power in the waning dark moon.
Plutarch wrote, "For the waxing moon is of good intent, but the waning moon brings sickness and death." In the alternation of the moon's
waxing and waning phases, later peoples saw the increasing phases of
the moon's growing light as beneficial, bringing life and growth. However, they had a very different attitude about the decreasing dark
moon, which they associated with death, destruction, and the forces
of evil.

The moon, with its repeating cycles of waxing and waning, became a symbol to the ancients for the birth, growth, death, and
renewal of all life forms. The lunar rhythm presented a creation (the
new moon), followed by growth (to full moon), and a diminution and
death (the three moonless nights, that is, the dark moon). Historian
of religion Mircea Eliade states that it was very probably the image
of eternal birth and death of the moon that helped to crystallize the
earliest human intuitions about the alternation of life and death; and
suggested later on the myth of the periodic creation and destruction
of the world.[2]

The moon, in her transformations, mirrors the same fluctuations
of increase and decrease that take place in the human body and in
the psyche. In our lives we experience these alternations of creation
and destruction, growth and decay, birth and death, light and dark,
conscious and unconscious. Unfortunately, in our society we have
been taught to fear and resist the decreasing energies represented by
the dark, by decay, death, and the unconscious. Thus we have lost our
knowledge of an essential part of cyclical life processes, symbolized by
the dark phase of the moon.

The purpose of the dark phase of any cycle is that of transition between the death of the old and the birth of the new. The dark time is a time of retreat, of healing, and of dreaming the future. The darkness is lit with the translucent quality of transformation; and during this essential and necessary period, life is prepared to be born.

The dark prefaces the light in the same way that gestation precedes birth and sleep allows for rejuvenation. In the human psyche we experience dark periods when we feel turned inward and nothing seems to be happening. However, in retrospect we often realize that these fallow times were germinal periods preceding outbursts of creativity and growth.

Without the time to withdraw, rest, and recuperate from the demands of the outer activities of conscious waking life, our bodies and minds cannot sustain their supply of vital energy. If we correctly understand the dark, however, we can use the cover of darkness to learn the magic of our own particular secret rites, which can lead to a revitalized and replenished life.

Unfortunately we have many confusing and negative associations with the concept of the dark. Darkness connotes that which is unknown, hidden, concealed, and evil. We have been taught to suspect and fear the unknown. The dark phase of the lunar cycle holds all that cannot be seen with the waking eye or understood by the rational mind. The contents of this phase of the cyclic process have been labeled "dark," perceived as threatening, and promoted as taboo. As the conscious ego rejects and denies the experiences and wisdom of the dark phase, these contents grow to embody our worst fears and assume the frightening form of the demonic "shadow" in individuals and society. Society's attitudes toward people of color, woman's sexuality, the occult, the unconscious, the psychic arts, the aged, and death itself are all manifestations of these fearful dark moon projections.

We are conditioned by our lack of night vision to experience the dark as terrifying. When we are unhappy, we say that we are going through a dark time, associating the dark with loss of love, fears of abandonment, alienation, failure, isolation, disintegration, and madness. The dark symbolizes our fears of aging, illness, death, and dying. It covers and hides our painful and shameful secret memories of traumas such as abortion, incest, rape, sexual violation, physical abuse, eating disorders, body dysfunctions, addictions. The dark keeps these secret fears buried deep in the unconscious mind.

Because our perceptions of the dark are filled with images of loss, pain, and suffering, we react with fear, panic, anxiety, confusion, depression, and desperation whenever we go through the many dark phase periods in our lives. Often what we have known in the past no longer exists, and what is yet to come has not yet appeared. We feel trapped in the chaotic, formless void of non-knowing. To the extent that we do not understand the true nature of the dark, many of us label these times as periods of depression.

The medical profession calls depression a devastating illness that affects perhaps 20 million Americans each year. One sufferer says, "I shut my eyes, I see nothing, and when I open my eyes, I just stare at the walls. And I just set and set and set because I figure there's just no use. I'm just hopeless. I don't see the future at all. None whatsoever." And psychiatrist Dr. Harold Eist comments, "It's a terrible, painful illness that interferes with motivation, that tangles their thoughts, that makes them hopeless, that fills them with despair, that fills them with self-hatred. And finally, the pain is so great, the only way out they can see is destroying themselves. There are very few illnesses of that magnitude."[3]

Most of us do not realize we all have many dark phase times in our lives, and that these are naturally occurring periods in any life cycle. We fail to understand that endings are the precursors to new beginnings; thus when our life rhythms move us into and through these dark phases, we are ignorant of what is actually happening. We find ourselves frozen in fear or panicking in desperation. We fear that henceforth the chaos, the uncertainty, and the pain are the way life is going to be. And this feeling engenders more fear and panic.

The intention of *Mysteries of the Dark Moon* is to revision the dark. It is hoped that the reader will come to understand that the dark phase of the cyclical process is a phase of healing and renewal rather than one of fear and unknowing; a time of mystery, wisdom, and healing power—all gifts of the Dark Moon Goddess.

The Moon and Her Lunation Cycle

The moon circles the earth every twenty-nine days. Each month the moon unfolds from the sliver of the waxing crescent moon, increasing in light, until totally illuminated at the full moon. Then, as the moon wanes, she gradually decreases in light until the dark phase, when she is invisible.

The lore of the moon has been intermingled with that of the sun; for if it were not for the sun's light, we would never see the moon at all. In order to fully understand the mysteries of the moon's dark phase, we first need to explore her intimate relationship with the sun. The sun and moon portray a cycle of relationship referred to as the lunation cycle. The lunation cycle is the cycle of the phases of the moon, unfolding from new to full to dark, which portrays her fluid and ever-changing relationship to the sun as seen from here on earth.

This relationship of the moon to the sun proceeds according to a wave pattern of increase and decrease in light, or separation and return to the sun.[4] Each night the moon reveals a different facet of her now luminous, now shadowy face as she reflects and distributes varying amounts of the sun's light. The moon herself does not change; her light does. What we earth beings see as the phases of the moon are actually reflections of the moon's changing relationship to the sun.

The sun and moon, referred to as "the luminaries," are the most prominent astronomical bodies in the sky. Together they embody the principle of polarity both in our physical world and in our psycho-

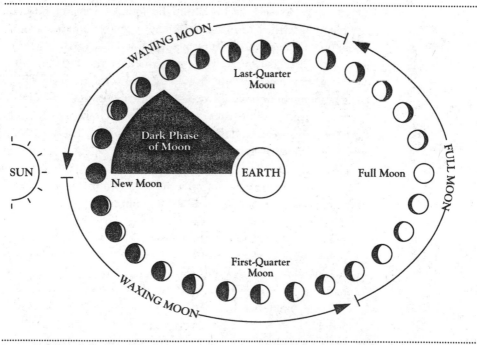

Fig. 1.1 The Moon's Lunation Cycle

logical nature. In our daily lives the alternating rhythms of the sun and moon regulate our day and night cycles. As the sun rules the daylight of consciousness and the outer objective world, the moon rules the night of the unconscious and our inner intuitive instinctual life. The darkness and light reflect our periods of receptivity and creativity and of contemplation and action.

The ancients personified these two lights as the Sun God and the Moon Goddess, who were seen to be the source of the masculine and feminine energies. The sun and moon are complementary opposites. As the masculine principle embodied in our notion of God and the feminine principle as Goddess, they are the polar manifestations of the same primal, undifferentiated divine force. They originate from and return back to the same source. When these two polarities are periodically united, portrayed in the Sacred Marriage of the God and Goddess, they create the mystical dimension known as One-ness, union, illumination. When these two polarities are periodically separated, they symbolically give birth to the Divine Child, the mystical dimension known as manifested life forms.

The sun, emanating bright light and warmth, projects its fiery, creative energy outward. The reflective quality of the moon distributes this light to earth during the night hours of dew and moisture, providing the fertile matrix out of which life can germinate and grow. The moon, as muse, mediates between the sun and earth. Earth beings cannot assimilate directly the powerful energies of the sun without being consumed in the flames of this constant high-voltage energy. The moon intervenes for us and distributes the sun's light in a rhythmic pattern of increase and decrease, which we experience in the tides of the oceans and the flow of women's blood. Thus the moon enables earth beings to gradually absorb the solar light and use it to create our organic and psychic life.

The sun and moon are not opposite forces, in the sense of being conflicting and irreconcilable. It is the continual interaction and interpenetration of the solar and lunar forces that creates the necessary conditions for life to exist here on earth. In their dance we can see them eternally drawing close to and moving away from one another, only to return again in the embrace of the sacred marriage. As we discuss the cycles of the moon in the remainder of this book, let us keep in mind that the symbolism revealed in the moon's phases arises from the mystery of her relationship with the sun.

The lives of the earliest peoples were very attuned to this rhythm of the soli-lunar relationship perceived as the moon's phases. Night after night they gazed upon the ever-changing silver lady in the sky and saw her alter place, shape, color, disappear and reappear. From her display the ancients gradually intuited the truths concerning the great mystery of life and death. The moon came to symbolize the themes of fertility and birth, time and destiny, change and transformation, the secrets of the unknown, and death and regeneration. The moon was perceived to be a gathering place of the dead, the storehouse of the seed of life, and accordingly a feminine being.[5]

According to the beliefs of early peoples, the moon was the force that fertilized and quickened all new life. Animal mating cycles and the seasonal nature of crop production, as well as women's menstrual cycles and pregnancies, represented the rhythmic ebb and flow of the moon's power of fertilization. They were also aware of the moon's relationship to the tides. The moon was thought to rule the waters of the oceans, the womb from which all life was said to have emerged.

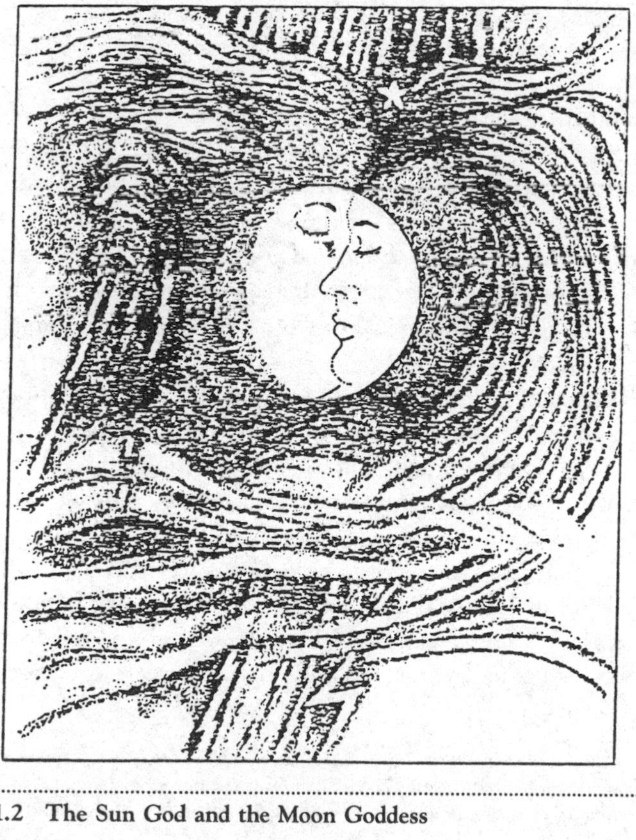

Fig. 1.2 **The Sun God and the Moon Goddess**

The moon has always been linked with time and destiny. The first calendars, dating to 33,000 BCE* during the Upper Paleolithic, were sequences of notches carved into bone and ivory that kept track of time according to the lunar phases. These calendars also marked the days of a woman's menstrual cycle, indicating the dates for conception, and then the lunar months of pregnancy until birth. Moon goddesses such as the Moirai (the Fates) were depicted as measuring the length of a person's life and weaving his or her destiny.

As ancient peoples watched the moon's capacity to show a different shape, place, and color each night, the moon came to embody the truth of change and transformation. The moon's constant movement through the heavens, alternating light and dark faces, taught people that nothing remained static, all was in a state of flux, rising and falling, dying and becoming reborn. The moon came to symbolize the cycle of transformation and the capacity for one thing to change into another. This power of transformation was seen to reside in women, who presided over the food mysteries: through cooking grain, grass became bread. When they internalized this power, women transformed their blood into milk to nourish the new life emerging from their bodies.

While the sun's light dominated the hours of the day and obliterated the passage of the moon across the sky, it was the moon who reigned supreme in the heavens at night. All things were concealed under the cover of the night's darkness, and so the moon came to be associated with all hidden things and mysteries of the unknown. The moon guarded over the secret teachings concerning sexuality, divination, and magic, and protected this knowledge from being abused by the uninitiated.

The greatest mystery of all, that of death and regeneration, was contained in the moon's most secret aspect, the dark phase. The three dark, moonless nights corresponded to the end of life, but on the fourth night the moon was reborn, signifying a new beginning. In the same way, the dead were also thought to find a new life. The ancients believed that the dead either went to the moon or to the underworld in Mother Earth to be given the necessary powers of regeneration.[6] The serpent, which sheds its skin and renews itself, like the waxing and waning of the moon, was seen to embody the

---

*BCE, "before the common era," is used in place of BC, "before Christ," to notate time in a manner that is inclusive of both Christians and non-Christians. Likewise, CE, "common era," is used instead of AD, *anno domini*, "in the year of the Lord."

mysteries of death and renewal. This lunar animal became the symbol of the transformative power of the feminine energy.

Noting the correlation between the twenty-nine days of the moon's cycle and the twenty-nine days of women's menstrual cycles, the ancients surmised that the moon must be feminine. And so they personified her as the Great Goddess. The Moon Goddess, in her bright phase, was a giver of life and all that promoted fertility. In her dark phase she was the wielder of the destructive powers of nature. Viewed from a modern, rational standpoint, a deity can either be friendly or malicious, but cannot be both.[7] But to the worshipers of the Moon Goddess, there was no contradiction in her dual nature. Both her light and dark sides, creation and destruction, were understood to be essential aspects of life processes.

The reproductive cycle of the universal Lunar Mother, as she turned from new to full to dark, mirrored the progressive phases of the birth, growth, death, and renewal of all life forms. As the Great Mother, the moon came to symbolize the great mystery of life and death; she was the fertile matrix out of which all life is born and into which all life is reabsorbed. Every living thing resonated to her instinctual rhythm of emergence, fulfillment, and completion.

As agricultural peoples discovered the vegetative cycle of plants, they saw the rhythm of the moon reflected in the growth cycle of

Fig. 1.3 The Lunar Phases and the Life Cycle of a Plant

their crops. We can better understand this process by comparing the phases of the moon to the life cycle of a plant.

The *new moon* corresponds to the germinating of the seed beneath the ground, when the vital force of the plant breaks through the seed casing. With the moon's increasing light, the first tender shoots push their way above the ground. The plant sends its roots downward to draw nourishment from the soil, and its stems and leaves reach upward to absorb the sun's light energy.

As the reflected light of the moon continues to grow, the buds contain the anxious expectation of the promise to follow. The *full moon* culminates with the maximum exposure of light, and the plant gives forth its flower and fruit. At this stage the fruit embodies the full actualization of the essence of the seed.

As the moon begins to decrease in light, the harvest is gathered and stored. During the waning *dark phase* of the moon's cycle, the fruit that has been left on the vine to go to seed withers and decomposes. The plant concentrates its remaining life force in the seed capsule that lies dormant in the dark underground. It awaits germination with the initiation of the next cycle and new moon phase.

Harmonizing to this lunar rhythm, all life emanates in spirals of circles as it cycles from new to full to dark, and then again to new. The essential movement of all life is cyclic in nature. The lunation cycle is the prototype for the process of progressive phases of the unfolding and continual renewal of all of life forms. The moon's lunation cycle carries the rhythmic beat of her dance with the sun. It taps out the recurring pattern of how life creates, fulfills, and destroys itself, only to be reborn anew.

The Dark Phase of the Moon

The dark phase of the moon, not to be confused with the dark side of the moon, occurs each month in the three days immediately preceding the new moon. At this time the waning crescent dissolves into blackness, and the moon disappears from sight. Because the light that we see as coming from the moon is the sun's reflected light, the dark moon is in a sense the moon's true face.

Each month, during the dark of the moon, the ancients in many lands experienced both fear and awe. During the absence of the moon's light, the dark phase of the cycle contained everything that they could not see with the waking eye nor understand with the rational mind. In the earliest of times, and even far into patriarchal times, the dark of the moon symbolized divination, illumination, and the powers of healing. Over the centuries, as people no longer worshiped the moon as goddess, the mysteries of the dark moon became imbued with terror and evil. Later peoples thought that the moon's disappearance was due to her being eaten up by a dark and demonic power. The waning moon came to represent a time when the destructive powers were at their height, and floods, storms, disasters, and pests were expected. It was considered unlucky for any enterprise, a time when all things were diminished and brought low. The dark moon was the captain of ghosts and the mistress of black magic. During her sojourn ghosts roamed about, haunting humans, and the powers of sorcery could be invoked to work their mischief unchecked.[8] The dark of the moon was also a time of nefarious deeds and an omen of death.

The serpent has always been associated with the dark moon mysteries; yet this lunar animal has been most vilified as a monstrous force of temptation and evil. The serpent, with its power to shed and renew its skin, was likened to the moon, who also renewed herself each month after her apparent death. Serpents live in dark holes, and the ancients believed their subterranean homes were located in the underworld. The dark phase of the moon was also linked to the underworld, and so the divinities of the dark moon often appeared in the form of snakes or with serpents in their hair.

In India, the serpent, coiled as *kundalini* energy in the seat of the sexual *chakra* at the base of the spine, symbolized the dark moon powers of regeneration through participation in the sexual mysteries. The gifts of inspiration, prophecy, and divination were believed to come from the dark moon, carried by serpents, whose venom was used to induce transcendent visionary states. It was also said that the serpent revealed to humans the mind-expanding virtues of the *soma*drink which contained the inspiration of the dark moon. In some myths the *soma*drink, to which the deities owed their wisdom and immortality, was brewed from the fruits of the mythical moon tree. The earthly counterpart of the moon tree was a plant growing in northwest India (*Asclepias Acida* or *Sarcostemna Viminale*), and from it a wine was prepared that had narcotic and intoxicating properties. Humans would partake of this draught in religious rites of communion with the divine spirit.[9]

In much earlier times, when societies were predominantly attuned to lunar rhythms, the role of the moon was both to be and to become. It underwent death and yet remained immortal; and its death was never an end but a pause for regeneration.[10] In her dark phase the moon was the land of the dead, the receptacle of souls between incarnations. She sheltered both the dead and the unborn, who were one and the same.[11]

The dark moon leads to the underworld, but it also makes transformation possible. Today the dark moon side of our psyche has become the region of individual salvation. It is through descent into our unconscious that we can find the secrets of renewal—secrets that are often diametrically opposed by conscious viewpoints.[12] At one time or another we will all enter into the waning dark moon phase of life experience. These periods of descent give us the opportunity to fertilize and germinate the seeds of our rebirth. The dark moon contains the power either to destroy, or to heal and regenerate—depending on our capacity to understand its meaning and flow with the rhythm. As Esther Harding says, "We must recognize that although the road of the crescent leads downward, yet it also may lead to transformation of the personality, to a real rebirth of the individual."[13]

The Dark Phase of Cyclical Process The dark phase of the moon is the closure phase of cyclical process, as well as the transition to the next spiral of unfoldment. All cycles have a dark phase, a naturally occurring recessive period where the continuing life entity experiences an essential mutation and regeneration of form. When life is perceived from a linear perspective, the closure phase signifies an absolute finality that gives rise to fear of the unknown. However, when life is understood as cyclic, the closure phase is known as the transition to renewal. In a cyclical cosmology the dark moon phase corresponds to the time when the continuing life impulse, under the

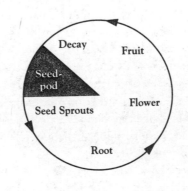

Fig. 1.4a The Plant Cycle

cover of darkness, goes underground to cleanse, revitalize, and re-generate its form and content.

In the seasonal and plant cycle the dark moon phase corresponds to the seedpod, which contains the plant's essence and is buried in winter's dark rich soil awaiting spring's germination. In the human lifespan we enter the dark phase through death, and subsequently gestate in its warm, dark, nurturing womb awaiting rebirth. The bear in hibernation, the chicken incubating in the egg, and the caterpil-lar wrapped in the cocoon all mirror the dark phase in the life cycles in the animal kingdom.

Regulated by the lunar cycle, the dark nights before the new moon have their equivalent in all natural earth cycles. In the alter-nating rhythms of day and night, the dark moon phase corresponds to the deepest part of night, the two hours before dawn. This is a time of deep inspiration, when we can be most receptive to the finely tuned vibrations of intuitions, visions, and insights through prayer and meditation. If we are asleep during this time before awakening, images of the future are revealed through our dreams.

In the yearly rhythms the earth revolves around the sun, giving us the turning of the four seasons. Spring germinates into the abun-dant fertility of summer, followed by fall's harvest. The dark moon phase in the seasonal cycle unfolds as winter takes life back into the warm, dark, protective underground to sleep and dream its new rebirth.

In the Celtic Wheel of the Year the dark phase begins at Hal-lowmas, known now as Halloween (October 31), when lore has it that

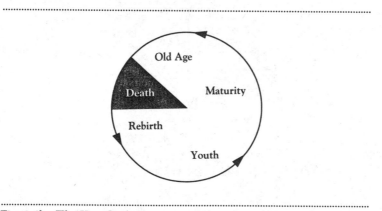

Fig. 1.4b The Year Cycle

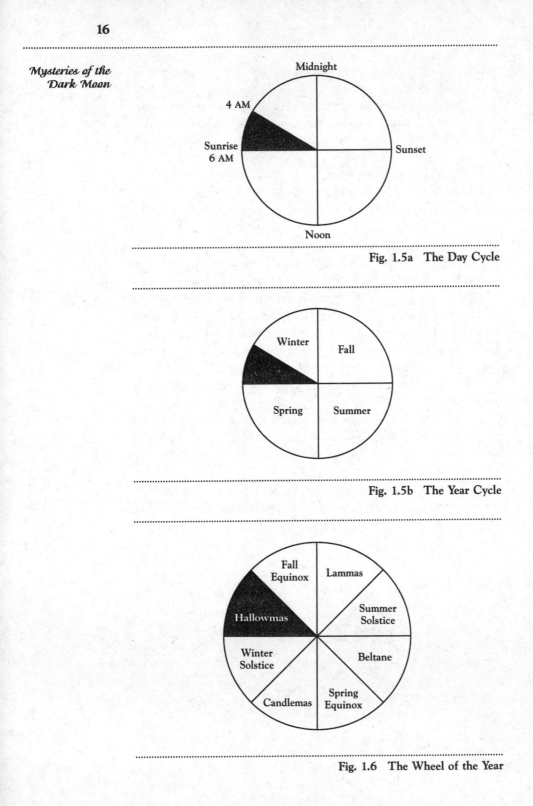

Fig. 1.5a   The Day Cycle

Fig. 1.5b   The Year Cycle

Fig. 1.6   The Wheel of the Year

the veil between the world of the living and dead is most transparent. This phase spans the shortest days of light until the birth of the sun at the winter solstice.

The Dark Moon Times in Our Lives

We experience the qualities of the dark of the moon at many times and in many ways. We periodically go through times lasting from several days, weeks, months, or even years where the dark moon closure phase energies are operative. These are the times for death and renewal transitions in our lives. There exist generic periods, when everyone experiences the dark phases at the same time or at similar ages. In addition there exist specific individual dark moon phase periods in our personal life cycles. Many esoteric traditions teach that it is possible through the ancient systems of astrology, tarot, and numerology to predict and identify the timing and duration of these closure phase transitional periods in our lives.[14]

In the same way that we go to sleep each night in order to feel rejuvenated for another new day, we sometimes need to let go, withdraw, pull inward, and renew ourselves in the dark stillness of other kinds of transitions. The opportunity for this inner work exists not only in the days preceding the new moon each month, but also every night in the last hours before dawn or awakening and, for women, every month when they menstruate and after menopause. The dark phase energies are also prominent each year in the month before our birthday, in the shortest days of sunlight in the weeks before the winter solstice, and in the last frozen part of winter before spring thawing.

The Dark Moon Phase and the Month before One's Birthday
The month before our birthdays is the dark moon phase of our yearly age cycle. At some point in midlife, instead of looking forward to birthdays with childlike anticipation, the mature adult begins to dread the approach of this day. There is the poignant awareness that we are another year older, another year has gone by when we have still not realized our hopes and dreams, we are another year closer to the end of our lives. People often feel lonely and overcome with despair during this time.

In our society aging is generally more difficult for women than for men. As men age society sees them as coming into their power and wisdom. As women age, however, society sees them as less attractive, less desirable, and less employable.

In the weeks before our birthday we fret over who is going to remember us with a card or gift and who else has forgotten us. Our birthdays, no matter how good they are, inevitably fall short of our unvoiced fantasies. The day after our birthday we breathe a huge sigh of relief that it is over and we can finally resume our daily life. In fact more suicides occur in the thirty days preceding the birthday than all the rest of the year.

It is important to realize that *most people* experience these emotions during the dark moon phase in the month before their birthdays. It is natural for feelings of uncertainty and fear to surface during this time. There *is* less energy available for outer activities and meeting the expectations of others, because the purpose of the dark phase is for focusing on the inner dimensions of our bodies and minds. If we can learn to attune ourselves to the natural rhythms of ebb and flow in our lives, we can use the intrinsic function of the dark times for healing and renewal. When we resist this inward motion in our psyche, then anxiety, stress, and fear are more likely to take hold of our emotions.

The Dark Moon Phase and the Winter Solstice   We can see the same themes appearing in our seasonal cycle, where the dark moon phase corresponds to the month before Christmas and Hanukkah. This is another time of high suicide rate, when many people are overcome with feelings of alienation or unconnectedness with a family or group. Others are driven by the anxiety of trying to meet the unrealistic expectations of their children's or partner's desire for gifts as proof of love.

The winter holidays occur at the winter solstice, when the sun's light is reborn. At this time Christianity celebrates the birth of the Son. In the month leading up to these holidays, the dark force predominates during these shortest days of sunlight. Again, the seasonal rhythm beckons us to hibernate and be still, gather our energies inward, withdraw, rest, and reflect. Instead we are pressured to go outward, frantically shop every weekend, spend money we can't afford, make and wrap presents, plan and attend parties, and perform endless preparations for the culmination of the big day. This is not to disparage the importance and joy of this celebration of renewal, but to recognize that the negative aspects of the dark emerge when we resist or go against the natural currents of cyclical process. If, as individuals and as a culture, we can remember a simpler way of honoring this time, one that is in accordance with natural rhythms, we can transform much of the insanity that now transpires during the holiday season.

The Dark Moon Phase and Menstruation, Pregnancy, and Menopause The dark moon phase is also linked to woman's menstrual periods. When the lunar cycle is overlaid on the menstrual cycle, the full moon corresponds to ovulation and the dark moon is analogous to menstruation (see Figure 7.1 in chapter 7). During the full moon ovulatory time, women are open, fertile, magnetic, receptive, and nurturing to the other. On a strictly biological level these emotional-chemical messages are conducive to facilitating sexual union, fertilization, procreation, and the continuity of the species. However, at the dark moon menstrual period, the life force is no longer other- and outer-directed, but rather self- and inner-reflective.

If women are attuned to their own body rhythms, when they bleed all they really want to do is to retreat to their bedroom, pull down the shades, climb into bed, and rest in the sweet, still silence of renewal. However, this response is generally not encouraged or supported by our society. Women feel forced to carry on as usual, pretending that nothing is different and feeling embarrassed if their "secret" leaks out. When we deny our menstrual needs, our unconscious self breaks through our socially conditioned personality as the raging bitch. She accounts for the pain, tension, tears, anger, hysteria, hypersensitivity, emotionality, and irrationality of PMS that we have come to associate with "the curse."

The ancient Goddess-worshiping cultures understood that the menstrual time is a woman's most powerful time of month, a time when her psychic and spiritual energies are most highly sensitized. It was for this reason that women retired to menstrual huts during their moon time in order that they might commune with the deities through meditation, prayer, and ritual to seek healing and truth. With the rise of the male god cultures, women continued to be separated and isolated during their moon time. But now it was not because they were holy, but because men feared their great psychic power during this time of the month. Menstruating women became taboo and were considered impure. This tradition survives today in many cultures, where menstruating women are barred from religious ceremonies.

Women no longer understand that the instinctive movement during menstruation is withdrawal in order to connect with powerful psychic energies to effect healing and insight in their lives on a monthly basis. Instead menstruation, as a dark moon phase, has come to be something that is painful, dirty, and embarrassing, leading to chaos, rejection, and isolation.

The last month of pregnancy is also a dark moon phase time. Amidst the joy and anticipation of a new child, many women also feel frustrated, irritable, immobilized by their huge and awkward body, and experience an indefinable anger. It is during this time immediately preceding birth that women are confronting their fears of the painful labor and the possibilities of their own or of the child's death in the process.

Knowledge of birthing, like that of dying, has been taken away from modern people. Most women going into their first labor have never seen or participated in another woman's birth experience. They have only heard whispers of the frightening stories of the anguish and suffering involved. Again it is our ignorance of the dark, which is the gateway between death and birth, that gives rise to our fears and contributes to our pain.

Menopause, which marks the final third of a woman's life, is the dark moon phase of her threefold sexual life cycle, which also includes menarche and birthing (see figure 7.2 in chapter 7). For many women menopause is a very sad and painful time. After they have raised their families, their children are grown, and their husbands are deceased, society tells them that they are useless and no longer wanted. The menopausal dark phase of a woman's life is characterized by loneliness, rejection, and lack of purpose.

In ancient cultures older women, as crones, were honored as wise women, the community elders. They were believed to come into their power as healers, seers, and magicians. However, modern society, in its failure to understand the value of the dark, has come to project many of its fears of the unknown upon older women who have passed through menopause. Today menopause signals the beginning of a woman's ostracism from society; now she embodies society's terror of the older woman's power during the dark phase of her life. And women themselves have forgotten that the rite of menopause initiates them into psychic maturation. If they can come to understand the true purpose of the dark, they can withdraw their energies from primarily taking care of others and devote them to nurturing their own mental and creative children.

In chapter 7 we will more fully discuss the themes of menstruation and menopause in relation to the dark moon.

The Dark Moon Phase and Aging and Death   The ultimate dark moon phase begins as we approach the end of our lives, where we often experience illness and increasing disability. We are confronted with the inevitability of our death and our beliefs about the hereafter. In Western cultures that scoff at the philosophy of reincarnation, death holds the fears of unending torture in hell or of a state of finality and nonbeing. It is partially for this reason that our society finds itself so distressed and uncomfortable to be around the aging and dying. Older people reflect the certainty of everyone's eventual death.

Society's collective denial of death has resulted in the majority of older people being removed from the mainstream. They are considered unemployable and taken out of the work force. While some are able to enjoy their retirement, many are frustrated with the limited outlets for expressing their wisdom, skill, and creativity, which has not diminished with age. For those people who are helpless in society's victimization of the elderly, old age becomes a dark cloud that envelops them as they sit in rocking chairs facing the television waiting to die. Older people are rounded up and put into senior citizen condominiums and villages or shut away in nursing homes. They are prevented from continuing to interact with the rest of the world.

Most modern people try to avoid any contact with death. The dying are isolated in hospital wards, often shunned by their families, and then shuttled off to the undertakers, whose job it is to disguise the face of death. Historically our knowledge of death has been obliterated by modern Western religious and philosophic concepts, and death is feared above all else. It is only in the last generation that we have had some clear information concerning what may occur during the death transition, such as Elizabeth Kubler-Ross's *Death: The Final Stage of Growth* (New York: Simon & Schuster, 1986). Research in this area has led to a more compassionate approach to the elderly and dying, and is helping to liberate people from their fears of the final dark moon phases of their lives.

The Dark Moon Phase and Personal Loss   In addition to these generic dark moon periods, we travel through a dark moon whenever we experience a personal loss and pass through a period of disruption and grief. We travel through the dark of the moon whenever we are immersed in the closure phase of a relationship, job, belief system, family, specific identity, responsibilities, living environment, or addiction; and whenever we face the loss of that form which has given our life a structure and sense of identity. Caught in the chaos of formlessness, we may experience free-floating anxiety. What has been is no longer, and what is to come has not yet appeared. We may feel overcome by an immobilizing depression, locked into the grief and mourning of our loss, or trapped in the madness of the uncertainty of our situation.

The results of recent social research have informed us that a normal mourning period can take up to two years, and even longer in some cases. Elizabeth Kübler-Ross has defined the stages of the grieving process—the denial, isolation, anger, bargaining, and depression that we pass through before we can finally accept the situation and move forward into a new expression of our identities and lives. If we do not allow ourselves this time of grieving and lying fallow, many acute problems can emerge later—such as cancer in our bodies or chronic depression and emotional frigidity in our psyches.

Finding Our Way through the Dark

When we enter into one of these dark moon periods, which may last from several days to several years, a vision of what to expect and how to best utilize the energies during the various stages of the process can enable us to move through this time with peace and faith rather than fear and panic. The dark moon phase corresponds to the closure phase of any cyclical process, when something in our life ends, and it spans the interval of our transition to something else that symbolizes a new beginning. In order to better understand the why of what happens during these dark times, it is helpful to understand the larger cycle that the dark moon phase symbolically draws to a close as well as the successive stages of the transformation process itself.

All life is composed of particles of matter in motion. Scientists know that all substance moves back and forth between its state of form, which is called matter, and its state of formlessness, which is called energy, in a continuous cycle of creation, preservation, and destruction. The point between destruction and creation, where matter becomes energy, is called the stage of transformation. Transformation occurs during the dark moon phase of cyclical process. Here matter, contained by a form that has fulfilled its function and used up its store of vital essence, disintegrates back into energy. The high-frequency vibration of this medium, the transformative process, cleanses and energizes this *prima materia*, or first matter, and prepares it for renewed and revitalized form making.

The new, full, and dark phases of the moon's cycle mirror the cycle of creation, preservation, and destruction as seen in the beginnings, middles, and endings in all of our life endeavors.

The cycle is initiated by an act of creation, corresponding to the new moon phase. Some kind of aspiration is birthed and released energetically as a thought form propelled by a motivation. For example, this aspiration could be an idea to acquire resources in order to build a house in which to raise a family. The waxing part of the lunar cycle consists of trying to construct some kind of form that can contain this impulse, dream, or sense of purpose. The raw, unformed energy gradually coalesces and assumes the shape of our aspiration.

Creation is followed by preservation. At the full moon stage of the cyclical process, it is time to infuse this form with content so that the meaning of the form can be fulfilled. In our example the carpenter builds the house, and this is analogous to the construction of the form. However, it is not until the family moves into the house

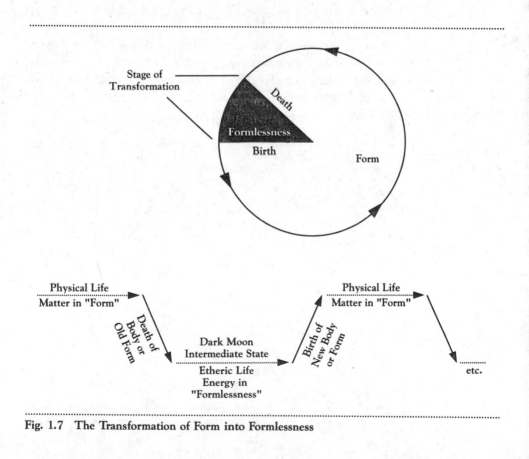

Fig. 1.7 The Transformation of Form into Formlessness

and transforms it into a home that the meaning of the house is fulfilled. Following the full moon is the time to actually live out the meaning and purpose of our aspiration. The children now grow and flourish in the home.

The waning part of the lunar cycle corresponds to destruction. What was wanting to happen has happened, the purpose has been accomplished, the function of the form has been fulfilled. At this point the form may be antiquated, run-down, useless, depleted of vital energy. The children have grown up and moved away. The large house is in need of more financial and physical maintenance than is feasible for the now aging parents. It is time to let go of a form that has fulfilled its function and no longer serves the purpose for which it was intended. It may be necessary to sell the old rambling house and move to a simpler and more appropriate life environment that better meets the changing needs of the parents.

It is at this point that we enter into the dark moon phase, the transition between the destruction of the old and the creation of the new. This process is called transformation, a process that occurs whenever any life form has fulfilled its purpose and used up its store of vital energy. It then becomes necessary for that form to be broken down in order to liberate the contained energy so it can be revitalized, recharged, and made available again to be infused into a new life form.

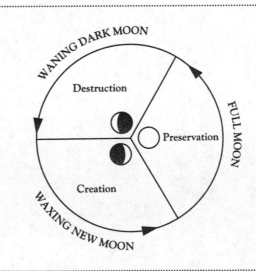

Fig. 1.8 The Cycle of Creation, Preservation, and Destruction

The dark phase of the cyclical process is where healing and renewal occur. During the dark time any form that has fulfilled its function and exhausted its supply of vital force lets go of the structure that has contained its energy. The matter then breaks up, dissolves, and is reabsorbed back into the formless state of nonbeing "from dust were you made and to dust you shall return" (Gen. 3:19) much in the same way that the universe falls back into the black holes. These forms can range from our personal or societal lifespan to those of our relationships, beliefs, and identities. In the dark phase the essence of that form is cleansed, distilled, reenergized, and dedicated with a vision that becomes the new form birthed at the moment of renewal.

The transformative process destroys old patterns of thoughts and behavior that hold us back. Old concepts and their corresponding life structures, which no longer serve a creative purpose or prevent growth, need to be eliminated. Much pain and agony may arise in the process of releasing our vital energy from useless forms or habitual nonproductive psychological patterns, but this is also the very energy that will nourish us and enable us to push onward toward new growth. The end results may not become apparent until we have clarified and enacted our new vision, and this often takes some time.

In this process it is inevitable that we face our terror of the unknown, which keeps us constricted in fear. Our images of the dark will also have to be revised. This is a courageous movement toward accepting the wholeness of our being that challenges our misogynic cultural conditioning of fearing the great dark unknown. An understanding of the Dark Goddess will help us develop our night vision, whereby we can discover a way through the darkness and know it as the place of our rebirth.

Journal Questions

1. Do I equate the concept of light with the forces of good, increase, and happiness? By contrast, do I associate dark with the forces of evil, decrease, and sadness?

2. Am I afraid of the dark? How do I feel when the power goes off and my house is plunged into darkness? Do I panic? Do I feel safer with a nightlight or porch light turned on all night? How do I feel about dark places in my environment, such as dark closets and basements? How do I feel about darker-skinned people?

3. How do I feel about growing old? Am I afraid of age, or of telling others how old I am? How do I respond when I see old people? Does

it make me uncomfortable or panicky? Have I ever been to a nursing home or old age home? Was I anxious to leave?

4. How do I feel when considering the prospect of my own or my loved ones' death? Am I afraid to die? Do I feel abandoned by the death or loss of loved ones? Can I express my anger and grief, and allow myself to mourn?

5. Do I go through anxiety, depression, and periods of darkness in the weeks before my birthday, during the winter holiday season, when I menstruate, or when I am faced with a major change in my security? Have I ever considered that these dark times in my life might be a naturally occurring part of the cyclical process and a necessary period to facilitate regeneration and the birth of something new?

Notes

1. Christina Rossetti, "Lady Moon," in *The Oxford Book of Children's Verse*, edited by Irma and Peter Opie (Oxford: Oxford University Press, 1872), 277.

2. Mircea Eliade, *Images and Symbols* (New York: Sheed and Ward, 1961), 71–73.

3. ABC News, "20/20," "Depression Beyond Darkness," transcript (New York: Journal Graphics, 1990), 2–3.

4. Dane Rudhyar, *The Lunation Cycle* (Santa Fe: Aurora Press, 1986), 37.

5. C. G. Jung, *Collected Works V: Symbols of Transformation* (Princeton: Princeton University Press, 1967), 317–18.

6. Anne Bancroft, *Origins of the Sacred* (London and New York: Arkana, 1987), 43

7. Esther Harding, *Woman's Mysteries* (New York: Harper & Row, Colophon, 1976), 111.

8. Harding, *Woman's Mysteries*, 26.

9. Harding, *Woman's Mysteries*, 53, 226–27.

10. Bancroft, *Origins of the Sacred*, 43.

11. Barbara G. Walker, *The Woman's Encyclopedia of Myths & Secrets* (San Francisco: Harper & Row, 1983), 671.

12. Fred Gustafson, *The Black Madonna* (Boston: Sigo Press, 1990), 96.

13. Harding, *Woman's Mysteries*, 151

14. In astrological cycles the dark moon phase refers not only to the natal and progressed balsamic phase, but also to void-of-course moon, lunar eclipses, and the twelfth house. Its qualities are operative in the transits of Pluto to sensitive points in the chart, the transits of planets through the twelfth house, and in the final year(s) of any planetary return cycle (the year before the Saturn return, and so on). The planetary significators associated with the dark moon phase energies are Pluto, the asteroid Lilith, the Dark Moon Lilith, the Black Moon Lilith, and other asteroid goddesses, such as Persephone, Hekate, Moira, Medusa, Nemesis, and Atropos. A forthcoming companion volume to *Mysteries of the Dark Moon* will explain to beginners how to determine personal dark moon times in your life by looking at your astrological birth chart. For information on how to obtain this book, send a SASE to Pallas Publishing Services, P.O. Box 405, Waldport, OR 97394.

2

The Dark Goddess
The Feminine Shadow

✦

It is not enough to say that we need a renewed
relationship to the feminine in our times.
What is needed is a relationship to
the dark side of the feminine.
—Fred Gustafson[1]

In the earliest societies that revered the moon as the Goddess, the third dark phase was personified as the Dark Goddess, wise and compassionate, who ruled over the mysteries of death, transformation, and rebirth. Over the course of many millennia, successive cultures gradually replaced the moon worshipers, and knowledge of the cyclical nature of reality, as mirrored by the phases of the moon, was lost.

Today, in our society, most people are unaware of the potential for healing and renewal that exists as an intrinsic quality of the dark moon phase of cyclical process. Instead we associate the dark with death, evil, destruction, isolation, and loss. In a society ruled by solar white consciousness, we have been taught to fear, reject, devalue, and disempower all that is linked with the concepts of the dark— people of color, women, sexuality, menstruation, nature, the occult, the pagan, night, the unconscious and irrational, and death itself.

Mythically we have embodied all of these fears of the dark into an image of feminine evil known as the Dark Goddess, who is intimately connected to the dark moon.

Over the course of history the original role of the Dark Goddess as a renewer was forgotten, and she came to be feared as a destroyer. Throughout many world mythologies she was portrayed as the Temptress, the Terrible Mother, and the Death-Bearing Crone. Her later biographers have recorded her as black, evil, venomous, demonic, horrifying, malevolent, fiery, and outraged. As patriarchal culture became more prevalent she came to be a symbol of a devouring feminine sexuality that causes men to transgress their moral and religious convictions, and then she consumes their vital essence and entwines them in an embrace of death.

In the mythic imagination of male-dominated cultures, her original nature became distorted and she took on horrifying proportions. As Kali she appears in cremation grounds adorned with a garland of skulls and holding the severed head of her mate, Shiva, dripping with blood. As Lilith she flies through the night as a she-demon who seduces men, breeds demons, and kills infants. As Medusa her beautiful, abundant hair becomes a crown of hissing serpents and the gaze from her Evil Eye turns men to stone. And as Hekate she stalks men at the crossroads at night with her vicious hounds of hell.

We might well ask why the Dark Goddess presents such a terrifying image. In what ways do she and her psychological counterpart, the dark feminine, threaten our security and create havoc in our lives? And how is her destructive power related to her healing qualities that bring renewal? In what ways has the Dark Goddess come to embody our fear of the dark, our fear of the occult, our fear of death and change, our fear of sex, and our fear of confronting our essential selves and our own interpretation of truth?

The answers to these questions can be found in the transition from matriarchal to patriarchal culture that occurred five millennia ago.[2] Current researchers into ancient history, working in the fields of theology, archaeology, art history, and mythology, are uncovering evidence that, starting around 3000 BCE, there occurred a transition in the predominant religious and political structures that governed humanity. Matriarchal societies, which had worshiped goddesses of the earth and moon such as Innana, Ishtar, Isis, Demeter, and Artemis, gave way to patriarchal societies, which followed the solar gods and heroes such as Gilgamesh, Amen Ra, Zeus, Yahweh, and Apollo.

Prior to this time an understanding of the connection between death and rebirth was the teaching of the cyclically renewing Moon Goddess who was worshiped by ancient peoples. The Goddess's teachings held that death was but the precursor to rebirth, and that sex can be used not only for procreation, but also for ecstasy, healing, regeneration, and spiritual illumination. When humanity shifted its allegiance to the worship of solar gods, the symbols of the Goddess began to disappear from culture and her teachings became forgotten, repressed, and distorted.

Contemporary scholars are now uncovering evidence of how the worship of the Goddess has been suppressed, her temples and artifacts destroyed, her followers persecuted and slain, and her reality denied. The new belief systems of the conquering patriarchal solar tribes denounced cyclical renewal, thereby disrupting the Moon Goddess's cycle of birth, death, and regeneration.

Let us now go into greater detail concerning the historical and psychological development of the Dark Goddess archetype, who was the third aspect of the ancient Triple Goddess. The Triple Moon Goddess, in her new, full, and dark phases, was a model for the feminine nature in her entirety as maiden, mother, and crone. In her original worship the Dark Goddess, as the third aspect of this lunar trilogy, was honored, loved, and accepted for her wisdom and for her mystery teachings of renewal. Through the course of patriarchal culture, however, she and her teachings have been exiled from legitimate society and banished to the dark corners of our unconscious.

The Worship of the Goddess: Her Story and Mythology

The story of the Dark Goddess begins thousands of years ago in a time before recorded history, when the moon was worshiped as a primary feminine divinity. Her tale takes us across much of the world, where the Dark Goddess is known by many names in different lands. She is called Kali in India, Hekate and Persephone in Greece, Lilith in the Near East, Eresh-kigal in Sumeria, Morgana in Britain, and Hel in Scandinavia. Moira, the Fates, the Furies, Medusa, Medea, Circe, Nemesis, Nyx, the Gorgons, the Sirens, the Black Madonna, Cerrwiden, Nephyths, Black Isis, Oya, Coatlicue, Mother Holle, Baba Yuga, the Black Dakini, the Terrible Mother, the Bad Fairy, and the Wicked Witch are some of her other names.

As far back as the beginning of the Upper Paleolithic, 40,000 years ago, there exists evidence that humanity worshiped a female deity who became personified in the symbolism of the Goddess. Ice Age peoples honored her image in their sacred art, sculpting the female form out of clay and carving it out of bone, rock, and ivory. These goddess-figures emphasize the breasts, belly, and vulva of the female body, signifying prehistoric peoples' reverence for the birth-giving and life-sustaining powers of the feminine. Over the last hundred years archaeologists have unearthed thousands of these statuettes and amulets spanning a range of territory from Spain, across Eurasia, to central Siberia.

During these ancient times humanity perceived the Great Goddess as an organizing principle of the universe who embodied all the forces of life, death, and rebirth within her figure. Her dominion encompassed not only the human world, but also the plant and animal realms, the earth and heavens, and the seasonal and sky cycles. The Goddess was the life force that animated all of existence.

These beliefs became the foundation for the worship of the Great Goddess of Neolithic times, which began in the ninth millennium BCE. Around 11,000 years ago the agrarian cultures settled the first year-round villages in the Fertile Crescent bordering the Mediterranean Sea, including Catal Huyuk, Jericho, and Halicar. They developed a complex cosmic religion that focused on the worship of the Triple Moon Goddess as Giver of Life, Wielder of Death, and Regeneratrix.[3]

This Neolithic Goddess embraced the constant and periodic renewal of life in which death was not separate from life. This religion displayed a deep respect for the natural cycles of women. The male principle was acknowledged and honored as the young horned God who was the son, lover, and consort of the Goddess. He also participated in the rites of birth, death, and renewal. Sexuality was sacred and celebrated as sensual, pleasure-giving, erotic, and healing.

The Great Goddess appeared in many different cultures throughout the ancient world. Known by many names, she was multifaceted and manifested in a variety of forms to satisfy the various needs of the peoples who called upon her wisdom and compassion. In the Near East she was worshiped as Innana, Tiamat, Ishtar, and Astarte. In Egypt she was venerated as Isis, Hathor, Neith, and Maat. In Greece she was revered as Demeter, Hera, Artemis, and Aphrodite. In the Far East she was known as Shakti, Adati, and Durga in India, Tara in Tibet, and Kwan Yin in China and Japan. This feminine deity later evolved into the Virgin Mary, Sophia, and the Shekinah of Christian and Judaic cultures.

The Goddess was immanent in all of nature, and people built shrines to honor and interact with her at springs, groves, caves, mountain peaks, hearths, and wells. In the societies where she was worshiped, women held exalted roles as priestesses, leaders, healers, midwives, and diviners. The sacred art of these peoples has been unearthed to reveal over 30,000 female images made of clay, marble, rock, crystal, copper, and gold from the nearly three thousand sites founded through Old Europe and the Near East during the last one hundred years.[4] The art, artifacts, and earliest writings of these peoples document that they were peaceful agriculturists, living harmoniously in matrilineal partnership societies.[5] In chapter 3 we will more fully discuss the prehistoric origins of the Goddess religion from a cyclical perspective.

The Triple Moon Goddess

The rhythm of the moon, whose phases resonated to women's menstrual cycles, held a special place in the myths, religion, and symbols of the Goddess. The ancients perceived the moon, which displayed the ebb and flow of birth, life, and death, to be feminine, and they personified her as the Great Goddess who ruled over these three great mysteries. As the moon turned from new to full to dark, it was

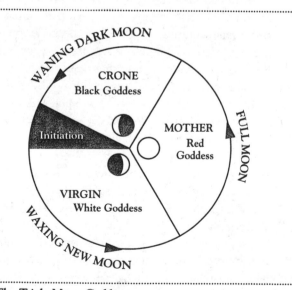

Fig. 2.1 The Triple Moon Goddess

worshiped as an embodiment of each of these three phases; hence the Triple Moon Goddess, who displayed herself on many levels as sets of three.

On the absolute energetic level, where our cosmos exists as particles of matter in motion moving back and forth between states of form and formlessness, the ancients conceptualized the triple nature of the feminine lunar energy as the cyclical forces of creation, preservation, and destruction that keep the universe in motion. As this energy begins to coalesce into the form realms, it was visualized as the deities who inhabit the heavens, and assumed the appearance of the virgin, mother, and crone aspects of the Goddess. And when the energy solidifies in the physical realm of human manifestation, the triple nature of the feminine lunar energy was experienced by early peoples as the three basic ages of a woman's life: the new moon as young maiden and bride, the full moon as fully flowered mother and wife, and the dark moon as wise grandmother and widow.

Each month the Triple Goddess revealed herself first as the White Virgin of the Waxing New Moon, who gives birth to new life and the promise of new beginnings. In her youth and innocence she rules over the season of spring and the upper air of the heavens. Filled with curiosity and excitement, the New Moon Goddess is adventurous, carefree, and enchanting, brimming with enthusiasm and unlimited energy.

She is the hunter and fighter and has dominion over heroic and dangerous animals, such as lions, tigers, panthers, cats, deer, and stags. Artistic representations of the New Moon Virgin sometimes depict her as a young, seminude maiden with a crescent moon-shaped headdress, a girdle around her loins, and adorned with jewelry. She is also portrayed as Lady of the Wild Beasts, or as the strong, fearless warrior maiden. Artemis, Diana, and Pallas Athena are some of the names of the New Moon Virgin Goddess

As the moon increases in light and size the Goddess grows into the Red Mother of the Full Moon, who nourishes and sustains life. In her fertility and productivity, she rules over the season of summer, with its abundant harvest, and the middle region of land and sea. The Full Moon Goddess is ripe, lush, full-blooded, and powerful, fiercely protecting all that she creates and loves.

She is a symbol of love and fertility. Her symbolic animals include all the nourishing animals, such as cows, goats, and sheep, as well as the animals of love, the doves and bees. In art the Full Moon Mother is often portrayed with a full, pregnant belly, giving birth between her generous legs, or nursing a child at her ample breasts. Goddesses such as Demeter, Isis, Aphrodite, Tara, and Kwan Yin embody the nature of the full moon mother.

With the diminishing of the moon's light she transforms into the Black Crone of the waning dark moon, who receives the dead and prepares them for rebirth. *This is the original derivation of the mythical Dark Goddess.* In her wisdom, which arises from experience, she encompasses the season of winter and the underworld. Grounded in her inner strength, the Dark Moon Goddess is filled with compassion and understanding for the frailty of human nature, and her counsel is wise and just.

She rules over the magical arts, secret knowledge, and oracles. Her animal totems are those which live below the earth—snakes, serpents, dragons—and animals of the night—owls, ravens, crows, and white and black dogs and horses. The Dark Moon Crone was artistically represented with the wrathful face of the goddess who devours life, and some figures also depict her vulva, symbolizing subsequent renewal. Queens of magic and of the underworld such as Hekate, Kali, and Eresh-kigal are symbols of the waning Dark Moon Goddess.

Among the most sacred customs of the Goddess, in all three of her manifestations, were the sexual rites in which her priestesses would have ritual intercourse with the members of the community who came to the temples to worship Her. These priestesses acted as channels to bring the Goddess's divine blessing of love and fertility into the lives of human beings. Warriors, returning home from battle, would first come to these priestesses to be ritually cleansed from the stains of having killed. The recipients of this blessing participated in a rite in which they could be purified, healed, and regenerated through the sexuality of the Goddess, which was enacted within a ritual context.

Thus was the Goddess seen in her cyclical turning of the moon's phases and the ever-renewing display of her light. She was loved and accepted in all three of her aspects, and her triple nature was woven into the beliefs about the nature of reality. In the realm of the Triple Goddess, the concept of time was cyclical rather than linear, and the cycle of the seasons, with its phases of waxing and waning, of life and death and revival, was the basic pattern of all thought.

The Ancient Dark Goddess During the worship of the Triple Moon Goddess, individuals understood the relationship of the dark phases of the moon's cycle as the prototype for death in the human lifespan. And they also understood the role of sex during the dark of the moon as the link to regeneration and rebirth. By observing the ever-renewing display of the moon's light, the ancients developed an intrinsic belief in rebirth.

They saw that just as the moon disappeared and then reappeared, so did the seed sprout, fruit, wither, disappear, and then reappear with new germination. There was no reason to think that human beings would be any different from the lunar and vegetative cycles with whose rhythms they lived in intimate harmony. As the moon's light reemerges after its period of darkness, so would individuals be reborn into the light. This was the law of the cycle and no power could prevent its turning.

The Dark Goddess, who is the embodiment of the dark phase of the moon's cycle, was thus honored for her role in presiding over the mysteries and initiations of the intermediary passage between death and rebirth. Her epithets include the Wise Old One, Crone, Grandmother, Queen of Shades, Guide to the Underworld, Mistress of Initiation, and Gatekeeper to the Realms of Spirit. She provided comfort, solace, and wise teachings to people as they approached the end of their lives.

As people approached their death the Dark Goddess was there for them with infinite compassion. She understood the cause of all of their mistakes and failures, and forgave their transgressions. Her devotees were respected as the funerary priestesses who instructed them for the experiences they would soon encounter during their journey into the darkness and back out again into the light.

The priestesses of the Dark Goddess cared for the terminally ill, sitting with the dying at the moment of last breath, preparing the bodies, presiding over the funeral rites, and counseling the grieving families. Old legends tell of the sexual passions aroused in dying people by the Dark Goddess at the moment of death, moving them into the death passage through orgasmic contractions not unlike the labor contractions at birth.

The ancients knew that as she died each month with the old dark moon, so would she be reborn at the new crescent moon. It was the Dark Moon Crone Goddess who took life back into her womb; but the ancients also understood that a New Moon Virgin Goddess would birth life back out again. The crone was the death-giver as the virgin was the birth-bringer. Reincarnation was represented by the refertilization of the crone-who-became-virgin. The continual interaction of destruction becoming creation is their eternal dance that maintains the cosmos.

The Dark Goddess eliminated and consumed all that was old, rundown, devitalized, and useless. She transformed its substance in her magical cauldron and offered it back as elixir. As portrayed in their secret initiation rites, ancient religions all shared the concept of an underworld where the Dark Goddess took the soul through the dark spaces of formlessness. Here she performed her secret powers of regeneration.

The English word "hell" comes from the land of the Scandinavian subterranean goddess Hel, but her underground was not a place of punishment. It was only the dark womb, symbolized by the cave, cauldron, pit, or well.[6] The Dark Goddess was not feared and her abode was not a place of torture. She awaited her initiates in graveyards, the entrance to her temple. Through death individuals entered the dark moon phase of their cycle; there they met the Dark Goddess, who led them through the intermediary passage back to birth.

When this closure and transition phase of the lifespan was understood and accepted, the Dark Goddess was honored for her wisdom and loved for her ultimate acceptance and compassion for the peoples of the earth. She was not feared by moon-worshiping peoples, who understood death as a recurring gap in the spiralic continuity through time.

The Turning Point in the Worship of the Goddess

The period around 3000 BCE is a critical time in the life cycle of the Moon Goddess and the peoples who worshiped her. It was a time when the goddess cultures that had flourished around the world for over 30,000 years began to decline. This period also marked the rise in the patriarchal tribes, who revered the solar gods, and the beginnings of humanity's recorded history, which was said to have originated in the civilization that was cradled between the Tigris and Euphrates river valley in the ancient Near East, present-day Iraq.

The beginning of the demise of the Goddess can be traced back to the closing of the Neolithic period and the advent of the Bronze and Iron Ages. Between 4000 and 2500 BCE successive waves of proto-Indo-European tribes from northern Europe and central Asia descended into western Europe, the Near East, and India. These light-skinned, nomadic, warlike peoples rode horses and fought with bronze weapons. They worshiped a Father God who came from the heavens above. In his fiery, light-bearing nature this solar god wielded bolts of lightning, which could be seen flaming on mountaintops and shining in the sky. The primary enemies of this God were the peoples of the Mother Goddess, and his followers invaded, conquered, and destroyed the indigenous Goddess cultures

These nomadic invaders, with their fiery solar gods, were ruled by priests and warriors. They were known as the Aryans in India, the Hittites and Mittani in the Fertile Crescent, the Luwians in Anatolia, the Kurgans in eastern Europe, the Achanian and later Dorians in Greece, and the Semites and Hebrews in Palestine.[7] The archaeological evidence indicates that from this time onward there existed patterns of disruption, including invasions and natural catastrophes that caused large-scale destruction of the Neolithic cultures of Europe and the Near East.

Mytho-historical sifting and archaeological digs tell of the violence and destruction that occurred during this transitional period in the habitats of Goddess-worshiping peoples around the world. They were raped and slaughtered, their homes and communities pillaged and burned, their values and beliefs suppressed. They were enslaved, exploited, and exiled. Women in these cultures were stripped of their positions of political authority and decision-making powers as leaders, and they were deprived of their spiritual authority as priestesses. Banned from functioning in their professional and healing capacities, they were progressively disempowered from expressing their sexuality, intelligence, and self-sufficiency.

The patriarchal tribes quickly rose to power, and built their civilizations upon the ruins of the peoples whose lives were attuned to the rhythms of the earth as Mother and the moon as Goddess. They imposed their ideologies and ways of life upon the peoples and lands they conquered. Riane Eisler writes that these invading tribes were based on a dominator model of social organization, and that they characteristically acquired material wealth not by developing technologies of production, but through ever more effective technologies of destruction.[8] The values of the Goddess religion, and the artistic and social contributions of women who were her priestesses and devotees, began to disappear from culture, and there was a regression of culture and civilization.

In the historical and mythical literature these events were depicted in the stories where the female deities of the Goddess religion

were replaced by the male divinities of the Indo-Europeans. The
sex of the primary deity was changed from the Great Goddess,
Mother of the Universe and all of creation, to the Great God, Father
of the Universe and of humankind, as in the transition from Tiamat
to Marduk, Gaia to Uranos, and Innana to Dumuzi.[9] The God,
King, Priest, and Father steadily assumed the roles and positions
of the Goddess, Queen, Priestess, and Mother. The Goddess was
renamed, and her myths were rewritten. What developed after 2500
BCE was a mélange of these two mythic systems, Old European and
Indo-European.[10]

The mythological tales of this transition between cultures tell of
the emergence of the young God, first as the son/lover/consort of the
Goddess. Then, as he grows in power, he eventually supersedes her to
become the God/King and her creator, husband, and father. The
myths actually relate how the conquering men supplanted the
women as religious and political leaders, and how they used the
queens and priestesses as pawns to establish the divine right of kings
and patriarchal succession and inheritance.

While originally the Goddess reigned supreme and alone, the
patriarchal cultures later relegated her to a position of secondary
importance as the mother of the God/King, such as Isis as the mother
of Horus, or Mary as the mother of Jesus. They also coerced her to
accept the reversal of this process. Now the God would become her
creator, as in the creation of Eve from Adam's rib. The goddesses were
also forced to accept gods as their husbands, without whom they were
powerless—such as the marriage of Hera to Zeus, and Isis to Osiris.
These forced marriages between the priestesses of the Goddess and
the leaders of the patriarchal tribes served to destroy the lineage of
matrilineal succession and transfer the royal bloodlines through
patriarchal descent. Priestesses who refused to marry were isolated
into enforced celibacy, such as the Roman Vestal Virgins.

The dependent status of the Goddess was later intensified when
she was made the daughter instead of wife of the omnipotent Father
God and inherited his characteristics.[11] This pattern was symbolized
in the birthing of Athena from Zeus's head; and she maintained her
elevated position as her father's favorite by denying that she ever had
a mother at all and by destroying her matriarchal antecedents, such
as Medusa and Pallas.

The final victories of this transition are found in the Indo-
European myths of rebellion, which abound with accounts of the
patriarchal solar heroes slaying the dragons and serpents. The serpent

and dragon are the primal animal representations of the Goddess or her son-lover, and are a symbol for the old religion of the Goddess. The serpent sons of Gaia, Typhon and Python, were killed by Zeus, wielder of the thunderbolt, and by the Sun God, Apollo. Marduk murdered his dragon mother Tiamat, Perseus decapitated the serpent-haired Gorgon Medusa, and Yahweh destroyed the serpent monster Leviathan.

This movement culminated in Judaism, Christianity, and Islam with the attempt to banish the Goddess altogether. In Deuteronomy 7:15, Yahweh issues a command to his people: "You must completely destroy all the places where the nations you dispossess have served their gods on high mountains, on hills, under any spreading tree; you must tear down these altars and smash their pillars, cut down the sacred poles, set fire to the carved images of their gods, and wipe their names from that place."

In the psychology of humanity there occurred a polarization between the male gods who came from above, bearers of the light, and the female divinities, who dwelt in the darkness of the caves and earth. Light was equated with good and dark with evil. The wars against the Goddess were conceptualized as battles between the forces of light and darkness. In India the light-skinned Aryans from the North took over the matriarchal dark-skinned Dravidians from the South. They instituted the caste system in order to keep the dark-skinned Goddess-worshiping peoples subordinated in the lowest castes.

As the Goddess became distorted from an image of the compassionate mother, the source and sustainer of all life, into a symbol associated with the forces of darkness and evil, women, her earthly manifestations, were likewise considered impure, evil, and guilty of original sin—people who must be punished. They became the property of their fathers and husbands. Women who had sexual relations outside of the patriarchal monogamous marriage contract threatened the certainty of patriarchal bloodline transmission, and were ostracized and killed as whores and harlots; their illegitimate children were deprived of all legal rights and social acceptance.

In classical Greece, hailed as the birthplace of democracy, women were deprived of their citizenship, of the right to vote, and the passing on of their names to their children. Ideal love was envisioned as the love between two men, especially between an older and younger man. Women were considered unworthy of meaningful emotional and intellectual relationships; their only function was that of bearing legitimate children who could inherit property rights.

The early Roman Christians methodically suppressed all information that did not originate from the church. They closed down ancient Greek academies and burned the books of great classical poets, philosophers, and scholars. The eternal flame of the Vestal Virgins in Rome was extinguished, and the great initiatory temple of Eleusis in Greece was smashed and the rites prohibited. In the fifth century the great library at Alexandria was razed, destroying the last repository of the wisdom and knowledge of the ancients.

The Papal Council of Constantinople, also in the fifth century, outlawed the concept of reincarnation and cyclical renewal. What became branded as paganism and witchcraft in medieval times was simply the folk customs of country people. They still related to the forces of the natural world and ritually celebrated the transitions of agricultural mysteries. The Inquisition and witch-hunts of the Middle Ages systematically eliminated all those who continued to remember, practice, and pass on knowledge of the old religion. Midwives, healers, and diviners, the ancient devotees of the Goddess, were branded as witches. They were persecuted, murdered, and their properties and holdings confiscated by the church.

Matriarchy and the worship of the Goddess were smothered into the dark of prehistory and the realm of fanciful legend. The remnants of the matriarchal teachings that survived can be found in the mystery religions of the cults of Demeter in Greece, Isis in Egypt, Kali in India, Cybele in Asia Minor, and the witches and fairies of Old Europe.

With the creative spirit now conceived as masculine, the new patriarchal religions moved increasingly toward monotheism and replaced the earlier pantheons of many gods, goddesses, and elementals. The one absolute Father God, derived from the male spirit, ruled alone and supreme in both heaven and earth, and he denounced all the old deities as "heathen idols." The final destruction of the ancient Triple Goddess transpired when her threefold nature became transformed into that of the Father, the Son, and the Holy Ghost.

In the new monotheistic cosmologies patriarchal culture tacitly acknowledged the first two aspects of the ancient Goddess trinity—the virgin and mother, now envisioned as an image of ideal feminine who gives birth to the Holy Son without the defilement of sexual intercourse. Woman's sexuality was accepted only for the purpose of creating offspring and continuing the race, and the memory of how the sexual energies of the Goddess were also used for ritual, healing, and regeneration was abolished.

The religious doctrines totally rejected the third, dark aspect of the Goddess, the wise crone who brings death. Humanity lost sight of the roles of sex and death as intrinsic parts of renewal that reside in the dark phase of cyclical process, and belief in cyclical renewal was tantamount to heresy. The Dark Goddess and her priestesses, versed in the arts of the funerary rites and of sacred regenerating sexuality, were feared and rejected.

The Development of the Left Brain and the Fear of Death

The demise of the goddesses and the rise of the gods can also be understood in terms of the changes that were occurring in the human brain during the period of transition. The mind, according to contemporary psychological and scientific theories, is said to have right- and left-brain functions. The right brain is likened to the feminine or *yin* polarity of energy, and the left brain to that of the masculine or *yang* polarity.

Princeton University professor Julian Jaynes, in his controversial study of human consciousness, suggests that ancient people did not "think" as we do today. People were "bicameral," directed by "voices" emanating from the right side of the brain and apprehended by the left side—voices that they treated as divine and obeyed unquestioningly until a series of natural disasters and the growing complexity of their society forced them to become conscious.[12] He suggests that people were not conscious beings, which he associates with left-brain functions, until around 1500 BCE. Here it should be noted that Jaynes reveals a misogynic bias in his definition of conscious as pertaining to only left-brain functions and the corresponding implications that right-brain processes are not conscious and therefore inferior. As we will see, this is certainly not the case.

The cosmology that developed during the reign of the Goddess arose from the kinds of thought processes that originate primarily out of the right brain. The right brain is feminine in polarity, circular in motion, intuitive in nature, and audial in emphasis. The right brain is relational and unifying; it focuses on a wholistic view of how things are similar and interconnected. When the right brain is predominant, then humans, animals, plants, and the physical world upon which they all live, the skies, the land and seas, the underworld, and the spiritual world of deities are all seen as interdependent aspects of one living being. The universe is alive, operating with intelligence, pattern, and purpose.

The right brain also sees time as cyclical. Humanity then worshiped a feminine lunar deity who circled and ever-renewed herself. She illumined the mystery where the end and beginning are the same point, touching back-to-back. Peoples thus understood death and sex as precursors to rebirth. And they did not fear the darkness of death, the ecstasy of sexuality, or the goddesses and her priestesses, who facilitated their transition between lifetimes.

While Jaynes does not discuss the changeover from the goddesses to the gods, he does document the catastrophes and cataclysms that started to occur in the middle of the second millennium BCE. In addition to the volcanic eruptions, tidal waves, and massive flooding, he sees widespread warfare and dislocation that we have previously identified as the patriarchal invasions. Jaynes suggests that the rational, logical, analytical mind, all functions of the left brain, was developed in order to assist humanity through the increasing complexity of their changing world. He presents evidence that the left-brain functions became more active at this time and grew to influence the ways in which individuals perceived reality.

The left brain is masculine in polarity, linear in movement, logical in nature, and visual in perception. It has been most prevalent in the analytical, technological, and scientific intellectualism of modern times. While the right brain focuses on how things are alike, the left brain emphasizes how they are different. It develops our capacity for analysis and discrimination, and in the process it perceives a distinction between subject and object.

This kind of dualistic view sees a separation between self and others, between us and them, and this perception inevitably leads to a war of opposites that yields an oppressor and victim. Our desire for self-preservation creates a fear of being overpowered by anything that we perceive as separate and external to us. This attachment to self, when taken to extremes, results in feelings of isolation and unconnectedness. This kind of thinking leads to a conclusion where individuals feel alienated in a lonely universe that is random, chaotic, and without underlying intelligence. The subsequent suffering causes an underlying, less conscious urge for reconciliation; thus the dynamic tension between pairs of opposites.

After 1500 BCE, when human beings began to operate primarily from the left brain, associated with the masculine principle, they began to see a distinction between themselves and the rest of all creation. Because they now feared the threat of being overwhelmed by external forces as something separate from themselves, there arose a desire to conquer the feminine principle, embodied in the Goddess, women, and nature, rather than to live in harmony with her.

In addition to fear of the other, the fear of death was a product of left-brain perception that denies cyclical time and instead sees time as linear. In linear time the end is no longer connected to the beginning. The end is the end, and death is the final conclusion of life. Life and death are not seen as the two alternating phases of cyclical existence, but instead are viewed as warring opposites. In a cosmology where death is linear and final, not cyclical and renewing, death is the ultimate terror. The pinnacle of Christian monotheistic religion was the concept of resurrection; the final triumph of eternal life over death.

The prevailing dogmas now taught individuals that they had but one life to live, and this life must be lived according to the new moral laws revealed by the solar gods. Disobeying these laws was to court a path of sin and punishment. To engage in sexuality for any other reason than procreation within legitimate monogamous marriage was now contrary to living a spiritual life. This denial of the ecstatic and healing powers of sexuality led to its becoming the ultimate temptation to holy men—ever wary of the seductive and licentious nature of women forcing them to weaken and sin. Unless they converted to the faith of the wrathful patriarchal god and prayed to him for forgiveness and salvation, they were fated to suffer eternally in the hellfire of damnation. There was no reprieve, no pardon, no opportunity to explain nor to learn from one's mistakes and make amends.

While the religion of the Goddess always included a concept of the underworld, it was not a place of punishment. It was simply the gap between lifetimes, the dark womb of the Goddess, where one went to be purified, healed, and prepared for rebirth. It was the patriarchal monotheistic religions, operating out of left-brain mentality, that conceived of a heaven and hell, with the corresponding associations of good and evil, reward and punishment. And the hell of this wrathful Father God was filled with unending sadistic torture and pervasive suffering.

Humanity then began to fear the darkness of death. Those who, during their lives, were not saved by a religious conversion to the Father faced a death of eternal torture and absolute finality. Their terror extended to the Dark Goddess of the Dark Moon, who was now only the death-bringer and no longer the renewer. When the Goddess became separated from her role in cyclical renewal, her third dark aspect became the horrifying image of feminine evil who seduced, devoured, and brought finality to the lives of human beings.

The dark aspect of the Goddess was then hated, persecuted, suppressed, and cast out into the predawn of history and into the depths of the unconscious. In exile the images of the Dark Goddess became repressed and subsequently distorted, and she grew to overpower humanity's mythic imagination in her capacity to destroy them.

As the left-brain energies became increasingly activated in the human mind, the masculine principle grew to influence the conceptual beliefs of humanity. Male gods and men rose to positions of power in worldly and spiritual affairs. With the diminishment of the right-brain perception of the cyclical nature of time, death was forgotten as part of cyclical rebirth. And the fear of death linked with the fear of sex led to the fabrication of the Dark Goddess as a malefic female destroyer with the resultant demonization of the dark aspect of the feminine as evil.

The Dark Goddess as the Feminine Shadow in the Modern World

Today the Dark Goddess, as the third phase of the ancient Triple Goddess, represents many of the rejected aspects of the trinity of feminine wholeness. The teachings of the Dark Goddess of the Dark Moon are concerned with divination, magic, healing, sacred sexuality, the nonphysical dimensions of being, and the mysteries of birth, death, and regeneration. In a similar manner these dark moon teachings, now called pseudo-sciences, have been rejected as legitimate areas of inquiry by modern religious and educational institutions.

For most people anything that takes them beyond the security of their conscious boundaries often evokes the compulsion to hold it back and deny its existence. The dark feminine and her dark moon teachings have been ostracized from the accepted dogma of patriarchal society. This rejection parallels the psychological development of the shadow in individuals and in society. Denial of an aspect of wholeness is the key ingredient in the formation of the shadow.

The shadow, according to Jungian psychology, is the dark, rejected part of the psyche. It consists of all those qualities that we, as influenced by the values of our culture, do not feel are desirable or acceptable to express as part of our personalities. The shadow contains what we do not like about ourselves, what we find threatening, shameful, and inadequate, as well as certain valued and positive qualities that we are pressured to repress and disown. Individually and as a culture we reject these denied and devalued parts of ourselves, exile them to the unconscious, and do not allow them to flourish as part of our conscious identity.

The shadow is also the messenger of the unconscious who, through dreams and images, reveals the workings of our inner being that operates beneath the threshold of the conscious mind.

The gods and goddesses of religion and mythology correspond to the archetypal personalities who inhabit our psyches and express themselves as the various forces in our personalities. As the collective culture has banished and defamed the mythical Dark Goddess and her teachings, so have we as individuals been conditioned to deny and detest the parts of our personalities that correspond to the qualities of the Dark Goddess. The Dark Goddess has come to contain the rejected aspects of feminine wholeness and, as such, she now symbolizes the feminine shadow. While the feminine shadow consists primarily of the magical and regenerating qualities of the Dark Crone Goddess of the moon's third dark phase, it also holds some qualities of the virgin and mother aspects of the Triple Goddess, such as independence, assertiveness, sexuality, power, and worldly accomplishment. To the extent that patriarchal cultures fear these aspects of feminine wholeness, women are pressured to devalue and disown these parts of themselves.

Whenever aspects of the wholeness of ourselves are not expressed and accepted but rather denied and rejected, they become distorted. When the shadow is confined to the dark realms of our unconscious, it becomes constricted, twisted, and deformed. As it festers, toxic by-products are released into our bodies and minds. These poisons contort our physical features, and they also obscure the mental lens out of which we perceive the world. Our view of ourselves, of others, and of the world is colored by these poisons in our mindstreams that are being generated by the rejected aspects of ourselves.

The inherent nature of the original Dark Goddess, who brought both death and rebirth, has been repressed and denied for thousands of years. Her toxic releases, festering in exile, have distorted and poisoned our perceptions of an intrinsic aspect of the feminine nature. The Dark Goddess was then conceptualized as malefic, and her teachings concerning the dark, sex, and death were distorted. Our mythical literature abounds with images of the Dark Goddess as feminine evil. She was feared as the Fates who, at the moment of our birth, determine the time of our death and whose decree is irrevocable; as Nemesis, the Goddess of Judgment and swift retribution; as the Furies, who will hound a man to madness and death. She also terrorized men as Medea, who killed her children; Circe, who transformed men into pigs; Medusa, who turned them into stone; the

Lamia, who sucked their blood; Lilith, who seduced them in order to breed demons from their sperm; and Hekate, Queen of the Witches, who snatched them into the underworld.

Through cultural conditioning we have all inherited these negative and false images of the dark aspect of the feminine. The kind of woman who is a threat to patriarchal culture is feared, ridiculed, and rejected for being covert, manipulative, jealous, greedy, pushy, demanding, wanton, and revengeful. Archetypally she has been imaged as the Bitch Queen, the Outcast Daughter, the Fallen Woman, the Terrible Mother, the Wicked Witch, the Wicked Queen, the Wicked Stepmother, the Domineering Mother-in-Law, the Bag Lady, and the Ugly Hag.

These distorted aspects of the dark feminine live within each one of us, male and female, as the negative thought patterns in our minds. They take on the form of our personal demons, which psychologists call our neuroses, complexes, obsessions, and compulsions. Our inner demons, both masculine and feminine, thrive in an environment of selfishness, guilt, shame, deceit, blame, and judgment. They fill our ears with whispered promises of failure, abandonment, unworthiness, and rejection. And they jealously guard us from exposing our shameful secrets, which surround us as addictions, dysfunctions, imperfections, violence, incest, abuse, and rape.

The shadow seems to flourish and acquire strength while in exile. It then acts in subversive ways to dominate our personalities. In our most vulnerable times of exhaustion or extreme stress, the shadow can suddenly burst forth from our unconscious with invectiveness and rage. When our inner demons are activated they erupt as our anger, hatred, jealousy, and greed, and cause us to act in violent, self-destructive, and obsessive ways that undermine our positive efforts and wreak havoc in our lives.

There exist times when we are pushed to the limits of our endurance, and our unconscious psyche can no longer contain the smoldering anger and resentment over all that we have denied, devalued, and disowned. At these times the shadow, now twisted and distorted due to repression, takes over our personality, and the conscious self loses control. While we may be shocked and horrified at what emerges from within us, we also feel powerless to halt our behavior. We can recognize the feminine shadow as it retaliates against individuals and a culture that oppresses certain aspects of feminine wholeness.

The feminine shadow appears in the obsessive, addictive behavior of the woman who loves too much, in the spurned mistress, betrayed wife, or crazy ex-wife. Hera, who was forced into a vow of monogamy and then betrayed by the infidelities of her husband, sought vengeance upon Zeus, his mistresses, and their children. Likewise our shadow self vents its rage and revenge against our partners and their lovers. Or like Medea, who killed her children to punish Jason for rejecting her for another, our shadow may take out its despair and anger upon our children. The behavior of the hysterical premenstrual woman, the eternally complaining and never satisfied menopausal woman, or the sexually manipulative or indiscriminate woman are all manifestations of a rejected feminine nature who is erupting uncontrollably with the anguish of her pain.

When the shadow is activated many painful and difficult situations arise that force us to confront these hidden and hateful parts of ourselves. We are reluctant to acknowledge the aspects of ourselves that are the cause of our shame, humiliation, or failure, and which we hope that no one will ever discover. We may rationalize our reaction, saying, "I just don't know what came over me; I wasn't my usual self," and dismiss our outburst as some kind of isolated aberration that will probably never happen again. However, this kind of response causes us to miss the opportunity to see and come to know the nature of our unconscious workings. What is important to realize about both our feminine shadow and the mythical images of the Dark Goddess is that they are not intrinsically evil; but, due to cultural conditioning and pressure, we have created their destructive effects through our denial and repression of the feminine aspects of wholeness.

While we may deny the shadow aspects of our being, it is impossible fully to disown this material; what is pushed down in one place will inevitably emerge in another. The shadow lives not only inside of us as our personal demons, it also has a seemingly independent life outside of us. When the shadow is not brought into light, we will project it onto others. The images in our mind's eye are the seed for the outer reality that we create for ourselves. When we project our shadow, we externalize these inner distorted images and then cast them onto others, thus undermining our capacity to form safe and honest relationships.

We then perceive the outer world through the inner filter of our negative emotions and thoughts. When our minds are full of fear and hatred, we then see others as the personification of what is most frightening and hateful to us. When the magical, sexual, and regenerating powers of the Dark Goddess were rejected, twisted, and distorted, they subsequently became projected as the demonic forces of evil. The dark became personified as the Dark Goddess, who was possessed by a destructive, furious rage trying to claim her due.

These rejected aspects of ourselves assume the forms of evil and temptation in our external world. They become all of our enemies—our abusers, rapists, terrorists, deceivers, and destroyers. Through our negative emotional states, we attract these kinds of people and situations to us. Furthermore, we also evoke and catalyze these negative qualities in others that are, in actuality, the reflections of our own unconscious denied self. Our shadow then becomes all that threatens our safety and security.

Edmond Whitmont sums up this phenomenon of shadow projection:

> This type of situation is so classical that one could almost play a parlor game with it—if one wished to court social ruin. Ask someone to give a description of the personality type he finds most impossible to get along with, and he will produce a description of his own repressed characteristics—a self-description which is utterly unconscious and which therefore always and everywhere tortures him as he receives its effects from the other person.[13]

This becomes especially dangerous when society collectively projects a shadow onto a group and fantasizes that it is the enemy. Societal prejudices against blacks, Jews, homosexuals, witches, aliens, Communists, or the Devil have all led to mass intolerance, and even to persecutions, inquisitions, and other manifestations of hatred all involving the sacrifice of a scapegoat. The Dark Goddess and her teachings have come to assume the shape of the collective feminine shadow of the patriarchy, who envisioned her as the enemy to be destroyed. It was this pattern of repression and projection that led to the demonization of the Dark Goddess and her teachings in the Middle Ages, when 9 million women were burned as witches.

The rigid sexual moral codes of patriarchal societies such as the Puritans, when repressed, distorted, and projected, were reflected back to them as the evil power of seductive witches who fornicated with the Devil and were a threat to the safety of the community. Arising from patriarchal fear of sexuality, the dark feminine shadow was perceived as the "temptress who bewitches." The woman who expressed her passion was denounced and ostracized as a seductress, whore, nymphomaniac, ball-buster, and castrator. Arising from their fear of death, the compassionate, wise crone was distorted into the hideous ugly hag and death-snatcher. The elderly woman, in the prime of her wisdom, was likewise cast out by patriarchal cultures as useless and grotesque.

In today's society a woman's expression of her independence, sexuality, and wisdom is becoming more acceptable. Maxine Harris, in *Sisters of the Shadow*, asks what then is the current content of the feminine shadow? She goes on to point out that many modern women disown their aspects of vulnerability, alienation, aggressiveness, and rebelliousness. As the archetypal victim, exile, predator, and rebel, it is homeless women who have now become the carriers of the denied and unlived aspects of female consciousness.[14]

It is important to realize that the shadow material is almost always unconscious, and intellectual reasoning or good intentions will not usually solve the problem of the unpleasant parts of our personalities or of societies. It is necessary that we become conscious of our own dark aspects in order to accept ourselves and others, and this effort requires commitment to inner work.

When we allow some inferiority to express itself in our personality, the shadow will be more balanced with the conscious self. However, when we are extremely righteous and rigid, the shadow will become exaggerated and destructive. Likewise, the more narrow and restrictive the society in which we live, the larger will be the collective shadow. The evil forces of the dark unconscious then take on huge, threatening proportions, which we must defend ourselves against by banishing and prohibiting their existence.

What teachings of the Dark Goddess have been feared by patriarchal culture, and how have these teachings been subsequently demonized as the shadow? As we explore these questions, let us keep in mind that it is these very same qualities that enable us to move through our unconscious and through the dark passageways of our transformation and renewal.

Our Fear of the Goddess's Dark Moon Teachings   Humanity, under patriarchal rule, forgot the mystery teachings of the Goddess concerning sex and death as intrinsic parts of cyclical process that lead toward renewal. These teachings were repressed into the dark realms of the unacknowledged and subsequently demonized as dark forces of evil. Today the images of the dark, of sex, of death, of magic, and divination encompass what is most feared and most misunderstood by modern people.

Patricia Weis, in an article about the Dark Goddess, comments,

> The dark, as we perceive it through our conscious rational minds, has come to represent all those forces that threaten our safety, security, and sanity in our world. Most people try to protect themselves from their fear by denying the dark. We deny our sexuality and bury it under layers of morality. We deny death by isolating our old and creating a cult of youth and physical beauty. We deny fear itself by creating an imaginary security around ourselves from life insurance to nuclear missiles.[15]

As we have learned to live in fear of the dark, patriarchal culture has fabricated images of a Dark Goddess who was associated with the sinfulness of sexuality and the terror of death. During the reign of the Goddess, death generally occurred from natural or accidental causes. It was not feared, because of the implicit understanding in rebirth. Under the rulership of the new gods, with their masculine left-brain mentality, death became feared above all else because, from the linear perspective, it was no longer seen as the preparatory stage for renewal.

The Christians outlawed belief in reincarnation and held that we have only one life to live. They conquered death with the promise of eternal (not cyclical) life in the Kingdom of heaven. However, this was only for those who had been saved through accepting the Father, the Son, and the Holy Ghost as their saviors; all others were doomed to never-ending suffering. The patriarchal societies in the Eastern religions that maintained a belief in reincarnation also maligned the positive value of cyclical renewal, proposing that cyclical existence is synonymous with the "suffering of *samsara*," that is, the physical world of phenomena. They taught that the goal of enlightenment was to escape from the wheel of rebirth and to transcend into the realm of the purelands, not unlike the heaven of their Western counterparts. And so death became feared above all else because it was severed from its positive and essential relationship to cyclical renewal.

The Bronze and Iron Ages flourished at the beginning of the reign of the patriarchy. At this time death took on ominous and frightening proportions. The worshipers of the solar gods developed technologies of destruction and lethal weapons with which to kill—not animals for food, but other people for power dominance. A warrior's courage to engage in bloody battles where he would court and defy death was glorified as heroic. And for those victimized and defeated in battle, in a linear cosmology where death was no longer connected to renewal, death became the ultimate threat whereby the dominator could extract surrender and submission.

As we revision the dark we will have to revise our beliefs about death. The Dark Goddess teaches us to understand death not as final and absolute but rather as part of the natural cycle of life constantly renewing itself. This knowledge can help us to dissolve the reign of terror unleashed by religious and political power structures that intimidate and control the peoples of the world through their fear of death.

In the attempt to deny the death-bringing Dark Goddess who also holds the sexual secrets, patriarchal culture has concealed from us the knowledge of the healing and rejuvenative gifts of her sexuality. Not only has this gross misunderstanding poisoned the relationship between men and women, but the rejection of feminine regenerative sexual power has also resulted in the stagnation and putrefaction of our bodies and of the earth.

Today the sexuality of the Dark Goddess is taboo in our culture. Women are made to feel ashamed of their raw, instinctive sexual desires and to feel that their menstrual blood is dirty and disgusting. And the snake, as a symbol of feminine sexual power, is hated for having caused our expulsion from Yahweh's Eden. Men have called the orgasm *le petit mort*—the little death, the diminishment of their vitality. They have twisted and distorted images of women and the Dark Goddess into terrifying images of sex and death. The regenerative qualities of the snake have become identified with a devouring feminine sexuality that tempts, seduces, and then dooms a man.

The ancient power of the Dark Goddess's capacity to heal, regenerate, and renew was centered in her ecstatic sexuality. In the transition to patriarchal rule, where men worshiped the new solar gods, it was necessary to turn people away from the sacred sexual rites of the Goddess. In order to do this the male-dominated cultures had to destroy and disassociate themselves from the power of women's sexuality. Feminine sexuality was then promoted as an evil temptation, the one exception being for procreative purposes within strictly defined monogamous boundaries. Women were denied sexual freedom and disempowered from expressing their instinctive sexuality.

As we have repressed her sexuality in ourselves and in society, we have cut ourselves off from her powers of renewal that allow our wounds to be healed so that we can become transformed and born anew. When wounds cannot heal they fester, autointoxicate, and weaken the entire system. These poisonous by-products distort our perception of the relationship between sex and death. The increase in sexually transmitted diseases, some of which are fatal, is the ultimate symbol of a society who fears and denies both sex and death. It is a cry of the Dark Goddess for us to reexamine and revision our attitudes and actions concerning two of the most powerful forces in our lives.

With the increase in degenerative, environmental, and auto-immune illness that lead to premature death, the inevitable ending of our lives is now entering into the mainstream of our consciousness. Our society can no longer deny its reality and presence. As we move into reclaiming our acceptance of death, the sexual energies of the Dark Goddess can be healed and empowered in each one of us. In order for this healing to be effective we must confront our deeply hidden fears of the Dark Goddess, which in patriarchal culture has become entangled with negative images of the relationship between sex and death.

Both men and women need to examine, heal, and transform their unconscious fears of being destroyed by sexual energies. These subliminal yet most powerful attitudes prevent us from fully opening up sexually and emotionally to another person. Our misperceptions also motivate us into using our sexual energies in ways that hurt, dominate, degrade, or destroy one another. The secret of sex and death as the regenerators of life is the secret of the Dark Moon Goddess that the patriarchy has tried to conceal from us in the name of taboo.

In addition to sex and death, the Dark Goddess's teachings concerning divination, magic, and the nonphysical dimensions of being have also been ostracized and suppressed. The dark moon phase exists as an aspect of all cycles of life and systems of understanding. Each month when the moon glides into the dark she conceals her mysteries behind the dark veil. The contents of the dark phase of cyclical process are the most hidden and difficult to access. Because we have been taught to fear that which we cannot see, we have regarded these repositories of secret wisdom as evil. Yet the initiates have traditionally used the special qualities inherent in this most secret time for healing and prophecy.

The essential qualities of the dark moon are change and transformation. Today we are afraid of many of the dark moon teachings, such as alchemy, astrology, and other spiritual or psychological disciplines, which reveal information about the unconscious or subtle dimensions of being. The Bible has told us that they are evil and contrary to the will of God. Educators tell us they cannot be validated by scientific inquiry and its practitioners are labeled quacks.

Yet it is these teachings, based on the timing of cyclical patterns, that give us the guidance that enables us to pass through the dark, nonphysical dimensions of being—of death and rebirth, endings and new beginnings, or spontaneous healings—with clarity and confidence instead of panic and terror. Philosophical traditions have repeatedly told us that the answers to the ultimate questions of life and death are found, not in the external world, but deep within the dark recesses of our own minds.

The dark moon teachings include knowledge of *karma*, reincarnation, and conscious dying. We can travel into the nonordinary realms through meditation, ritual, shamanic journeys, and other trance techniques that bridge the conscious and unconscious dimensions of reality. The intuitive psychic arts, such as astrology, tarot, and numerology, provide a window into the mysteries. The wisdom of the dark can be accessed through channeling, psychic visions, and oracular prophecy. In women's spirituality, initiation rites and blood mysteries are contained within the dark moon phase. The elusive esoteric and mystery traditions such as the Eastern Tantra, Western Hermetics, Middle Eastern Sufis, the Gnostics, the Druids, the Rosicrucians, the Essenes, the Pagans, the Cabbalists, and many others hold the secrets of transformation and renewal.

In psychology the dark moon areas of the unconscious are reached through psychotherapy, dreamwork, hypnosis, regression, bioenergetics, and breathwork. Many of these techniques receive only borderline acceptance, if any at all, by the established medical societies. Just recently there has been reluctant recognition of the success of programs like the Twelve-Step process that can take us through our addictions and wounds into our recoveries.

But what is even more concealed and filled with apprehension is the dark slice within each of the dark moon teachings. Astrologers flinch when they see planets in the twelfth house, the dark moon phase of the cycle of houses. Tarot readers dread having to explain the meaning of the Death key when it comes up in a reading. In women's blood mysteries menstruation is the curse, and talk of the healing and magical powers of the menstrual blood causes people to feel embarrassment and disgust. In seasonal rituals Hallowmas is the celebration of the awesome Dark Goddess, and she has been denigrated to the black witch associated with Halloween. Snakes and spiders, the animal totems of the Goddesse's mysteries, still bring up irrational terror. The snake is linked as the perpetuator of evil in the Garden of Eden, and the spider as a harbinger of hideous death.

In all of these systems we have been conditioned to fear and devalue the dark of the moon, as symbolized by the deepest part of the night, the wisdom of our night dreams, the death phase of cyclical life, the shadow of the unconscious, menstruation and menopause, magic and divination, the barren desolate season of winter, and the harvest of our old age. As we revision the dark it is the dark slice within each of the dark moon teachings that also needs to be divested of fear.

Healing the Dark

The images of the Dark Goddess and her associations with the dark moon teachings that exist within the collective unconscious also exist within the personal unconscious of each of us. In our attempt to reclaim the healing and regenerative powers of the Dark Goddess we must develop a positive relationship with the feminine shadow as it operates within each woman and man. As humanity came to perceive the dark feminine as threatening to the conscious, rational ego-self and the established social order, each of us likewise has denied and suppressed these very qualities in ourselves. In the process we have cut ourselves off from acknowledging and expressing our complete psychic reality. This severing has led to a deep wounding and illness in our souls.

For some individuals the Dark Goddess archetypes, as contained in the feminine shadow, are significant themes throughout their lives, and these issues come up again and again with different people and situations. For others the eruption of the feminine shadow material is confined to only several out-of-control blackout times in their lives, and it operates primarily in hidden and subversive ways that are for the most part unconscious.

While the shadow holds many of the rejected parts of the psyche, it is also the messenger of the unconscious. It pressures us from deep inside to purify our toxins and to clarify our mental and emotional images and concepts in ourselves, in our relationships, and in our world. To the extent that we experience the Dark Goddess issues in demonic, violent, painful, destructive, and frightening ways, what can we do to understand, cope, and perhaps transform this negativity that threatens our sense of well-being?

When we are engulfed in the kinds of traumas that are colored by the projection of feminine shadow material, we can alternately be the one who is doing the projecting or the one being projected upon. In either case the results are often disturbing and it is difficult to untangle the ensuing confusion. In the first instance we may be casting the projection of our own disowned and hated parts upon other people. Here we toxify our psychological environment as we force others to carry our shadow material, and we inadvertently cause them to act in ways that are most threatening and uncomfortable for us. Our relationships become chaotic, filled with mistrust, disappointment, betrayal, and blame.

In the second situation, when we are out of touch with our own wholeness, we become vulnerable to being the recipient of another person's projections upon us. Here we accept their hated and disowned material and come to believe that it is truly part of ourselves. We are trapped in a web of ensuing self-hatred and poor self-esteem. Healing the dark feminine requires that the recipient of the projection acknowledge and return the disowned shadow material to the sender, who must then reclaim and integrate these denied parts of the personality into the wholeness of his or her self.

The most important concept to realize is that the malefic nature of the Dark Goddess, as she is embodied in our psyches as personal demons contained within the feminine shadow, is not by nature inherently evil. Nor does she have an independent reality outside of us apart from our mind's projections. The negativity and evil associated with the dark feminine is not her true essence; it has only become distorted in this way through our personal and cultural repression.

The dark becomes frightening and destructive only when we deny and disown it. When we deny that sexual abuse ever happened in childhood, we may grow up emotionally frigid or paranoid. When we deny that an alcoholic family was a factor in early life, we have difficulty trusting or believing our partners and friends. When we disown some aspect of ourself, it comes back to haunt and torment us in the guise of other people. Denial of some aspect of the past that is now forgotten and unconscious, or rejection of some aspect of our personality that is unacceptable to us, plays a crucial role in the problems we later face. These may range from depression and sexual inhibitions to childhood scripts, pregnancy fears, and blocks in creative inspiration.

Jungian psychology tells us that in order to heal the wounds and suffering caused by denying and rejecting aspects of our wholeness, we must first enter into our unconscious and develop a relationship with our shadow. It is necessary to recognize that all of these hated and ostracized parts of ourselves have a legitimate need to exist and to be expressed. If we can affirm the full range of our essential human nature, acknowledging both the desirable and undesirable qualities, then we have the option to transform the more problematical energies that cause our pain and suffering into constructive activity that will benefit our lives and relationships.

As we become less fearful and allow ourselves to look at what we have hidden, we can begin to reclaim the dark feminine and heal our psyches. When we embark upon the healing journey into the realm of the feminine shadow, it is important to approach her with honor, respect, and kindness. When we first confront the shadow we may feel overwhelmed by the sadness and pain of the outcast parts of our being. We must admit to the suffering that we have kept hidden from ourselves and others. In our suffering the boundaries of what we thought we could bear are greatly stretched; and this expansion makes us open and vulnerable to larger forces.

As we experience the pain that arises from rejecting parts of ourselves and our traumatic memories, we can release the blocked energies that lie festering in the unconscious. We can initiate a process of healing the wounds in our soul by purifying the toxic by-products of the negative emotional patterns that have accumulated in our minds over years and even lifetimes of repression and false beliefs. In going through our pain and fear, the Dark Goddess strips away all our inauthenticities, our illusions of false security, our adaptations to society's standards; and she exposes the strength and essence of our true nature, which lies in the dark core of our being.

In the process of reclaiming the Dark Goddess and the feminine shadow, it is important to extend compassion to the weak and undesirable aspects of our personalities that we had previously despised and rejected. It is ultimately through accepting and empathizing with the hated and denied parts of ourselves that we can transform and heal the wounds of the shadow self.

In Tibetan Buddhism demons are explained as the unreal apparitions that assume the forms of our mind's anger, hatred, greed, pride, and ignorance. In the teachings of this philosophy and religion, there exists a meditational practice of the Black Mother, an Oriental image of the Dark Goddess. Revealed through Machig Lapbron in the eleventh century CE in Tibet, the purpose of this practice is to appease and exorcise the demons who arise from our negative emotional patterns. It is called *Chod*, which means to cut at the root of fear and delusion. The essence of this practice implies that the correct procedure to exorcise the demons is not to kill, banish, or destroy them but rather to invite them to a great feast as the honored guests.

The *Chod* practice calls for visualizing and preparing a great accumulation of food and other desirables, which include one's own ego attachments, that are offered to the demons. These hungry, needy, deprived, rejected aspects of ourselves come and partake of this feast until they are completely fulfilled and satisfied. Once the demons are fed they are pacified and disappear as demonic destructive influences in our lives.

Tibetan Buddhist teacher Tsultrim Allione, in *Places Where She Lives*, advises, "If we feed our demon anger and frustration, it will continue to bother us; if we feed it love and compassion, it will evolve. By loving the demon, it melts. The tension is in the duality and pushing the demons away makes more suffering. . . . Eventually through love and compassion, the demons evolve and are liberated."[16]

In the same way, we need to go into our darkness and make our peace with all the lost parts of ourselves in order to redeem the healing and renewal that reside in the dark. We must call our demons in from the backyard where they've been starved and banished into the leaking doghouse. We must welcome them in the warmth of our kitchens and feed them the foods that will heal their wounds of rejection. As we cleanse our inner images of the Dark Goddess through loving and accepting her, we will notice a corresponding decrease in the fear, anger, rejection, failure, disappointment, deception, and hatred that we experience as part of our outer reality. In this way we reach the original true essence of the dark feminine that exists within us, an essence that is unclouded by layers of distortion.

As the fairy tales have instructed us to kiss the frog in order to turn him into the prince, we can transform the beast into the beauty by reclaiming the lost and rejected parts of ourselves and integrating them into the wholeness of our being. It is often through another person seeing the worst part of us and loving and accepting us nevertheless that we can accept our shadow selves. In the process we effect a healing and transformation. In this way we can reclaim the healing and regenerating potential of the dark moon energies. We are then able to access the Dark Goddess, who offers us her gifts from the unconscious: gifts of healing, prophecy, ecstatic sacred sexuality, regeneration, and spiritual growth.

The hero or heroine's journey into the underworld to reclaim the stolen treasure from the monster is not an easy quest, and it is one fraught with many dangers. To enter into our darkness, to confront the beast within ourselves, to reclaim the dark and take back the night demands much courage, inner strength, and commitment to the process of physical well-being, psychological wholeness, and spiritual growth. As we move toward accepting the wholeness of our beings, we will inevitably have to revise our fears of the dark.

And so we must invoke and praise the Dark Goddess, who has been banished to the neglected corners of our psyches. Her ultimate function is to facilitate the transformation that occurs in the dark. She provokes the death of our ego selves, of our old forms, and of our false assumptions, so that we can give birth to the new.

When we embrace the dark and allow ourselves to enter into the unknown dimensions of our minds, we can be led toward our healing, salvation, transformation, and renewal. The guidance of many psychological, spiritual, and support-group programs can help us confront our denial and recognize the reality of our unconscious attitudes and projections, which have contributed to our life as it is. As Ariadne's ball of twine revealed the way through the mysterious labyrinth, we can follow this shimmering thread of change as we wind our precarious way through the dark. Here courage is essential to knowing that we will return to the light.[17]

The healing that occurs in the dark precedes renewal, and we do emerge back into the light with the wisdom of change. Our personal healing experiences then become the training ground for the compassion that permeates our potentialities as a wounded healer.

The Secret of the Dark Moon Goddess

What then is the secret teaching of the Dark Moon Goddess, who has become the shadow demon of patriarchal culture and whose wisdom has been concealed from us in the name of taboo? What stands behind our fear of the eternal darkness of death and nonbeing that patriarchal institutions have used to intimidate, terrorize, and control the masses?

Behind the luminous dark veil it is the activity of the Divine God and Goddess in sexual union that creates and animates the world. As they make love, their orgasms ripple out like waves gathering into the tidepools where life emerges. When the Moon Goddess each month draws into her dark phase, she reposes between the Earth Child and Sun God. Her illuminated face is toward the sun and her dark face is toward the earth.

This is the dark time that straddles the gap between the old and the new moons. This is the rest time that allows for purification and regeneration. This is the death time that ensures renewal.

The mystery of the Dark Moon Goddess is that death and birth are the twin faces of her cosmic orgasm with the Sun God each month at the new moon conjunction. Fulfilled in love, she then circles, ever turning around the earth, and sends forth a shower of blessings with the knowledge that there is no annihilation.

Journal Questions

1. When I went to school, was I ever taught about the existence of the earliest civilizations, who worshiped a feminine deity? What was my reaction when I first heard about this idea? Did I think it blasphemous that in the beginning God might have been a woman? How do others react to me if I present this idea to them? If I have heard of the phrase the Dark Goddess, did I associate this with an image of feminine evil?

2. Do I have dark secrets that I have never revealed to anyone? What qualities do I most dislike in other people? If I look closely, will I recognize any of these qualities in myself? How does even the possibility of this idea make me feel right now? The thought of what circumstances or kinds of people bring up the greatest fears in me? To what extent are my fears part of my reality, either as phobias or actual situations? Am I paranoid that others are out to get me, and that I must therefore protect myself?

3. Am I attracted to dark lovers or to those partners who will take me to and through the dark spaces of my emotions and sexuality? How do I feel about my sexuality? Do I see it as a source of healing and renewal in my life? Do I feel uncomfortable or ashamed about sexuality, or that sexual organs are dirty, dark, or disgusting? How do I feel about oral sex and the ingestion of sexual fluids?

4. What are my beliefs concerning the afterlife? Do I believe that death is a finality and nothingness? Do I think that I will go to heaven or hell? Do I believe in reincarnation and cyclical renewal?

5. Do I believe in or practice any of the psychic arts such as astrology, tarot, palmistry, numerology, ritual, trance, magic, witchcraft, paganism, crystal healing? Am I afraid to acknowledge or reveal these

interests of mine to others? If I am skeptical of or denounce these studies, what are my opinions of the people who follow these paths?

Notes

1. Fred Gustafson, *The Black Madonna* (Boston: Sigo Press, 1990), 96.
2. Information documenting the shift from matriarchal to patriarchal cultures can be found in the following works: J. J. Bachofen, *Myth, Religion, and Mother Right* (Princeton, NJ: Princeton University Press, 1967); Riane Eisler, *The Chalice and the Blade* (San Francisco: Harper & Row, 1987); Eleanor Gadon, *The Once and Future Goddess* (San Francisco: Harper & Row, 1989); Monica Sjöö and Barbara Mor, *The Great Cosmic Mother* (San Francisco: Harper & Row, 1987); Merlin Stone, *When God Was a Woman* (New York: Harvest/Harcourt Brace Jovanovich, 1976): Barbara G. Walker, *The Woman's Encyclopedia of Myths and Secrets* (San Francisco: Harper & Row, 1983).
3. Marija Gimbutas, *The Language of the Goddess* (San Francisco: Harper & Row, 1989), xix.
4. Marija Gimbutas, *The Goddesses and Gods of Old Europe: Myth and Cult Images* (Berkeley: University of California Press, 1982).
5. Eisler, *The Chalice and the Blade*.
6. Barbara G. Walker, *The Crone* (San Francisco: Harper & Row, 1985), 85.
7. Eisler, *The Chalice and the Blade*, 44.
8. Eisler, *The Chalice and the Blade*, 45.
9. Heide Gottner-Abendroth, *Matriarchal Mythology in Former Times and Today*, translated by the author with Lise Weil (Freedom, CA: The Crossing Press, 1987), 4.
10. Gimbutas, *The Goddesses and Gods*, Preface.
11. Gottner-Abendroth, *Matriarchal Mythology*, 10.
12. Julian Jaynes, *The Origin of Consciousness in the Breakdown of the Bicameral Mind* (Boston: Houghton Mifflin, 1976).
13. Edmond Whitmont, *The Symbolic Quest* (New York: G. P. Putnam's Sons, 1969).
14. Maxine Harris, *Sisters of the Shadow* (Norman, Oklahoma and London: University of Oklahoma Press, 1991).
15. Patricia Weis, "The Dark Goddess," *Women of Power* 8, Revisioning the Dark (Winter 1988): 44.
16. Tsultrim Allione, *Places Where She Lives* (forthcoming), quoted in the *Tara Foundation Newsletter* (April 1990).
17. Sarah Scholfield, *The Four Directions* (Yachats, OR: Self-published, 1989), 9.

3

A Lunar Her/Story of the Feminine
The Birth, Death, and Rebirth of the Goddess

✦

The naked awareness of the Dark Goddess is to see
the destruction and death of the old
and joyfully embrace it as a sign of imminent renewal.

The Goddess is essentially a personification of the moon's lunar energies. In the same way that the moon cycles from new to full to dark and back again to new, the Goddess herself has life cycles of birth, growth, death, and rebirth. During the dark of the moon each month, the moon disappears from sight for several days. After this period of dormancy and darkness, at the new moon, the moon's light emerges as the slim, young crescent phase. Her light grows and culminates at the full moon, gradually decreases, vanishes altogether, only to reappear again.

In this chapter I am proposing an original theory that came to me while walking along the ocean beaches of the Oregon Coast, where I live. As I thought about the moon and the Goddess in a place where her tidal rhythms ebb and flow every day, I began to wonder if there might be any connection between the disappearance of the Goddess and the dark phase of the moon.

I began to question whether the disappearance of the Goddess during the last five thousand years of patriarchal rule might not have been due to her suppression and destruction by the patriarchy, but was in fact her natural withdrawal into the dark moon phase of her own cycle. Perhaps it was simply that the inevitable time had come in her own lunar cyclic process to let go and retreat, so that she could heal and renew herself. And now she must be reemerging at the new moon phase of her cycle with the promise and hope that accompany the rebirth of the light.

Furthermore, in the cycle of precessional world ages, humanity now stands at the cusp between the closure of the Piscean Age and the dawning of the Aquarian Age. The cuspal periods spanning world ages can last for around five hundred years, and they are times of great transformation. We are currently in the dark moon phase of the Age of Pisces; and according to some astrological historians, this time period is not only the closure of the 2,300-year Piscean Age, but also of an entire 26,000-year polar precessional cycle. If this is so, then we are in a most powerful dark moon phase in the history of humanity.

The essential mystery teachings of the Goddess concern death and rebirth. The Goddess has been reborn during a transformational dark moon phase period of the precessional age cycle in which massive death is pervading the earth. Everywhere the old is dying in order to give birth to the new. This is evidenced in the pollution and dying of the forests, soils, waters, atmosphere, wildlife, and the escalating rate of degenerative diseases in human beings. The Goddess has returned to the peoples of the earth at a critical time in a large-scale cosmic cycle in order to share her wisdom and vision of how best to pass through the dark corridor of death toward healing and renewal.

Let me again emphasize that the views and suggestions in the following discussion are speculative and based on my own musings. I offer them to you not as irrefutable fact, but rather as insights to ponder in the attempt to revision the dark. Try to intuit if these ideas strike a chord of resonance within you. Ultimately it is only within ourselves that we can ascertain the truth of a matter in the absence of incontestable, accurate, and unbiased historical documentation.

Society is currently witnessing a global women's movement and an ecological movement, which many people are referring to as the "Return of the Goddess." Since the beginnings of the Women's Liberation Movement and the rebirth of women's spirituality in the early 1970s, individuals are reawakening to the beauty, wisdom, and strength of the feminine. We are now discovering and remembering her myths, symbols, and rituals.

Along with the rebirth of the Goddess, a more knowledgeable and compassionate approach to death and dying has been entering the mainstream of consciousness due to the efforts of such healers as Elizabeth Kübler-Ross. Our sexuality is also emerging, coming out of the closet of repression. Increased information and a fuller expression of our multifaceted sexual nature are liberating men and women from societal and religious patterns of denial and guilt over this most potent life force. This movement also entails the awakening of healing energies within our planet and within individuals as we realize our interdependence with the ecology of the Earth Mother whose body supports our existence.

Confusion exists in the contemporary literature as to whether this arising of womanspirit is due to an awakening of a new feminine center of consciousness in the human psyche, or if this is an arousal of an ancient, slumbering power. In the course of the following discussion we will discover that it is both. The feminine principle has been reborn on another turning of her evolutionary spiral where currently, at the new moon phase, she has released a new vision that is now germinating in the mindstream of humanity.

In the discovery of the Goddess's ancient herstory, as we have discussed in chapter 2, many feminist scholars have concluded that the matriarchal Goddess cults and women of power were suppressed and destroyed by patriarchal god cults. According to Merlin Stone, "Archaeological, mythological, and historical evidence all reveal that female religion, far from naturally fading away, was the victim of centuries of continual persecution and suppression by advocates of the newer religions which held male deities as supreme."[1]

Overwhelming evidence all points to this conclusion, which is most obvious to the conscious mind. However, when we expand our perception to include the long-term cosmic cycles that the earth and moon partake of, the disappearance of the Goddess can be viewed within the context of the Goddess's own lunation cycle.

If we propose that the Goddess and her ancient teachings concerning death are now reemerging, then it behooves us to ask the questions, *"Who was she before she disappeared, why did she vanish, where has she been, and what is causing her to reappear?"* In this chapter we will explore the link between the symbolism of the moon's cycle and the moon's identification with the Goddess. This correspondence can serve as a model that will illumine the mystery of the cyclical birth, death, and rebirth of the Goddess. We will also discuss the demise of the Goddess against the backdrop of the changing precessional ages.

Before we proceed let us briefly mention something about the symbolic meaning of cyclical patterns. There seems to exist a correspondence, which is not necessarily causal, between transitions in cosmic planetary cycles and changes in the religious and cultural symbols that appear on earth during various times.

Psychoanalyst Carl Jung used the term "synchronicity" to shed light on the mystery of meaningful coincidence—related events that occur simultaneously across boundaries of time and space, and that have no direct cause-and-effect relationship. The attempt to understand why these kinds of correlations occur, beyond the realm of random coincidence, has intrigued people for thousands of years. While we do not know why this works as it does, synchronicity points to an underlying connection of intelligent patterning in the universe.

There exist many different recurring cycles that correlate to the unfolding of human and planetary evolution. In science we recognize the periodic changes that occur in the earth's environment due to the Ice Age cycles, sun spot cycles, eclipse and tidal cycles, and weather cycles. In the esoteric disciplines we are aware of the many different planetary and numerological cycles that form a backdrop against which to better understand the course of developments in the history of individuals and humanity.

When viewed within a cyclical context, discrete, seemingly unrelated events form patterns of meaning and are seen as being related to each other. Each cycle has its own timing of initiation, culmination, and completion that brings endings, change, and new beginnings. While each cycle has its own rhythm and duration, the various cycles overlap one another. Sometimes two or more cycles peak at the same time during critical points in their individual unfoldment. This kind of juxtaposition often brings significant changes that are even more powerful than usual. This is what transpired in the time period around the disappearance of the Goddess and what is occurring now, at the end of the twentieth century.

The Lunation Cycle

All life forms have cycles of birth, growth, death, and renewal that are mirrored in the progressive phases of the moon's cycle. Many cultures, in an attempt to conceptualize the wholistic meaning of the moon's cycle, have subdivided it in terms of three phases and four quarters. The threefold division, based on the triangle (which is a feminine polarity image), consists of three phases: the waxing new moon of increasing light, the full moon that is totally illuminated, and the dark waning moon of decreasing light. The fourfold division, derived from the square or cross (which is a masculine polarity

Revisioning the Dark: A Lunar Her/Story of the Feminine

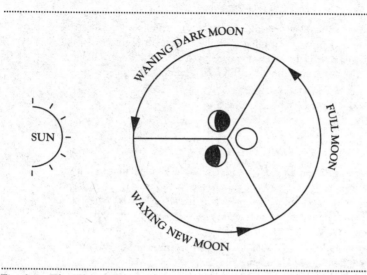

Fig. 3.1   The Three Phases of the Moon

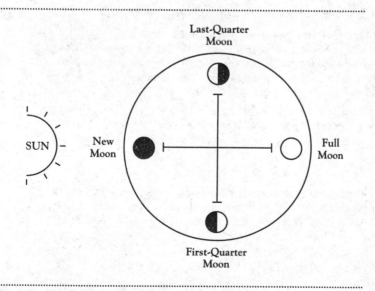

Fig. 3.2   The Four Quarters of the Moon

The Eight Lunation Phases

Dark Dawning

I. At the **New Phase,** the flow of solar-lunar energy emerges, initiates and projects the seed impulse in an instinctive and subjective manner that will fulfill and complete a purpose as the remaining cycle unfolds. In the absence of light, the vision is felt, not seen. The symbolic seed germinates underground.

- Moon rises at dawn, sets at sunset
- Moon is 0–45 degrees ahead of the Sun
- Up to 3½ days after official New Moon

Light Quickening

II. At the **Crescent Phase,** the life impulse encounters a challenge as it must struggle away from the inertia of the past cycle, mobilizing its energy and resources and moving forward. As the light is stirring, first glimpses of the vision may be perceived. The symbolic seed breaks out of its seed casing and pushes its first shoots above ground.

- Moon rises mid-morning, sets after sunset in the western sky
- Moon is 45–90 degrees ahead of the Sun
- Between 3½ and 7 days after New Moon

Light and Dark in Balance, Light Ascending

III. At the **First-Quarter Phase,** the life force must firmly establish itself in its environment and take direct action to build the organic structure that is to become the vehicle for the life purpose. With the light gaining, the structural outline of what is to be comes into form. The symbolic seed establishes its root and stem structure.

- Moon rises at noon, sets at midnight
- Moon is 90–135 degrees ahead of the Sun
- Between 7–10½ days after New Moon

Light Dominant

IV. The **Gibbous Phase** necessitates analyzing whatever was developed in the previous phase, and perfecting the form so that it can operate efficiently and effectively. As the light becomes dominant, there is a questing for revelation. The symbolic seed buds.

- Moon rises at mid-afternoon, sets around 3 A.M.
- Moon is 135–180 degrees ahead of the Sun
- Between 10½ and 14 days after New Moon

Light Peaks

V. The **Full Phase** is the flowering of the cycle when the meaning of the life purpose is revealed and must be infused into the structure built during the waxing half of the process. If the form is inadequate to contain the meaning, or the meaning is not worthy of the form, there can occur a breakdown, abortion, or dissolution of the life impulse at this point. This is the peak of the light and total illumination of the vision is the promise of this phase. The symbolic seed flowers.

- Moon rises at sunset, sets at dawn
- Moon is 180–135 degrees behind the Sun
- 15 days after New Moon

First Stirring of Dark

VI. The **Disseminating Phase** corresponds to the fruition of the cycle. The seed germinated at the New Moon has now become what it was meant to be. The life impulse must fulfill its purpose by distributing the energy and disseminating the meaning. With the first stirrings of darkness, there becomes an urgency to live out and share the value of the meaning. The symbolic seed fruits.

- Moon rises at mid-evening, sets at mid-morning
- Moon is 135–90 degrees behind the Sun
- Between 3½–7 days after Full Moon

Light and Dark in Balance, Dark Gaining

VII. At the **Last-Quarter Phase,** the life impulse has completed its mission and now begins to reorient to a dimly intuited future. Rebellion against old patterns and breakdown of old useless forms characterizes an inner revolt and crisis in consciousness. The dark becomes increasingly dominant as the life force turns away, diminishes, and composts the old. The symbolic seed withers on the vine and decomposes.

- Moon rises at midnight and sets at noon
- Moon is 90–45 degrees behind the Sun
- Between 7–10½ days after Full Moon

Depth of Dark

VIII. At the **Balsamic Phase,** the life impulse distills and concentrates the wisdom of the entire cycle into a capsule of seed ideas for future visions. During the dark of the moon, the life force transforms the past into a mutation of the future and makes a commitment to seeding new concepts within old structures. The symbolic seed once again turns back into itself.

- Moon rises at 3 A.M. and sets at mid-afternoon
- Moon is 45–0 degrees behind the Sun
- Between 10½ days after Full Moon up until the next New Moon

symbol), yields the first-quarter moon, the full moon, the last-quarter moon, and the new moon, which is back-to-back with the dark moon.

When the fourfold division of the moon's monthly cycle around the earth is again quartered, it yields eight distinct lunar phases. They are named the new, crescent, first quarter, gibbous, full, disseminating, last quarter, and balsamic. Each lunation phase represents a certain quality and kind of energy that is utilized at the various stages in the growth and development of any organic form. When astrologer Dane Rudhyar rediscovered the ancient lunation cycle, he reinterpreted these eight phases in the light of personality functions and types using the metaphor of the growth of a plant to illustrate the process.[2]

Let us now briefly review the successive stages of the cyclical unfolding of any life form as depicted in the symbolism of the moon's eightfold phase lunation cycle (shown in The Eight Lunation Phases

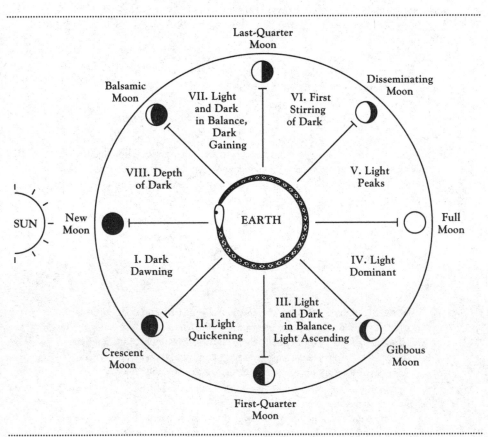

Fig. 3.3   The Eightfold Division of the Moon's Cycle

table). The process begins at the new moon phase when a seed, containing a new vision infused with an intention, germinates in the darkness. With the light of the waxing crescent phase, the first tender shoots of this vision have struggled to push themselves above the ground. During the first-quarter phase the life force of this vision takes root by establishing itself; its stem and leaf structure give shape to a strong, definite form.

The waxing gibbous phase corresponds to the development of the buds with the promise and expectation of the flower that blooms during the full moon phase. Now, halfway around the lunar cycle at the full moon, the vision is fully illuminated and infused with meaning and content. The waning gibbous phase, also known as disseminating, corresponds to the fruition of the cycle, when the vision is acted on and lived out through the lives of humanity, thereby fulfilling its purpose.

The last-quarter phase refers to reaping the harvest of the crop, when we ingest and assimilate what we have realized throughout the cycle. The essence of the vision is then distilled into a seed capsule that is buried underground during the final dark or balsamic phase of the cycle, where it is nourished and prepared for rebirth. This germinal idea is subsequently released with the initiation of a new cycle.

This eightfold division of the lunar cycle correlates to the solar symbolism of the European pagan Wheel of the Year. The Wheel of the Year, upon which the ancient agricultural mysteries were based, is derived from the two solstices, two equinoxes, and four cross-quarter days. These seasonal holidays are:
- Yule, at the Winter Solstice (December 20–23)
- Candlemas (February 2)
- the Spring Equinox (March 20–23)
- Beltane (May 1)
- the Summer Solstice, also known as Midsummer's Night (June 20–23)
- Lammas (August 1)
- the Fall Equinox (September 20–23)
- Hallowmas (October 31).

This cycle of the sun's increasing and decreasing light from the sun's apparent annual motion north and south of the equator indicates the rhythm of the seasons, the ebb and flow of nature. The ancients celebrated these eight holy days, believing them to be times of power when there existed a crack or opening between worlds. At these times the sacred energy of the cosmos could fully enter into the earth plane.

When the rhythm of the lunation cycle, with reference to the moon as a feminine being, is reflected in the Wheel of the Year, the Goddess is annually reborn at the Winter Solstice (new moon). She is a fragile, new hope at Candlemas (crescent); and a child at the spring equinox (first quarter). The maiden discovers her sexuality at Beltane (gibbous); and becomes the mother of all life at the Summer Solstice (full moon). At Lammas (disseminating moon) she ripens into the maturing matron; reaches menopause at the Fall Equinox (last quarter); and completes her life cycle as the ancient crone preparing for death at Hallowmas (dark balsamic moon).[3]

The story that the moon tells is of birth, growth, fullness, decay, disappearance, with rebirth and growth again. In every cycle there is a naturally occurring dark phase when the life force seems to disappear for a period of time. This recessive part of the cycle occurs under the cover of darkness, where it is invisible to the conscious, waking

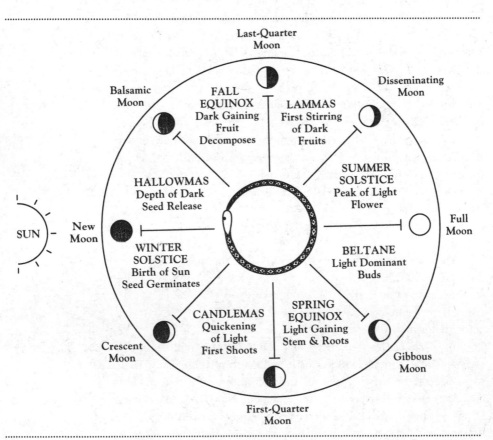

Fig. 3.4 The Lunation Phases and the Wheel of the Year

eye. Here is where life cleanses, revitalizes, and transforms itself in its evolutionary development, spiraling toward attunement with its essential nature.

If the Goddess is true to her own essential nature, she will resonate in attunement to the moon's rhythms of ebb and flow, and like the moon, will periodically withdraw into the dark phase of her cycle. Here she performs her mysteries of renewal. *If we look closely at the rhythm of the moon's cycle, we may perceive that the development and flowering of the Goddess, her subsequent disappearance, and her current reemergence may be due to her natural cycle of waxing and waning phases.*

The Birth and Growth of the Goddess

The Moon Goddess is an embodiment of the continually self-renewing energy symbolized in the lunation cycle and celebrated in the Wheel of the Year. Resonating to the cyclical rhythm of increasing and decreasing light, the Goddess herself has cycles of increase and decrease that transpire over generations of time in the cultural evolution of humanity.

We will now look again at the historical rise and fall of the Goddess culture and religion. Our query this time around the circle is to see if we can discover any correspondences between the life cycle of an evolving feminine principle and the symbolic meaning of the successive phases of the lunation cycle.

We know that the Goddess culture began to decline around 3000 BCE. Our fairy tales tell us that Snow White and Sleeping Beauty were poisoned by the Wicked Stepmother and Bad Fairy, and then fell into long swoons encased in a deathlike sleep. These stories carry the mythic image of the Goddess and the feminine, who also have been in a deep slumber. The mythological tales repeatedly tell us of the moon goddesses who periodically disappeared to bathe in the sacred springs in order to renew their virginity and be born anew. We now see, as we approach the year 2000, that the Goddess is definitely reborn. We can see this evidence in the current proliferation of her circles, stories, chants, images, and rituals.

During the period of her dormancy, the images and symbols of the Goddess have been virtually absent from culture, except those occasional springs of her waters bubbling up for short periods of time during various periods and places. While five millennia may seem to be a long time, one which in fact encompasses all of written history, it is a relatively short span in terms of human development (2.5 million years) and the geological formation of our planet (6 billion years).

We can estimate that the feminine energies virtually disappeared from culture for about five thousand years. If we place this period of dormancy within the context of the lunation cycle, this would correspond to a five thousand year (3000 BCE–2000 CE) dark phase of a historical cycle. If the dark balsamic phase comprises one-eighth of the lunation cycle, then the entire previous lunar life cycle that relates to the Goddess must be (8 × 5000) or 40,000 years in duration.

According to our hypothesis, an evolving feminine principle embodied in the symbolism of the Moon Goddess also has cycles of birth, growth, death, and renewal. The duration of the previous cycle of her development lasted 40,000 years. If this is the case, then we can propose that in about 38,000 BCE a new vision and aspiration of the feminine principle was birthed and released at the beginning new moon phase of one of her life cycles.

We will now explore this long-term evolution of a feminine principle. First, we will present an overview of the Upper Paleolithic era to show the major themes in the birth and development of the Goddess culture. Second, we will delve more deeply into the specific sub-ages that correspond to the phases of the lunation cycle. Let us now superimpose our theoretical model of the lunation cycle of the Goddess over the timetable of distinct archaeological periods of the prehistoric ages.

Figure 3.6 depicts the dates and names, assigned by paleo-anthropologists, for the divisions of the Upper Paleolithic and its

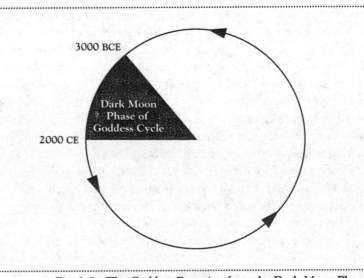

Fig. 3.5 **The Goddess Emerging from the Dark Moon Phase**

sub-ages in Europe. These divisions are based on the different kinds of artifacts found that were a product of various races, and of peoples who had different tools, languages, stories, and economics.[4] (There also exist variations in this dating system, which are used by other paleo-anthropologists.)[5] These divisions are circumscribed around

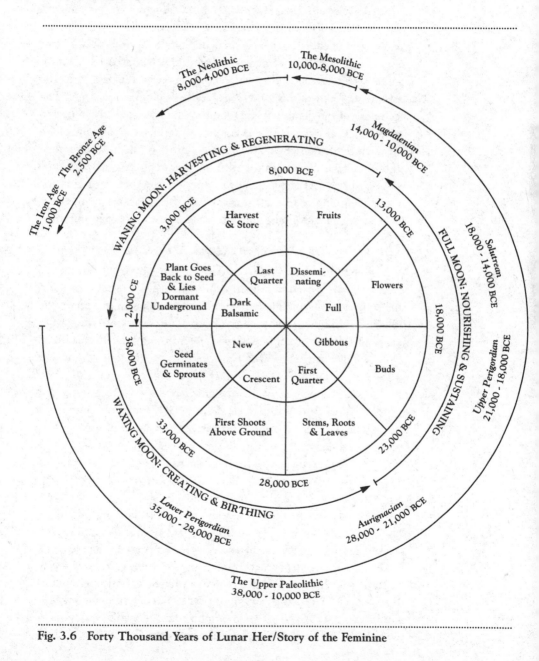

Fig. 3.6 Forty Thousand Years of Lunar Her/Story of the Feminine

the time scale for the eight lunation phases of a 40,000-year Goddess cycle that began in 38,000 BCE.

Referring to Figure 3.6, we find that 38,000 BCE, the proposed beginning of the Goddess's life cycle at the new moon phase, is also the date that scholars define as the beginning of the Upper Paleolithic. At this time *Homo sapiens*, anatomically modern people with vastly enhanced intellectual powers from whom all present-day humanity is descended, first appeared in Europe around 40,000 years ago. The Upper Paleolithic lasted until the Neolithic Revolution beginning around 8000 BCE, which corresponds to the date when the last-quarter phase of this 40,000-year cycle would have occurred. The beginning of the demise of the Goddess cultures is clearly indicated by 3000 BCE, and this period is analogous to the dark balsamic phase of the cycle. And circa CE 2000, which currently heralds the return of the Goddess, aligns with the next new moon phase signifying some kind of rebirth. Let us see if we can discover any themes originating at the beginning of this cycle that, over the duration of the entire cycle, grew to fruition and impacted the course of human culture.

Overview of the Upper Paleolithic

According to Randall White, the dawn of the Upper Paleolithic was a revolutionary period in human achievement, when there was a virtual explosion of symbolic behavior.[6] "There emerged in Europe the fully modern human, and with the birth of our own kind, came what has been called a creative explosion—an outburst of inventiveness and sensibility entirely without previous parallel in the long history of the human family."[7]

Three developments of major significance marked the transition into the Upper Paleolithic. First, there suddenly appeared in Europe a new species, *Homo sapiens*, who carried new kinds of tools. Their emergence coincided with the disappearance of the previous inhabitants, the Neanderthals, whose ancestors had populated the world for the previous half million years. Second, it was these new peoples who first demonstrated a skill in making images and symbols, and this capacity blossomed into astonishing artistic accomplishments. Third, archaeological evidence from the art and artifacts these peoples created and engraved affirms that they worshiped a female deity.

The great advances in technology and culture that marked the Upper Paleolithic stand in sharp contrast to the very slow growth in the ages that preceded this period. Fossil evidence has now made it quite clear that the genus *Homo* originated from apelike ancestors in sub-Saharan Africa around 2.5 million years ago. For nearly 1 million years human evolution was infinitesimally slow. Then, about 1.6 million years ago, early hominids became *Homo erectus*. Humankind was still primitive, but they tamed fire and developed more advanced hunting and gathering techniques. About 1 million–700,000 years ago, *Homo erectus* radiated out of Africa into the Near East, Europe, Asia, and Indonesia. In Eurasia, *Homo erectus* evolved into Neanderthal around 125,000 years ago.

While the Neanderthals were skilled hunters and able to survive the hazardous conditions of the Ice Age, they made little or no attempt to modify the world in which they lived. Their technology, which they inherited from *Homo erectus* half a million years before, was limited to slow changes in basic tools. They lacked the ability to conceptualize visually and were probably unable to communicate with fully articulate speech. However, the nature of Neanderthal was not that of a brute; evidence does indicate that they were a compassionate people who cared for their ill and buried their dead.

With the sudden appearance of *Homo sapiens* in Europe, the character of the human population radically changed. These new people were anatomically similar to modern populations and were the first ancestors of our modern lineage. They were intelligent, technologically skilled, and culturally sophisticated. There exists much controversy surrounding their origin and whether they evolved in one place or in many areas.

One prevalent view among paleo-anthropologists maintains that all modern human populations can trace their origins to 1 million years ago when our hominid ancestor *Homo erectus* first left Africa and traveled to other parts of the world. Called the Candelabra hypothesis, this theory suggests that in each place *Homo erectus* gradually became fully modern *Homo sapiens*, developing independently in several different regions more or less simultaneously. However, many other scholars disagree, and proponents of what is called the Noah's Ark theory argue that our immediate ancestors evolved only in Africa and radiated out from there to other parts of the world. According to this view, the anatomically modern people who appeared in Europe at the dawn of the Upper Paleolithic were not descended from Neanderthals, nor did they evolve in Europe. Anthropologist Brian Fagan believes that the European Neanderthals were not in the direct line of evolution to modern humans. In his view, they became extinct, overtaken by a new, rapidly developing Stone Age world.[8]

Then, in 1987, a controversial new theory concerning our origins was proposed by a team of biochemists in Berkeley, California. Based on the rate of genetic mutation in the mitochondria of DNA, the new theory concluded that every person on earth today can trace back their ancestry to a single woman, quickly dubbed Eve, who lived in Africa some 200,000 years ago. Therefore, according to the Eve hypothesis, our direct ancestors, who emerged in Europe at the beginning of the Upper Paleolithic, were the descendants of this one African female, the mother of us all—the most recent common ancestor for all present-day humanity.[9]

These new people became more and more abundant over the next few centuries, and the Neanderthal people disappeared entirely. What separates our lineage from Neanderthal is our capacity for creativity and inventiveness. According to Randall White, "From these peoples, we have inherited the capability to speak and comprehend symbolically based language, the capacity to monitor and adjust behavior according to a framework of shared norms and values, the ability to imagine things that have never been observed, and the ability to externalize physical skills in the form of tools."[10]

The last several glaciations took place during the Upper Paleolithic. Over the course of this period the human population expanded into most of the world's habitable areas, including what is now North and South America and Australia. These peoples developed a wide range of technological innovations. Many important inventions appeared at this time, including needle and thread, skin clothing, hafted stone and bone tools, the harpoon, spear thrower, and fishing equipment. Archaeological diggings show, at least from 27,000 BCE, the existence of human dwellings consisting of subterranean pit houses and huts made from skins, mammoth bones, wood, clay, and stone as shelter against wind and snow.

Societies became reorganized, with larger more complex groups who traveled less frequently and for shorter distances. There were changes in the kinds of food people ate and in the ways they obtained their food. And of prime importance and interest is the sudden and widespread appearance of figurines, paintings, sculptures, carvings, musical instruments such as bone whistle and flute, and other artifacts that reflect a creative development of art, dance, ceremony, and ritual.[11]

While no written records of these Ice Age peoples exist, evidence of their beliefs remains as the artifacts found in the ruins of their dwelling sites across Eurasia from the Pyrenees in Western Europe to Lake Baikal in Siberia. Additional information about their values is contained in the rock sculptures and massive paintings discovered on the walls of their caves hidden in the forested, mountainous regions of northeastern Spain, southwestern France, and in southern Germany and Czechoslovakia.[12]

The archaeological evidence indicates that the peoples who suddenly emerged at the beginning of the Upper Paleolithic displayed a reverence for the feminine. Hundreds of small sculpted, carved, and engraved female images and amulets, dating to at least 25,000 BCE, have been uncovered at sites all across Eurasia. These statuettes, which have come to be known as Venus figures, emphasize the parts of the female body associated with sexuality and fertility. They portray images of faceless, full-breasted, and lush-bodied goddess/women.

In addition thousands of breast, vulva, and buttocks amulets that date back to an even earlier time have been found in the occupational layers of the prehistoric ages. The research of Marija Gimbutas shows how these artifacts, as a whole, represent women's power as life-giving, fertility-giving, and birth-giving. The continuity and proliferation of these images prove the persistence of Goddess worship for nearly 30,000 years.[13]

According to our model of the Goddess's lunation cycle, at the beginning of the Upper Paleolithic the evolving feminine principle gave birth to a vision that would unfold over the course of her 40,000-year life cycle. This vision was to be realized and expressed through the development of *Homo sapiens* who appeared in Europe at this time. The kernel of this seed vision was a reverence for the mystery of the life-giving powers of the universe, and an intention to decipher the secrets of how it is that life is created, sustained, and regenerated. This veneration for life included not only humans but also plants, animals, the earth upon which they all resided, and the heavens, which linked them to the universe.

This reverence for the life force carried over into a reverence for women. While there is evidence that early peoples understood men's role in procreation, it was the changes in the female body—which appeared to create and nurture life—that exemplified the mystery. The feminine was thus honored for her seemingly miraculous ability not only to birth new life from her vulva, but also to feed and nourish it with milk produced in her breasts. Furthermore, women could bleed without being wounded, heal themselves at every moon, and their menstrual blood contained the power to regenerate themselves and others.

Along with the mysteries of birth and life that were held in awe by our early ancestors, those of death and resurrection were venerated. Their funerary customs pointed to their belief in an afterlife. They buried their dead ceremonially, often under the floor of their living spaces, surrounded the bodies with vagina-shaped cowrie shells, and adorned them with red ocher to symbolize the life-affirming qualities of blood. In this way Paleolithic people hoped they could draw the life force back into the deceased and bring them to rebirth.

The body of the earth was also perceived as feminine, with paired sets of mountains as her breasts, the valleys as her vulva, the caves as her vagina, and the rivers as courseways carrying her blood. The original shrines were built at these sacred sites that paid homage to the sexual life-sustaining powers of the Earth Mother. And the moon who circled in the heavens, marking the rhythm of women's menstrual cycles, was worshiped as the Goddess displaying the divine aspects of the feminine.

For prehistoric peoples the ability to secure a stable food supply determined whether or not life could survive. And so part of the quest of the evolving feminine principle was the search for the means by which to keep the life force alive and continuous. The female body contained the secret to produce the food for the infant child; what was the key to unlock the mystery of the earth's body to produce the same relatively predictable, secure source of food in order to sustain her adult human children? The technological advances in the first half of the Paleolithic were focused on inventing and refining tools to better hunt, skin, and prepare the animals, their primary food source.

The Fruition and Harvest of the Evolving Goddess: The Discovery of Agriculture The fruition phase of the Goddess's lunation cycle occurred around 11,000 BCE. At this time it was women who were said to have discovered the secret of agriculture and the invention of cooking, transforming the seed to grain and then into bread.[14] The capacity to produce food rather than simply to hunt and gather it was the apex of the Goddess's cycle. This achievement led to a harvest period during the Neolithic era, one in which civilization could be created. This, then, was the climax and major contribution of the Goddess culture to the evolution of humanity—agriculture, which erected a foundation upon which future civilizations could be built.

The vision that is recorded in the art and ceremonies of the Upper Paleolithic people is that of a reverence for creation of life embodied in the sacred nature of the earth, the moon, and the feminine. Their cyclical understanding of reality also included the mystery of death and the promise of renewal, where the decaying compost provided the fertile soil in which the dormant life force can be regenerated.

These beliefs became the foundation for the worship of the Great Goddess during Neolithic times. The Neolithic period, when the first settled villages that grew into thriving, prosperous cultures were developed, corresponds to the harvest phase of the Goddess's lunation cycle. The major themes of the all-powerful Neolithic Triple Goddess can be traced back to the earliest bone, ivory, and stone sculpted images and symbols of the feminine, which first appeared 35,000 years ago at the dawn of the Upper Paleolithic.[15]

The Goddess's Lunation Cycle

Now that we have taken an overview from the new to last-quarter phases of the Goddess's lunation cycle, we can delve more deeply into each specific sub-age. We will see how the progressive stages of the development of Upper Paleolithic peoples mirrored the cycle of unfolding lunar phases.

New and Crescent Phases: The Lower Perigordian Referring to Figure 3.6, we can see that the first sub-age of the Upper Paleolithic, the Lower Perigordian (35,000–28,000 BCE), approximates the first two phases of the lunation cycle. It corresponds to the new and crescent phases, when the new life vision bursts forth from its seed capsule and emerges above ground. The first representatives of the new species were called Combe Capelle, and they resembled the smaller-boned races who inhabit today's Mediterranean world. This sub-age is characterized by the invention of the flint blade and other specific tools, as well as the earliest musical instruments, such as the flute. The oldest art objects on earth have been uncovered at the site dwellings from this period. They include dozens of engraved and sculpted images of female breasts, vulvas, buttocks, and small goddess figurines.

One of the earliest of these figures, the "Venus of Willendorf," dating to 33,000 BCE, was discovered in Austria. She is naked, with pendulous breasts and a swollen belly, and is still marked with traces of red ocher symbolizing the life-giving or menstrual blood. In Paleolithic art the sexuality portrayed in the imagery is not meant for erotic or obscene purposes, but rather it is a symbol for the generative life force. At this point in the unfolding of the seed vision, the great Mother Goddess and her earthly representatives, the women, were understood to be the very source of this life force.

The First-Quarter and Gibbous Phases: The Aurignacian and Upper Perigordian In our analogy, by the first-quarter phase of cyclical process the vision takes firm root, anchoring its life force. The first-quarter phase of the Goddess's lunation cycle would have begun around 28,000 BCE. This, in fact, is the date given by scholars of prehistory to the second major sub-age of the Upper Paleolithic, the Aurignacian period (28,000–21,000 BCE), and the third sub-age, the Upper Perigordian (21,000–18,000 BCE), which span the next two lunar phases, the first quarter and waxing gibbous. The Cro-Magnon people, tall, large-boned, powerful, and similar to modern northern Europeans, became predominant during this time period. They developed the first straight-backed knife and modified the flint blade into a beveled chisel, which helped to create a whole new series of tools made from animal bone and horn.

The archaeological finds from this period indicate the presence of many pieces of notched, scratched, and decorated bone, horn, ivory, and stone. Alexander Marshack believes that these marks are notational and represent time-factoring devices. In his exhaustive research Marshack explores the possibility that these incised objects served to track time by means of a lunar phase calendar. He further speculates that they also indicate a framework for the stories and mythologies of their rituals, which were based on lunar and seasonal cycles.[16]

One bas-relief sculpture from the Aurignacian sub-age is the "Earth Mother of Laussel" (ca. 25,000 BCE), which is carved on a limestone slab on the entrance to a rock shelter in Dordogne, France. She has a swollen belly, indicating that she is pregnant; her left hand points to her vulva, and in her right hand she holds a notched bison horn, which may represent the crescent moon symbolic of new life. The thirteen lines incised in the horn may mark the thirteen months of the lunar calendar, and also may be a lunar pregnancy record showing that conception takes place on the fourteenth day after a woman's moon time.

Transition from Waxing to Waning During the waxing first half of the lunation cycle, which unfolds from the new moon to the full moon, the seed that is released as an idea develops its structural form. Something spontaneously grows and develops because the organic need exists for what the seed can potentially become. The proliferation of female images from Aurignacian-Perigordian peoples demonstrates their growing awareness of how new life emerges from the female body, and an increasing skill in expressing their knowledge in artistic symbolic images. The birthing, nurturing, and renewing qualities inherent in the evolving feminine principle were celebrated and exalted.

During the waning second half of the lunation cycle, which spans from the full moon back to the dark moon, the meaning is infused into the form and the vision becomes actualized. The last two sub-ages of the Upper Paleolithic, the Solutrean (18,000–14,000 BCE) and the Magdalenian (14,000–10,000 BCE), approximate the time scale for the full and disseminating (waning gibbous) lunar phases. These phases mirror the stages when the seed vision flowers and fruits. The Magdalenian culture has been described by archaeologists as the Golden Age of the Paleolithic, a "peak of true culture in the history of humanity."[17] (In alternate dating systems, the Magdalenian period began around 18,000 BCE.)

The Full Moon and Disseminating Phases: The Solutrean and the Magdalenian   The climate of the Solutrean culture was intensely cold, and the settled life of the previous inhabitants in the warmer conditions of the Aurignacian-Perigordian age gave way to nomadic hunters who followed the migrating herds. There is some indication that this period was dominated by northern horse hunters who invaded Europe along the open grasslands, and that these peoples were a warlike race. This time is noted for the finest examples of flint workmanship of the Paleolithic of western Europe, such as the laurel leafed points.

At the full moon Solutrean period, the lunation phase analogy initially becomes perplexing because there exists little evidence of goddess figurines dating to this time. In fact, examples of all Solutrean art are rare; they consist primarily of bas-reliefs and incised stone slabs. However, what does begin to flourish is the deep cave paintings that portray horned and hoofed animals such as the bison, bull, and buffalo. The various animals represent the masculine principle of vitality, and they were depicted with a beauty of form and a grace of flowing movement. Recent research proposes that some of the animals portrayed in the cave paintings were pregnant, and the notched calendar bones record the pregnancy cycles of these large animals.

In cyclic process the full moon phase corresponds to union with the other. In women's menstrual cycles it is analogous to ovulation, when the optimal conditions exist for fertilization. In a similar fashion it is necessary to pollinate the blooming flower in order for it to bear fruit. I offer the conjecture that the evolving feminine principle in the mindstream of Aurignacian-Perigordian peoples, who had exalted the symbols of female sexuality in the creation of thousands of goddess figurines, was now, at the full moon Solutrean stage, fertilized and impregnated by a masculine principle depicted by the animal symbolism of the cave art. Among the earliest images are those of pregnant women dancing with the animals, some of which are also pregnant. Engraved upon a small piece of reindeer bone is a scene portraying the hind legs and phallus of a reindeer standing over a naked, pregnant woman lying on her back.

The final culture of the Upper Paleolithic, the Magdalenian, corresponds to the fruiting phase of the lunation cycle. The Magdalenian is noted as a golden age, and the richness and diversity of remarkable art forms attest to this pinnacle in the development of prehistoric art. The most outstanding feature of the Magdalenians was the magnificent cave art in which the great animals—the bison, horse, reindeer, mammoth, musk ox, ibex, and stag—were exalted in paintings, engravings, and sculptures.

Scholars have yet to fully penetrate the meaning and purpose of the cave art, but it is speculated that the caves were their religious temples, not their living sites. Many of the paintings are executed in remote, almost inaccessible spots such as rock ledges and hidden recesses in the inner sanctuaries. Only toward the end of this period did the cave art emerge toward the outer entrances and in rock shelters, places illuminated by the daylight.

Andre Leroi-Gourhan, a leading authority of the cave art and symbols of Ice Age Europe, proposes that the cave paintings were organized according to some preconceived plan. They conveyed beliefs and told a story whose significance was clear to both the creators and viewers of the art. He further suggests that there existed an underlying sexual structure that divided the various signs and animals into male and female groups. The male symbols included the barbs, short strokes, and dots, and the horse, ibex, stag, and reindeer; the female symbols included the triangle, rectangle, and oval as vulvas, and the bison, oxen, and mammoth.

Certain animals/signs were consistently associated with other animals/signs. For example, the horse was almost always paired with the bison. The male signs and animals appear at the entrances, in the passageways, and in the deep recesses of the caves, while the male/female pairs dominate the great central chambers. Leroi-Gourham proposes that this structure indicates that Magdalenian people held a philosophic and religious view of the world as divided into two opposing and complementary principles that became the foundation for many of the other great religions based on similar principles of duality.[18]

In the cosmology of the earth as sacred living mother, the caves were seen as her vagina, which linked the inner womb to the outer world. They were believed to be the passageways between the realm of the dead and unborn and that of the living. Deep within their recesses, the union of the feminine egg and masculine sperm were fused and life was conceived. Therefore the caves were the perfect sites for the initiation rites that revealed the great secrets of birth and death.

The abstract signs and symbols that accompany the cave art are also believed by some scholars to be inscriptions of early written language, implying that the Magdalenians were a literate people.[19] During the middle period a rich and spectacular body of smaller portable objects and elaborate, specialized bone and antler tools have been uncovered. Eighty percent of all known Upper Paleolithic art dates to the Magdalenian period, and many female images reemerge during this time.

Many scholars of prehistory, conceptualizing out of the patriarchal mindset, see prehistoric peoples as aggressive, primitive, and barbaric, giving them labels such as "man the hunter," "man the tool-maker," and the "killer ape." It is these historians who also dismiss Paleolithic art as totemism and sympathetic magic. They suggest that the female figurines and amulets were simply erotic-pornographic fetishes of a fertility cult, and that the animal paintings in the caves were hunting aids. These views are unrealistic, as the animals are portrayed in peaceful attitudes with no signs of wounds or deadly weapons. The notchings on bone and ivory that have previously been described as spears, harpoons, and barbed arrows are now understood to be plants, not weapons.[20]

Recent archaeological discoveries, when viewed from a feminine, cyclical perspective, suggest the Venus figures and cave paintings of the Upper Paleolithic peoples were part of their sacred art. These images played an intrinsic role in their rituals and ceremonies that honored the feminine and the masculine principles as manifested in humanity, the earth, the animals and plants, the sun and moon, and all of sentient life that participated in the great mystery.

By the end of the Upper Paleolithic, the Old Stone Age, humanity had invented most of its fundamental tools; they had learned to provide shelter and warm clothing, had finely wrought weapons, and were well equipped to hunt the most powerful animals. In their cosmology the key symbols that carry the underlying meaning of the Goddess religion were already articulated in the Ice Age art and ritual. The framework of the myth of the sacred female that evolves into the Great Goddess of Neolithic culture was already in place.[21]

Transition: The Mesolithic A short transitional period, called the Mesolithic (10,000–8000 BCE), bridged the Old (Paleolithic) and New (Neolithic) Stone Ages. The skills, lore, and tradition brought

brought out by the Upper Paleolithic (which included the mating, migrating, calving, sprouting, and fruiting lore), as well as the notational, storytelling, and symbol use, would develop dramatically in a few thousand years into true writing, true astronomy, true husbandry, true agriculture, true arithmetic, and into highly organized comparative religion and myth.[22] It was during this transitional period that the lunation cycle of the Goddess reached its apex and the seed bore its fruit.

At the end of the last Ice Age, about 10,000 BCE, the glaciers retreated and the climate warmed up. The herds of horses and reindeer followed the ice northward, and many Magdalenians followed them. There is some speculation that it was these Magdalenian peoples continuing their culture in the colder climates who were the ancestors of the "hordes from the north" leading the patriarchal invasions into Southern Europe, Asia Minor, and India in the third and fourth millenniums BCE. By the tenth millennium BCE, the culture of the Magdalenians in Europe had declined. Those who remained behind became known by other names, and these cultures ushered in the Mesolithic—the Middle Stone Age, which spanned the next two millennia (10,000–8000 BCE). The milder and moister weather allowed abundant flora and fauna to develop in the woods and waters, and this new environment set the stage for radical changes in the lifestyle of humanity.

Surrounded with a larger and more easily accessible food supply, Mesolithic peoples made tremendous improvements in hunting and food-gathering techniques. They established the first year-round settlements; and they learned to dry the surplus fish and meat and to store other foods, such as seeds, nuts, berries, and fruits, that appeared seasonally in certain locations.

At this point, as Mesolithic people became increasingly involved in the vegetative cycle of wild foods, their understanding grew. It was then a simple leap to the most decisive achievement in human history—the discovery of agriculture. They realized that they could plant the seed of the wild grasses and cultivate that seed to a plant, which they could then harvest and store. There are suggestions of simple agriculture that began to be practiced in primitive forms. At one early cave site of this era, archaeologists found the remains of 10,000 miniature knives covered with grass resin that were used for cutting the wild grasses. Mortars and pestles used for grinding the grain were discovered nearby, as well as the charred remains of fires in which bread was baked.[23]

The discovery of agriculture is the fruit of the seed vision that was germinated at the beginning of the Upper Paleolithic. Twenty-eight thousand years after the evolving feminine principle initiated a new cycle of growth, the reverence for the birth-giving and life-sustaining powers of the Great Goddess yielded the secret of a stable and predictable food source from the body of the Earth Mother herself.

The Last-Quarter Phase: The Neolithic Revolution The last-quarter phase of cyclical process corresponds to reaping the harvest. In the Goddess's lunation cycle it dates to 8000 BCE. This is the time period that historians cite as the beginnings of the Neolithic, the New Stone Age. The Neolithic cultures developed and refined the art of agriculture, and they also began to domesticate farm animals. Freed from the unpredictable, seminomadic existence of having to hunt and gather food in order to survive, Neolithic peoples were able to remain fixed in one location and to produce and store their food. A more settled life and stable food supply provided people with the leisure time to engage in other activities—religion, politics, trade, science, and the arts; in short, to create civilization. This fateful moment in the history of humanity is known as the Neolithic Revolution.

Riane Eisler writes that all the places where the first great breakthroughs in material and social technology were made had one thing in common: the worship of the Goddess.[24] However, the Goddess and women played a far greater role than just mother and food source. Early descriptions of goddesses ranging from Celtic Britain to Greece, Rome, the Near East, and India describe them as the bringers of civilization.

Scholars of prehistory (or her/story) are now beginning to credit women with the discovery of agriculture and the invention of cooking. It was women who planted the seed; tended, harvested, husked, and ground the grain; and baked it into bread. Seeds from many different plants were cultivated; and it was women who learned to spin the fibers from flax and cotton, incorporating hair and wool from their farm animals, and weaving the threads into cloth. They also learned to make pottery durable by firing it in kilns.

Weaving and pottery are considered gifts of the Goddess, and became the vehicles for the development of new artistic forms. Workshops that include looms and kilns have been discovered in shrines to the Goddess. The temples of the Goddess were the original storage bins for the grain and honey, the bounty of the Earth Mothers' offerings to humanity. The priestesses of these temples developed a system of notation and mathematics for recording the distribution of foodstuffs to the members of the community. And as they settled disputes, the priestesses of the Goddess also laid the foundations for law and justice.

In the turning of the Goddess's lunation cycle, we can see that this Neolithic Goddess that flourished during the revolutionary changes heralded by the discovery of agriculture was the culmination of a growing awareness imaged in the earliest female figurines of the Paleolithic art. Working from a different contextual system, Alexander Marshack reaches a similar conclusion. He asks, "Could it be that the origins of time factored multi-storied agricultural 'mother goddess' appear in the Upper Paleolithic, thousands of years before agriculture? Could the time factored lore and rites of the 'goddess' be one of the cognitive, intellectual threads leading to and preparing the way for agriculture?"[25]

He goes on to say,

Then is it possible . . . that the goddess with the horn ["Earth Mother of Laussel"] is a forerunner of later Neolithic, agricultural variants. She was the goddess who was called "Mistress of the Animals," had a lunar mythology, and had associated with her signs, symbols and attributes, including the lunar crescent, the crescent horns of bull, the fish, the angle-signs of water, the vulva, the naked breast, the plant, flower, bird, tree and snake. This later goddess was associated in story with a consort or mate who was also part of the seasonal and calendric mythology, a hunter of bull and lion, stag and ibex, as well as mythical animals whether in the labyrinth, depths, or in sky. In story he was often the "sun" to goddess "moon." These later cultures also depict images of men and women in attitudes of reverence, with arms raised toward either the god, sky, or animal images. They also present images of hunters engaged in mythological and ceremonial hunting, killing or combat.[26]

A seed vision of the feminine principle as the source, sustainer, and regenerator of life released at the new moon phase in the beginning of the upper Paleolithic, now by the last-quarter harvest phase of the Neolithic, had developed into a complex set of religious beliefs. Three-quarters around the span of the Goddess's lunation cycle, people could now see the vital connection between the mystery of life, the role of women as birthers, nurturers, and renewers, and the earth and moon as sacred feminine. Neolithic peoples assimilated these beliefs about the nature of reality and expressed them through the creation of their art, culture, civilization, and religion, which venerated the Goddess, women, the earth, and moon as simultaneous manifestations of the all-powerful Mother.

In the ruins of the earliest Neolithic settlements, such as Jericho (9500 BCE, Catal Huyuk (6500 BCE), Halicar (5600 BCE), and southeastern Europe (7000 BCE), are found numerous testimonies to the worship of the Goddess. The architecture of the sites, unfortified and built in feminine shapes, the numerous shrines, the votive figurines, the art and artifacts—all indicate that Neolithic people had a pivotal and profound relationship with the Goddess. As the creative source, the feminine principle expressed herself not only as birther and sustainer of children and their food, but also as the birther of mental and creative children. Her reverence inspired an outpouring of painting, sculpture, pottery, weaving, music, dance, song, poetry, and story that sang her praises. The tremendous display of creativity that archaeologists such as Marija Gimbutas document in goddess figurines and artifacts found in Old Europe between 9000 and 4000 BCE attest to the lush and bountiful harvest period of the Goddess's lunation cycle.[27]

As the activities and manifestations of the Goddess became numerous and diverse, she began to be conceptualized in a triple form, mirroring the three phases of the moon and the three worlds—heaven, earth, and the underworld. Multifaceted, she presided over all of the myriad displays of her creative essence. Hailed as Lady of the Wild Things, she was often portrayed as mistress of the animals, flanked by wild lions, wolves, deer, snakes, birds, and bears that recall the Goddess with the animals in the Magdalenian cave paintings. The Paleolithic Goddess's intimate relationship with the male animals had by Neolithic times evolved into the young horned and hoofed god, King of the Stags, who becomes her son, lover, and consort.

While the feminine principle was primary, the importance of the male principle was also recognized. The fusion of male and female energies, resonating to the cyclical rhythms of birth, death, and renewal, became incorporated into a body of ceremonies and rituals that were celebrated as the major transitions in the seasonal and lunar calendars. A religion developed, symbolized in the Wheel of the Year depicting the annual solar cycle, where the dying and resurrected young god, known in various cultures as Tammuz, Adonis, Dumuzi, Baal, and Dionysus, also followed the Goddess's vegetative cycle.

In this tradition the Wheel of the Year symbolizes the story of the birth of the Son from the Great Moon Mother at the winter solstice, the emergence of the reawakened Goddess as daughter at Candlemas, and their growth together through the spring equinox rebirthing the world. At Beltane the lovers celebrate the rituals of the Sacred Marriage, and consummate their union in the fertility of the earth at summer solstice. At Lammas the mature god dies and goes into the grain that is harvested at the fall equinox. By Hallowmas, the dark phase of the solar cycle, the Goddess of the Moon mourns his sacrifice and she ages, but then she once again becomes pregnant with him. He is reborn along with the rebirth of the sun's light at the winter solstice Yule.

The Neolithic cultures honored the feminine and masculine principles as co-creators in this mystery of the renewal of life. Riane Eisler's research documents the many societies where peoples of both sexes coexisted peacefully during this time. When all of life and its inhabitants are valued, there is no need for any one person or single nation or culture to enforce and maintain a stance of superiority and domination.

In all of the archaeological finds of the Neolithic era, there exists no evidence of war, violence, or cruelty in any of the ancient cities. There are no images of warriors, no scenes of battle, no lethal weapons such as spears or swords, and no depictions of captives or slaves. There is an absence of military fortifications. We can therefore surmise that these peoples, who for 35,000 years revered the cyclically renewing Goddess, were peaceful and egalitarian.

All of this began to change with the advent of the final phase of the lunation cycle, the dark phase, which began around 3000 BCE. This time period is referred to by historians as the beginning of the Bronze Age. In the Near East people discovered they could make an alloy from tin and copper, a new metal that produced excellent weapons. The Bronze Age, at the beginning of the dark phase of the Goddess's lunation cycle, demarcates the transition between the demise of the goddesses and the rise of the gods. This is when the patriarchal nomads first invaded the lands of the Neolithic Goddess.

The Dark Moon Phase: The Death of the Goddess

In chapter 2 we chronicled the events that led to the eventual abolition and death of the Goddess, the suppression of women, and the devaluation of nature and the feminine. In this section we see how the lunation cycle of the Goddess explains why, in the third millennium BCE, the feminine principle decreased as a major cultural influence and the masculine principle subsequently increased as the predominant governing force in religion and society.

As mentioned earlier, the obvious conclusion is that the matriarchal cultures who venerated the Goddess since the Upper Paleolithic were conquered and destroyed by patriarchal warlike races who carried superior weapons. Was the nature of the peoples who followed the solar gods inherently violent, destructive, and ruthless against the worshipers of the moon goddesses? Or might there exist larger forces operating on cosmic levels that can give a broad perspective to the monumental changes that transformed the face of the earth at this time?

From our analysis of the Goddess's lunation cycle, we can now propose that the decline of the Goddess was a natural factor of the decreasing and withdrawing energies that are an inherent aspect of the dark moon phase of cyclical process. The evolving feminine principle embodied in the symbolism of the Goddess that had initiated a new cycle of growth at the beginning of the Upper Paleolithic had, by the end of the Neolithic, actualized the seed vision. The mystery of life was decoded in the relationship between the male and female energies, preparing the way for the discovery of agriculture and the creation of civilization—that is, politics, trade, the arts, law, and science.

As discussed in chapter 1, when the form fulfills the purpose of the cycle, it is then necessary to let go of the old form. The Goddess, true to her third aspect as Goddess of Death, embodied her mystery teachings that destruction precedes regeneration. And so she entered into her dark moon phase, where she retreated and disappeared in order to heal, transform, and renew herself for another round of growth.

The third millennium BCE was the critical transitional period between matriarchal and patriarchal cultures. It marked not only the dark moon phase of the Goddess's 40,000-year lunation cycle, but it also coincided with a major shift in another large-scale 26,000-year cycle, the precessional age cycle. Here, the Age of Taurus gave way to the Age of Aries. It is the juxtaposition of critical turning points in both of these long-term cosmic cycles that gives the full understanding of what happened in the death of the Goddess. This occurrence can be understood through both cyclical processes—the lunation cycle of the Goddess and the precessional age cycle. Before we continue to pursue the unfoldment of the dark phase of the lunation cycle, let us briefly digress by seeing how the decline of the feminine can also be explained by another cosmic planetary cycle that was operating at that time.

Precessional Motion and the World Ages

In addition to the more obvious motions of the earth, namely rotation and revolution, it has a third motion that is detectable only over long periods of time. This motion, called precession, requires 26,000 years to complete one cycle. Precessional motion is a slow, swinging motion of the earth's axis of rotation. This wobbling, gyroscopic movement, much like a child's spinning top, is due to the gravitational forces that the sun and moon exert upon the protuberant matter at the earth's equator.

Because of precession, the axis of the earth, over a 26,000-year period, describes a circle in the sky pointing to different pole stars. While our north celestial pole star orientation is now approaching the star Polaris in the constellation of Ursa Minor, the Little Bear, this was not always the case. In 14,000 BCE the pole star was Alpha Cephei; in 8500 BCE it was Vega; and in

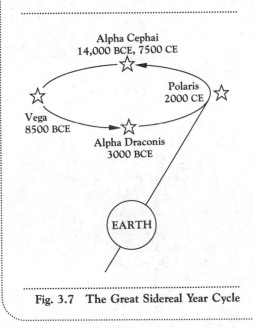

Fig. 3.7 The Great Sidereal Year Cycle

3000 BCE it was Alpha Draconis. In the future our axis will come back to these positions (Alpha Cephei in 7500, Vega in 14,000, Alpha Draconis in 21,500, and Polaris again in 28,000).

The changing location of the north celestial pole is not the only result of precession. This cycle also governs the precession of the equinoxes through the twelve zodiacal constellations that determine the world age in which we live. While many people have some concept of the world ages, aware that we are now entering the Age of Aquarius, most are unfamiliar with the astronomical background of this phenomenon of the "changing of the ages due to the precession of the equinoxes."

The zodiac is the band of twelve constellations (many of which depict animals) that encircles the earth. They are named Aries the Ram, Taurus the Bull, Gemini the Twins, Cancer the Crab, Leo the Lion, Virgo the Virgin, Libra the Scales, Scorpio the Scorpion, Sagittarius the Centaur, Capricorn the Mountain Goat, Aquarius the Water Bearer, and Pisces the Fish.

Although these twelve constellations constitute only a narrow segment of the dome of stars that surround us, they stood out with great prominence to the ancient stargazers. As viewed from the earth, it was along this path of zodiacal constellations that the sun seemed to travel in its annual journey around the earth.

This path is called the ecliptic. The planets and moon also move along both sides of the ecliptic in a band about 20 degrees wide. The ancient people who tried to decipher the mysteries of the universe observed that most of the movements of the planetary bodies in our solar system occurred against a backdrop of the zodiacal

Precessional Motion and the World Ages

constellations. In order to specify the location of a particular planet or star, it was necessary to define a starting point for the measuring system.

This starting point, called the vernal equinox, is the point where the ecliptic, or sun's path, intersects the celestial equator (an extension of the earth's equator). This is the position where the sun stands on the first day of spring, March 21. The vernal equinox point is seen against the backdrop of the constellations. Due to precessional motion, the vernal equinox point also moves westward in the sky throughout the circle of the zodiacal constellations at the rate of approximately fifty seconds of arc per year.

The constellation in which we see the vernal equinox determines the world age we live in. Since one complete cycle of precessional motion requires approximately 26,000 years, the vernal equinox spends about 2,300 years in each of the twelve signs of the zodiac. The vernal equinox has been passing through the constellation of Pisces the Fish since the Christian era. Because of its westward motion, the vernal equinox will move into the constellation of Aquarius early in the twenty-first century, at that time ushering in the "Age of Aquarius."

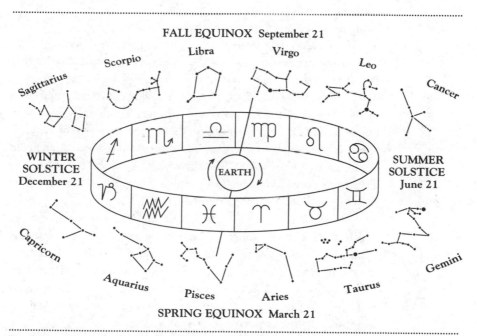

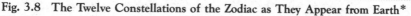

Fig. 3.8   The Twelve Constellations of the Zodiac as They Appear from Earth*

*The twelve "tropical signs" of the zodiac, upon which the seasonal cycle is based, should not be confused with the twelve "sidereal constellations" of the zodiac. At one time, around 600 BCE, the signs and constellations were aligned. Since then, due to precessional motion, these two bands have pulled apart by around 23 degrees. This means that the first degree of the sign of tropical Aries is now aligned to 23 degrees of sidereal constellation of Pisces.

The Decline of Feminine as Explained by the Precessional Age Cycle   The precessional age cycle is derived from the slow, swinging motion of the earth's axis, causing it to trace a circle in the sky that takes approximately 26,000 years to complete. As it does so, the earth's axis points to different pole stars, and this precessional motion gives us the twelve world ages. This astronomical phenomenon is explained in the box, and referring to it will assist the reader to better understand the following text. Let us now examine how the precessional age cycle sheds light on the major changes in the predominant cultures on the earth starting in the third millennium BCE.

While Polaris is currently our celestial north pole star, this was not always the case. In 2750 BCE, our critical time period, the earth's axis pointed to the star Alpha Draconis, also called Thuban, in the constellation of Draco the Dragon. For the people living then, this star seemed to be fixed in the sky as the earth appeared to revolve around it. This must have given the Dragon supernatural significance as it looked down upon the earth. In ancient Egypt Thuban was used to determine the orientation of the pyramids to face north, and its light shone directly into the entrance passageways.

The Dragon is a derivative of the old Mother Serpent. The serpent was believed to embody the Goddess's mysteries of death and renewal. In the ancient star lore Thuban was associated with the dragon/serpent Ladon, who guarded the golden apples of immortality in the Garden of the Hesperides. The Arabics called Thuban "The Subtle," which links it with the subtle serpent who was the tempter of Eve in the Garden of Eden, urging her to eat of the forbidden apple of the tree of knowledge. Thuban was also known as the dragon Tiamat, the ancient Mother Goddess of Sumeria-Babylonia, who was slain by the Sun God Izhdubar or Marduk.

During the patriarchal transition, serpents and dragons, animals which symbolize the Goddess's mysteries, were conceptualized as monsters. The mythological tales of the solar gods and heroes defeating the monsters record the violent battles and transitions between the old order of goddesses and the new order of gods. The Greeks tell of Thuban as the dragon Typhon born of the Earth Mother Gaia, a fierce, fire-spitting protector of the old goddesses.

One legend tells that the patriarchal gods of Olympus once had to flee to Egypt trying to escape the pursuit of Typhon, the scourge of humankind. When Typhon suddenly came upon them, they changed themselves into all kinds of animal shapes in order to save their lives. Zeus altered himself into a ram, which Typhon overlooked completely. Zeus then immortalized the ram in the constellation of Aries, the sign of the conquering patriarchy.

Another story describes the battle for supremacy of the universe between the old Titan gods and the new generation of Olympian gods. It was said that Minerva, daughter of Zeus, while fighting for the Olympians, seized the dragon by the tail and hurled it into the sky. As the dragon sailed into the dome of the stars, it became twisted, tangled, and froze as it came close to the cold celestial north pole.

The Dragon/Serpent, who represents the mysteries of the Goddess, encircled the fixed north celestial pole during the reign of the matriarchal societies of Neolithic times. The mythical tales of the transition period describe how the serpent was denounced, defeated, and cast out at the end of the long and fierce wars that spanned the demise of the goddesses and the victory of the triumphant gods.

Age of Taurus During the time period when the celestial Serpent/Dragon constellation circled directly overhead in the night sky, the vernal equinox point was passing through the constellation of Taurus the Bull. This period marked the culmination of the Neolithic era, when the Goddess reigned supreme. After 2700 BCE the earth's polar orientation started to swing away from Thuban and began its gradual approach to Polaris in the constellation of the Little Bear. By 2300 BCE the vernal equinox point had left Taurus and entered into a new constellation, Aries the Ram, the animal symbol of the patriarchal invaders.

In the ancient science of astrology, the sign of Taurus is said to be feminine in polarity and is the place of the Moon's exaltation. The

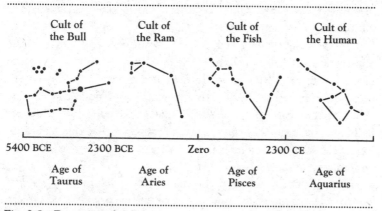

Fig. 3.9 Precessional Ages

sign of Aries is masculine in polarity, where the sun is exalted (that is, finds its full expression). Furthermore, Taurus is ruled by the planet Venus, principle of peace and harmony, while Aries is ruled by Mars, principle of warfare and conquest.

When the vernal equinox point passes through each zodiacal sign, the symbolism of that sign is reflected in the religious and cultural images of that corresponding world age. Esotericists and astrologers explain this phenomenon in the belief that there exists an intelligent patterning in the universe and the various constellation groups symbolize different mental constructs or thought forms. When the earth is attuned to a particular constellation, these constructs act as a filter through which we receive and interpret the universal energies of the cosmos.

During the precessional age of Taurus the Bull, ca. 4200–2300 BCE, humanity worldwide revered the Holy Cow, the Golden Calf, and the Heifer. Krishna appeared in India spreading the cult of the cow; the Semites worshiped the bull god El; and in Crete it was Europa, who as a cow gave birth to the Bull King Minos. The Egyptians believed that their god Ptah, creator of all, incarnated on earth in the body of a special individual bull, Apis. The Great Goddess Hera was revered as the cow-eyed queen, Hathor as the celestial cow, and across the Mediterranean islands Cypress, Malta, and Sardinia, the peoples all practiced the cult of the cow and bull.

In relation to the four elements of fire, air, earth, and water, Taurus is connected to the earth element. The earth Age of Taurus corresponded to advances in farming by domesticating oxen and the growth of agriculturally based societies. The horns of the bull were seen to reflect the lunar crescent. As the moon is exalted in the sign of Taurus, the worship of the Neolithic Moon Goddess permeated the land during this world age.

Age of Aries   The vernal equinox point began moving into the constellation of Aries the Ram in the middle of the third millennium BCE. This event is depicted in the Old Testament when Moses went up to the mountaintop and saw the revelation of God in the burning bush. He then came down and proclaimed the change in world ages by blowing the ram's horn and warning people that they could no longer worship the Golden Calf, but instead must offer the sacrificial lamb to honor the gods.

The Egyptians instituted the cult of the solar ram-headed god Amen-Ra, and the Israelites that of the Passover lamb. The Greeks set out in the solar boat in quest of the Golden Ram's Fleece, and they had to challenge its former guardians, the never-sleeping serpent and the fire-breathing bulls. Pallas Athena, the most elevated goddess in the Olympian patriarchal pantheon, dressed in the armor of a soldier with a ram's horn helmet. Mithra, the Sun God of Persia, who used to be called the sacred bull, now became the slayer of the bull. Apollo, Sun God in Greece, was now the patron of shepherds and flocks.

Aries is related to the fire element and the fiery sun. During the Age of Aries religious worship shifted from the moon mother goddesses to that of the father sun gods. Aries is ruled by Mars, God of War, and this time period saw the rise of priest-kings as shepherds and warlords. Nomadic ruling societies moved about vanquishing, conquering, and forcibly converting the indigenous agrarian peoples.

Twenty-three hundred years later, as the vernal equinox entered the constellation of Pisces the Fish, the Christ was the Messiah who ushered in the next world age. He gathered together his fishermen disciples and performed his miracles with the loaves and fishes.[28] Pisces is a feminine polarity sign where the planet Venus, associated with the Goddess of Love, is exalted. However, while Christ's message of love, compassion, and surrender (all Piscean themes) was released during this time, it was not fully realized by the peoples of the earth. This was partially due to the fact that the feminine principle continued to be dormant in a dark moon phase throughout most of the Piscean Age, while the masculine energy proceeded to ascend unrestricted.

The closing years of a world age are analogous to the dark moon phase of that age. The transition period between two world ages, several hundred years in duration, is called the "cusp of the ages." The period around the demise of the Goddess cultures was a cuspal time between the world ages of Taurus and Aries. Cusp periods are always times of intense change where the old is dying in order to give birth to the new.

Transformation also occurs on large-scale collective levels where humanity, as a whole, experiences the death and rebirth process. Much of the death that permeates individual and collective reality during the cusps of the ages stands back to back with the rapid emergence of radically new ways of operating in the world. This present time period, during the closing of the second millennium CE, is also identified as the cusp of the Aquarian Age. We are currently living in such a time of global transformation.

We can now view the apparent death of the Goddess against the backdrop of the precessional age cycle. The earth's axis pointed to the

star in the constellation of the old Mother Serpent, signaling the
timing for the periodic shedding of her skin and renewing herself.
Then, as the world ages changed from feminine Taurus to masculine
Aries, the religious cosmologies of humanity shifted from the culmination of the worship of the moon goddesses grounded in the fertile
earth as mother to the rise of the solar gods, venerated as father, who
came from the heavens above.

In the political realm the peaceful, agrarian matriarchal cultures
gave way to the warlike, nomadic patriarchal cultures. As the feminine principle drew inward into its dark closure phase, the masculine
principle moved outward to shape the conceptual beliefs of humanity; male gods and men rose to positions of power in spiritual and
worldly affairs. And in the evolution of the human brain, the pre-
dominance of feminine polarity, circular right-brain processes was
replaced by increasing activation of masculine polarity, linear left-
brain functions. In a new linear worldview, cyclical renewal was
denied and the darkness of death became feared.

From this larger perspective of changing precessional world ages,
the decline of the Goddess in the third millennium BCE can be seen
as part of the rhythms of alternation and change inherent in cosmic
planetary cycles and indeed in all cyclical processes. Now let us return our attention to the dark moon phase of the Goddess's lunation cycle.

Revisioning the Dark Moon
Phase of the Goddess

If we can consider the possibility that the disappearance of the Goddess was not solely due to a conscious and intentional destruction by
the patriarchy, but was more a factor of her natural cycle of waxing
and waning phases, then many profound insights can arise from this
alternate view that probes the reasons for her decline. First of all, we
can realize that the destruction of the Goddess culture was a necessary prelude for her subsequent regeneration, and this process was
built into her cosmology of death and rebirth. Second, because
knowledge of cyclical renewal had diminished over the years, the violence, brutality, and chaos that did in fact occur were the reaction of
people panicking as they passed through a dark moon phase of the
feminine cycle. And third, for all of us who carry the feminine principle, we can be released from our attitudes of victimhood, which reinforce our sense of powerlessness.

As we develop these themes, let us keep in mind our understanding of cyclical process and long-term cosmic cycles. And let us also recall how it is our fear of the dark that creates the pain and suffering associated with our dark moon phase periods and our denial that creates the shadow. This expanded view can help us to alter our perceptions and conclusions concerning the death of the Goddess, and to develop our forgiveness and compassion as we participate in the vision for her rebirth.

Feminist scholars are now uncovering the early history of the Goddess and stripping away the layers of patriarchal suppression that deny her existence. These revelations are having a huge impact on women's consciousness and the feminist movements, encompassing many area of expression including politics, ecology, economics, professionalism, education, spirituality, psychology, healing, and the arts. However, some of the conclusions that we have come to have trapped us in the very patriarchal, dualistic conceptual system from which we are struggling to break free.

Many people conclude that the Goddess culture was destroyed, and the patriarchal conquerors forcibly usurped power and position from women. This was an intentional, negative, and evil act, and the suppression of the values of the Goddess has led to a decline in the quality of life on earth and our present-day crisis. As a result of this disempowerment, it is proposed that now women must reclaim their lost power and recapture their birthright in every strata of their lives.

To the extent that this perception is fueled by anger, vengeance, and retribution, we maintain the tension between an oppressor and a victim. The distinction between "us" and "them" as separate is the root cause of *samsara,* the Buddhist term for the suffering and misery that pervade humanity. The twin forces of attachment to protecting the self and aversion to anything that threatens the self lead to the creation of a hostile reality in which most people feel frightened and alienated. This is the inevitable outcome of left-brain masculine, dualistic thinking that perceives our self or our group as different and better than the other with the subsequent necessity to protect it.

Here we need to acknowledge that, on an outer level, the violence that was unjustly inflicted upon peaceful peoples was real, and women and the feminine have indeed suffered greatly during the period of patriarchal supremacy. And it is our responsibility to ourselves, to others, and to the well-being of the planet that we secure freedom, justice, equality, and protection for women. It is important for women to come into full participation in mainstream society;

to have equal access to all aspects of employment, education, citizenship, public service, and family life; and to take action to reestablish feminine values in the world.

However, in order to truly reconnect with the egalitarian and synthesizing values of the Goddess, we must make a fundamental shift in our conceptual outlook. Women must release their concepts of "us" as good and unfortunate victims and "them" as evil oppressors, and begin to move toward seeing the unity of all humanity and sentient life. In the heart of the Goddess all beings are equally loved, accepted, understood, and forgiven in the great bosom of the Mother's compassion.

As we reclaim the mystery teachings of the Goddess and revision the patriarchal distortion of the dark, we accept that dissolution and decay are essential and necessary stages that prepare the way for renewal. And so the disappearance and death of the Goddess were at one with her rhythms of ebb and flow. Heeding the signal from the star in the serpent constellation, she magnetically withdrew into the recessive dark moon phase of her cycle.

In their mythical tales the Greeks told that the Moon Goddess Hera, Queen of the Heavens, periodically ran off and hid during the dark of the moon. She wrapped herself in mourning clothes and performed her most secret rituals of renewing her virginity. With the new moon she emerged as Anandos—the Goddess arising, and returned to her people and her husband as virgin and bride.

During the closure phase of a 40,000-year cycle, the evolving feminine principle as the Goddess entered into a deep, incubatory sleep. Here she went into the darkness in order to distill the wisdom of the cycle into a new seed. The composting decay from her disintegrating culture provided the fertile soil to nourish the unlimited possibilities of the developing embryo. The ancient Eleusinian Mysteries tell us that the Divine Child is conceived in the underworld. This allegory alludes to the fact that the conception of the vision-to-be-realized in the future cycle occurs in the dark moon phase of the previous cycle.

During the last five thousand years of her disappearance, the Goddess was preparing for her rebirth, regenerating her body and mind, revitalizing her emanations. And now she has come full circle with her recent rebirth.

An acceptance of the cyclical nature of the Goddess's unfoldment over time and space releases us from the judgment that what happened was a mistake, a bad thing, and that someone else is to blame.

Letting go of our attitudes of judgment and blame toward others can help us to transcend the dualistic reality that keeps us oppressed. The ultimate solution to peace between individuals and between nations is not a political one, but a spiritual one. It involves recognizing that others are not separate from oneself.[29] The next step in our process is to see if we can develop any feelings of compassion and forgiveness for those who enacted the brutality and violence that erupted during the transition.

To the extent that we resist letting go of the old and accept a change that is inevitable, our unconscious self will create an even more powerful opposing force in order to break us free from our attachment and liberate us. We will more fully discuss this concept in chapter 9. From a cyclical context, the fight for survival needs to be balanced by a realization of the impermanence of all things, and an awareness of the regenerative potential of destruction and death.

When the Goddess withdrew, people reacted with all the fear and panic that accompany our dark moon phase periods, when all we see is the loss and destruction of our life structures and identity and we do not remember that death of the old is the precursor to rebirth of the new. Individuals, no longer attuned to the Goddess's cyclical ways, perceived her disappearance as desertion and they felt abandoned by the Great Mother. They did not have the perspective on the shifting world ages coinciding with the dark phase of the Goddess's lunation cycle. Nor did they fully comprehend that the polarity changes in their brains affected the way they perceived reality. They may have felt that the Goddess who had supported them was no longer there. Her priestesses, despite prayers and offerings, could not invoke the oracle of the Goddess to give them sound and helpful advice. Her rulers could no longer provide a structure of safety and security, nor protect them from the brutal onslaught of the invaders. The old ways and beliefs no longer sustained them, and the world as they knew it was breaking down.

Riane Eisler poignantly expresses the confusion, fear, and horror of this time, when people were in the midst of massive slaughter, destruction, suppression, and exploitation.

All over the ancient world populations were now set against populations, as men were set against women and against other men. Wandering over the width and breath of this disintegrating world, masses of refugees were everywhere fleeing their homelands, desperately searching for a haven, a safe place to go. But there was no such place left in this new world. For this was now a world where, having violently deprived the Goddess and the female half of humanity of all power, gods and men of war ruled.[30]

What could have caused this fury directed toward the feminine? Perhaps it is the same fury that wells up in a child who feels abandoned or rejected by his or her mother. All we know is that the poisonous by-products of hatred fashioned a distorted image of the third, dark aspect of the Moon Goddess as Mother Death, a horrific female destroyer. And the peoples of the new gods became obsessed with obliterating the memory of a mother who deserted them, and to punish her earthly representatives, the women, for her act of leaving them.

As people denied and suppressed all that was associated with the Goddess, this repressed material festered in the collective unconscious. It then violently erupted as the demonic shadow, in the guise of the great monster death, and unleashed a reign of slaughter and terror upon the lives of humanity. People became caught in the frenzied madness that arises when their reality is being shattered and destroyed, and they are battling against the demons of their unconscious projections.

Caught up in a left-brain, dualistic reality, individuals saw self as separate from other polarized into male against female. The oppressors brutalized the victims, each one projecting the essence of its own worst fears upon the other. Our unconscious collective memories of the horror of this time continue to affect the ways in which men and women (and the male and female within each person defined by the Jungians as animus and anima) react to one another today. This is the wound that is seeking to be healed in the next turning of the Goddess's cycle. As Beauty must first love the Beast in order to redeem him, the way to dissolve the malefic nature of the demon is to love it.

In Chinese philosophy the health of an organism depends upon the integration and balance of *yin* and *yang*, the feminine and masculine polarities. The evolving feminine principle, by 3000 BCE, had completed her developmental phase as a self-contained entity. She interacted with the masculine mainly as a means to create and continue the flow of life. The notion of building a primary relationship with the masculine, based on mental, emotional, and spiritual equality, was not a priority of this cycle of the evolving feminine principle. With the coming of the solar gods the masculine *yang* energy (re)entered into the planetary biosphere as a force in its own right, establishing its presence and function in the larger whole. At this time it became imperative for the feminine to relate to the masculine in a new way and to develop forms of interactive, cooperative, and loving relationships. This then became part of the seed kernel that was to be nourished during the dark phase and given birth with the Goddess's reemergence.

During the Middle Ages the mythological wisdom of the ancients was encoded into the fairy tales. The human princess Psyche must go into a deathlike trance before she can be transformed into a goddess and heavenly bride of Eros. Sleeping Beauty and Snow White go through the same incubation sleep before being reawakened and brought back to life by the kiss of the prince. When the evolving feminine principle went into her dark moon phase, one of her intentions was to transform, sensitize, and strengthen the feminine etheric channels so she could receive the powerful force of the masculine without being overwhelmed and destroyed.

The myths repeatedly warn that for a mortal to look upon the face of a deity directly results in being burned up in the brilliance of the light. The tale of Eros and Psyche told of the transformation of a mortal, Psyche, into a deity after she had transversed through the underworld, and her subsequent union in a divine marriage. During her dark phase of transformation and renewal, the feminine principle created a new energetic body that will allow for a fusion and integration with the masculine force. In this new cycle, conscious relationship with the other will be one path to spiritual and evolutionary development.

The healing of wounds that exist between men and women is contained within the seed vision of the New Moon Goddess. This healing also entails balancing the polarization between the masculine and feminine principles within each person seeking wholeness within herself or himself. It also addresses these polarities as they operate within gay and lesbian relationships. It is important that we transform the power-struggle mentality that defines our values. As each individual man and woman, each person and his or her enemy, reconcile differences and heal wounds, this healing extends outward to reconcile the opposing and antagonistic forces arising from a dualistic perception. In this way the Goddess can restore balance, wholeness, and well-being to the earth and her inhabitants.

The Rebirth of the Goddess

An ancient Chinese curse says, "May you be reborn in interesting times." Those of us living at the end of the twentieth century have indeed been born into a momentous time at a critical juncture in two great cosmic cycles. We are standing at a point that straddles the beginning of a new 40,000-year lunation cycle of the Goddess and the ending of the 2,300-year Piscean world age, and perhaps the closure of an entire 26,000-year precessional age cycle. Following swiftly upon the heels of the rebirth of the Goddess will be the dawning of the New Age—the Age of Aquarius, which, according to some astrological scholars, will be the inception of another great precessional cycle.

According to astrologer Daniel Giamario, the major clue suggesting the inception of another great precessional age is based on the belief held by many calendric and medicine traditions that winter solstice points mark the ends and beginnings of calendars. In 1998–99, for the only time in a 26,000 year cycle, the winter solstice point will precess to exactly align with the intersection of the Milky Way (our galaxy) and the Zodiac (our solar system). (In occult traditions, the galactic center was said to be one of the gateways whereby departing souls leave incarnation.) Another factor in the star lore that is said to determine when a cycle ends and begins is the date at which there is a precise north star. In 2100 Polaris will be as close to the north point as is possible for any star to be precisely north.[31]

Remembering that the mystery teachings of the Goddess concern death and rebirth, it is most fortuitous that her rebirth at the beginning of a new lunation cycle coincides with a time when we face massive death and destruction—a sign that the dark closure phase of the precessional age cycle is indeed occurring. The current stages of these two cycles account for the seemingly contradictory feelings that are engulfing many people at this time. One stream of feeling is the hope and optimism for the rebirth of womanspirit and the possibilities of the New Age. The other stream is the overwhelming despair at the hopelessness of our dying planet and peoples. In the following discussion we will address both of these themes, and ask the Moon Goddess to illumine within us a sense of understanding.

Snow White and Sleeping Beauty eventually awaken from their long sleep and assume their rightful roles as queens. The ancient devotees of the Goddess, during the current century, are participating in her reawakening, acting as midwives at her rebirth. The return of the Goddess is evidenced in the discovery of herstory and the revival of her worship. Women's spirituality is the cosmological belief system that stands behind the global women's movement that is seeking economic, political, and sexual justice for women. It is also the source of the current healing and recovery movement that is an affirmation of life, and the ecological movement (eco-feminism) that recognizes the earth as the body of the Great Mother who sustains our existence.

In esoteric astrology the sighting of new planets in the solar system corresponds to an activation of a new center of consciousness. More specifically, the mythological archetypes who share the same name as the planetary body become active forces in culture and psyche. In 1801 the first of many asteroids (located between Mars and Jupiter) was discovered and named Ceres (Demeter) after the Greco-Roman Great Mother. In the following years Pallas Athena, Vesta (Hestia), and Juno (Hera), all great goddesses of antiquity, were seen, identified, and awakened in the human psyche.[32]

In the early nineteenth century Ceres, Pallas Athena, Juno, and Vesta led the procession of the reawakened feminine energy, signifying the beginning of a new lunation cycle. The first wave of feminism was marked by the 1848 women's rights convention in Seneca Falls, New York, addressing the issues of women's equality, the patriarchy, and women's spirituality. The timeless stories of these goddesses speak to the pressing psychological issues of our times that are seeking healing in our movement toward recovery. These issues include eating disorders, codependency, sexual abuse, dysfunctional families, chemical dependencies, love addiction, changing relationships, women's professionalism, domestic violence, sexual freedom, quest for meaningful work, and new spiritual directions.

These psychological issues are symptoms of a dysfunctional society that is trapped in dualism, the great separation of self from other that also leads to the splitting off of mind, body, emotions, and spirit within each individual. With the rebirth of the Goddess people are now addressing social problems concerning war, rape, hunger, homelessness, animal rights, the well-being of the planet, sexism, and racism.

The Goddess has emerged, purified and regenerated. Having renewed her virginity in the dark phase, like a youthful maiden, she once again comes forth—vibrant and expectant with visions for a future of open possibilities. Look around you. See her pictures. Hear her songs. Dance in her circles. Women are bonding with one another in large, national conferences and festivals as well as small, local groups and circles. Women are reempowering each other, reaffirming the strength and beauty of the feminine, and trying to live out the values of the Goddess to create a better world. The flow of the creative feminine energy is once again pouring through women artists, writers, musicians, and healers who are remembering the ways of expressing her beauty, wisdom, and healing powers.

This awakened feminine energy is having an equally profound impact on the lives of men. The rise of patriarchy did not only overshadow the feminine, but with its emphasis of domination and destruction, it also obliterated the life-affirming qualities of the natural masculine who tilled the earth and tended the domesticated animals. The patriarchy should not be perceived as synonymous with men, but rather with a distorted side of the masculine. In the Celtic tradition the positive side of the masculine was symbolized by the myth of the green man who is the counterpart of Mother Nature. The rebirth of the Goddess is also heralding a reemergence of the life-affirming qualities inherent within the masculine principle that likewise had been suppressed during the dark moon phase.

With the growing awareness and pressure for them to express their feelings and intuitions, men are confronting not only changing women, but also their relationship to their own psyches. Men's consciousness groups, their participation in childbirth, single-parenting, and domestic role reversals are several areas where, in a rapidly changing society, the awakened feminine is transforming their lives. In the raising of both men and women's consciousness, the healing of all our various relationships has become a major theme in the recovery movement.

The recently activated feminine energy, which is linked to right-brain functioning, is contributing to the growth of many consciousness-expansion movements. Wholistic health and education, spiritual and psychic awareness, and the vision to co-create our reality are some of the current expressions of increasing right-brain processes.

And yet for all the positive signs and hopeful possibilities that the New Moon Goddess brings with her reemergence, she has been reborn at a time when humanity is faced, as never before, with massive threats of total annihilation. Death looms everywhere—in the storehouse of nuclear arsenals, in the deadly radioactive particles contaminating the soil, waters, and atmosphere, in the toxic environmental pollutants, in the dire earthquake, ozone hole, and global warming predictions, in the vanishing rainforests, in famine and population explosion, and in the degenerative and auto-immune diseases that are increasing in epidemic proportions.

The pessimistic pragmatist within us wonders how humanity can possibly survive this projected scenario of destruction and holocaust, one whose clocks are drawing ever closer to the midnight hour. It is not unreasonable to assume that human beings may not survive. In the 6 billion-year history of the planet, many species have arisen. Because they could not adapt to changing environmental conditions, they have become extinct. Are human beings any different from any of the other species of sentient life that have inhabited the earth?

According to Buddhism it is only within the human body that enlightenment is possible, and it is for this reason that human life is so precious. It is said by esotericists that all evolution is preceded by mutation that is caused by radiation. In this context mutation does not refer to something defective, but rather to an essential, irreversible transformation of the old into something altogether new. According to the recent scientific Eve hypothesis, it was such a genetic mutation that produced modern *Homo sapiens*. And transformation is the key purpose of the dark moon phase of cyclical process.

Let us hope that, during the Goddess's long sleep, she has effected a transformation at the deepest level of the feminine energy that will allow us to pass through the destruction of the old order and, like a Phoenix, rise out of the ashes to soar. It is said that the cockroach has the capacity to survive nuclear radiation. If even one life form has developed this capacity, then the imprint exists as a possibility for other life forms. And it may well be that the radiation we so greatly fear may in fact be the very agent of our mutation and possibility for evolution. Transformation can only occur in the dark. In the coming darkness of the closing precessional age, we can hope that humanity can achieve some kind of essential mutation that will allow our species to continue living in what might be a radically different environment.

For those who are not aware of cyclical process, it may seem contradictory that the life-negating specter of death exists simultaneously with the promise of renewal heralded by the rebirth of the Goddess and the dawning of a new age, the Age of Aquarius. However, from a cyclical; perspective, we now know that death stands back-to-back with birth. As we give birth to the New Age, we need to remember that preceding any rebirth, the old must first die. This is the law of the cycle. As we look at the doom and gloom facing the world as we have known it, it may not be totally appropriate for us to try to hold back the forces of destruction. Having faith in the cycle of the Moon Goddess, perhaps we should welcome the death of the old order and embrace the darkness that the Moon Goddess offers as a passageway to renewal.

This is not to imply that we should give up our concerns and efforts for the health and continued well-being of the planet. The growing environmental and ecological movements that are seeking to save the earth in the face of a task that seems hopeless and beyond repair are not in vain. They may be part of the seed vision that is being inculcated during the dark moon phase of the Piscean Age. Hopefully, with the dawning of a new precessional age, a reverence and care for the body of the earth will be imprinted in the consciousness of all humanity.

While the dark moon phase officially ends at the new moon conjunction, there still exist one and a half nights of darkness before the slim, sliver crescent appears in the night sky. In the rebirth of the Goddess, it is important to not become discouraged by the confusion, lack of unity, and clear vision that characterize the struggles of a fledgling feminine movement emerging into mainstream consciousness. As the child crawls and stumbles before he or she walks and runs, the New Moon Virgin Goddess, for all her active, exuberant activity, is yet young in her wisdom ways. However, we need to witness with certainty her return. Look at the moon cycle and have faith, without judgment or preconception, in her gradual unfoldment.

Also, know that the Goddess was not a victim. Know that she did not have her power taken away, and that she did not relinquish it. Women are not victims, and they do not have to make war to reclaim their power. Women have always had their power, and now it is once again fully available, recharged, and revitalized for them to express it in the outer world. We need to recognize the new face of the young Goddess as the face of the old one we last remembered, before she went into her dark moon phase.

But now she has, in fact, returned, her wisdom illuminating our lives. To see the destruction and death of the old and joyfully embrace it as a sign of imminent renewal is the naked awareness of the Dark Goddess. The work of our psyche necessitates that we cleanse and purify our distorted images of the Dark Goddess and of death. Through patriarchal culture these erroneous images have affected our bodies, minds, and environment, and have impaired our relationships with the other. As we revision our understanding of the dark, part of our soul task is to become skillful artists who image and fashion this renewed creative feminine energy.

Now our journey turns to evoking, honoring, and reclaiming the Dark Goddess and integrating her into the wholeness of our being.

Journal Questions

1. If I am aware of the Goddess herstory, do I think that women were innocent victims of the patriarchy's brutal aggression? Do I think that women must rise in anger to protest this injustice and to reclaim what was forcibly taken away from them? Do I perpetuate a tension between a victim and oppressor in my attitudes toward protecting myself against the potential threat of those who are more powerful?

2. After reading this chapter, can I consider the possibility that the disappearance of the Goddess was overshadowed by cosmic planetary cycles and part of a natural process of renewal that occurs in the darkness? What comes up for me and in what ways does this challenge my previous beliefs?

3. Do I have hope in the possibilities of the New Age? Do I feel despair over the dying environment of the planet or see it as a hopeless task? Do I feel moved to try to save the earth? Can I see the death of the old as the precursor to the birth of the new?

Notes

1. Merlin Stone, *When God Was a Woman* (New York: Harcourt Brace Jovanovich, 1976), xiii.

2. Dane Rudhyar, *The Lunation Cycle* (Santa Fe: Aurora Press, 1986), and *Astrological Aspects* (Santa Fe: Aurora Press, 1980).

3. Diane Stein, *Casting the Circle: A Woman's Book of Ritual* (Freedom, CA: The Crossing Press, 1990), 93.

4. Editors of Time-Life, *The Epic of Man* (New York: Time-Life Inc., 1961).

5. Randall White, *Dark Caves, Bright Visions: Life in Ice Age Europe* (New York: American Museum of Natural History, 1986), 30. Chatelperronian, 35,000–30,000 BCE; Aurignacian, 34,000–30,000 BCE; Gravettian, 30,000–22,000 BCE; Solutrean, 22,000–18,000 BCE; Magdalenian, 18,000–11,000 BCE; Azilian, 11,000–9000 BCE. Dates are approximate and vary from region to region.

6. White, *Dark Caves, Bright Visions*, 13.

7. White, *Dark Caves, Bright Visions*, 10.

8. Brian Fagan, *The Journey from Eden: The Peopling of Our World* (London: Thames & Hudson, 1990), 89.

9. James Shreeve, "Argument Over a Woman: Science Searches for the Mother of Us All," *Discover* 11, no. 8 (August 1990): 52–59.

10. White, *Dark Caves, Bright Visions*, 14.

11. Robert J. Wenke, *Patterns of History: Humankind's First Three Million Years* (New York: Oxford University Press, 1984), 117.

12. Elinor Gadon, *The Once and Future Goddess* (San Francisco: Harper & Row, 1989), 4.

13. Marija Gimbutas, *Goddesses and Gods of Old Europe: Myth and Cult Images* (Berkeley: University of California Press, 1982), Preface.

14. Elinor Gadon, *The Once and Future Goddess* (San Francisco: Harper & Row, 1989), 22.

15. Marija Gimbutas, *The Language of the Goddess* (San Francisco: Harper & Row, 1989), xix.

16. Alexander Marshack, *The Roots of Civilization: The Cognitive Beginnings of Man's First Art, Symbols and Notation* (New York: McGraw-Hill, 1972).

17. D. De. Sonneville-Bordes, "The Upper Paleolithic: 33,000 BC–10,000 BC," in *France Before the Romans*, edited by S. Piggot (London: 1973), 30–60.

18. Andre Leroi-Gourhan, *Treasures of Prehistoric Art*, translated by Norbert Guterman (New York: Harry N. Abrams, 1967).

Mysteries of the Dark Moon

19. A. Forbes, Jr., and T. R. Crowder, "The Problem of Franco-Cantabian Abstract Signs: Agenda for a New Approach," *World Archaeology* 10 (1979): 360–66.
20. Marshack, *The Roots of Civilization*, 173.
21. Gadon, *The Once and Future Goddess*, 20.
22. Marshack, *The Roots of Civilization*, 342.
23. Evan Hadingham, *Secrets of the Ice Age* (New York: Walker, 1979).
24. Riane Eisler, *The Chalice and the Blade* (San Francisco: Harper & Row, 1987), 9.
25. Marshack, *The Roots of Civilization*, 314.
26. Marshack, *The Roots of Civilization*, 335.
27. For a full description of Neolithic cultures, see Gadon, *The Once and Future Goddess*, and Gimbutas, *The Language of the Goddess*.
28. For more information on precessional ages, see Alan Oken, *The Complete Astrologer* (New York: Bantam, 1980).
29. Chagdud Tulku Rinpoche from a talk entitled, "Peace in Personal and Interpersonal Relationships," given in Eugene, Oregon, October 1990.
30. Eisler, *The Chalice and the Blade*, 58.
31. Daniel Giamario, personal communication, September 1991.
32. Demetra George, *Asteroid Goddesses: The Mythology, Psychology and Astrology of the Reemerging Feminine* (San Diego: ACS Publications, 1986).

✦ PART II ✦

Goddesses of the Dark Moon

*To the Magic, Mystery, and Healing Power
of the Dark Goddess*

The Guardians of the Unconscious

In Part II we will turn our attention to the mythological tales of goddesses who are associated with the dark of the moon and who express the dark moon archetype. We will explore the mythical biographies of Nyx, Mother of Night, and her daughters, the Fates, the Furies, the Hesperides, and Nemesis. This will be followed by a look at three other dark goddesses, Hekate, Lilith, and Medusa. In the process we will try to see how their timeless stories are relevant to the kinds of issues, operating primarily in the unconscious, that continue to confront men and women today.

I have chosen these particular goddesses of the dark moon because several planetary bodies in the asteroid belt have been named after them. In my work as a mythologist and astrologer, I have repeatedly seen that when a heavenly body is prominent in the sky at the time of a person's birth, the mythological story of the god or goddess who shares the same name as the planet becomes a major theme in that individual's life. I have had the opportunity to study how the archetypal principles carried by these dark goddesses are experienced in the lives of individuals.

Before we begin our mythological exploration of these dark goddesses, let us briefly consider our beliefs concerning the word "myth." In our society the word myth has come to mean something that is not true. However, to the ancients, the myths were the repositories of their traditions and wisdom. On an outer level the myths were the oral legends that conveyed the stories of their creation and the history of humanity. This oral tradition, preserved by the bards and storytellers, was the primary means of communication in a time before reading, writing, and books were accessible to most people.

On an inner level the myths depicted the psychology of the human condition. The stories of the gods and goddesses represented the basic archetypal scripts and characters that were available to individuals, and through which they could live out the meaning of their lives. These stories contained the divine inspiration that could aid people in their search for self-knowledge, healing, and growth. In the ancient healing temples of Asklepius, part of a person's cure involved attending a dramatic performance in the Theater of Dionysus. The different plays, in which the gods and goddesses had major roles, addressed the psychological issues behind a person's physical ailment.

Carl Jung called myths "the eternal patterns in our soul" that continue to live on in our dreams, fantasies, symbols, and in the interactions of our daily life. Psychologists are just beginning to discover that myth is the natural language of the collective unconscious. Joseph Campbell added that "all the gods and goddesses live within us" as the forces of our personality, and their stories represent the mythic themes that shape our lives. Our view of mythological deities has evolved over the millennia from personified gods and goddesses to properties of the psyche. The changing images in the transformations of myths over time parallel the emotional and mental development of the corresponding archetype in the psyche of humanity.

The Dark Goddess and the Unconscious

In the ancient cosmologies all mythic geography came to be projected onto celestial planes, the sun, the moon, the Milky Way. According to this system the moon was described as the Land of the Dead or as the regenerating receptacles of souls.[1] All the goddesses of the dark moon are associated with death and regeneration. From a modern psychological point of view, the underworld is a metaphor for the unconscious, and these deities reside in the unconscious sphere of our psyches.

However, the ancients did not have notions of the psyche, the inner realms of consciousness or of the unconscious. This idea was not even conceptualized until the middle of the nineteenth century with the publication of Sigmund Freud's theory of the unconscious. The ancients expressed their awareness of the conscious and unconscious spheres of reality, that which was known and unknown, and of the interface between them in the three primary creation legends of the Greek cosmology. Each legend begins with a different Great Mother who gave birth to the world.[2]

In one legend the Homeric tales sing that it is the Sea Goddess Tethys who is the Mother of the World.

In a second legend Hesiod gives this role to Gaia, the Great Mother Earth.

And in a third legend the Orphics tell that it is Nyx, Goddess of the Dark Night, who lays the Cosmic Egg out of which the world is born. Hermetic scholar Adam McLean sees these three versions of creation as the three facets of the Triple Goddess, each one corresponding to one of the three aspects of consciousness in the human mind.

The deities who arose from Gaia-Mother Earth are associated with those aspects of the psyche that operate more in the light-filled dimensions of consciousness. Our conscious mind gives us information through our five senses that allows us to perceive a solid, tangible, and earthy world. The children born from Nyx, Queen of Night, lead us down to the dark unconscious. This formless, nonphysical realm is the source of our hidden treasures and hidden enemies. The gods and goddesses who emerged from Tethys, Mistress of the Sea, link the dark subterranean depths of the ocean with the surface waves upon which the light can play. They are the mediators who move back and forth between above and below, between the conscious light sphere and unconscious dark sphere in our psyches.[3]

The ancients did not image the unconscious as a hidden part of their own psyches, but as something outside of themselves. Their awareness of an unknown and mysterious region was envisioned as the hidden, terrifying depths of the underworld, the place where all spirit things dwelt. The underworld was an actual geographical place to which they could take a journey.[4] And it was the goddesses of the dark moon who presided as queens of this underworld.

These awesome queens wielded the power of death, destroying all that was created in their upper-world activities; and they also controlled the powers of rebirth and immortality, of the life that arises from death. The dark goddess of many names was the prophetess and holder of mysteries. She bestowed dreams, visions, and magical knowledge whereby one could fathom the mysteries of the unknown, and this understanding of secret and hidden things brought power in itself.

For the ancients a safe and helpful relationship to the powers of the underworld was to be gained through a right approach to the Dark Goddess.[5] Contemporary psychology reframes this ancient wisdom in suggesting that a safe and helpful relationship to the powers of the unconscious is to be gained through a right approach to the shadow. Nyx, the Goddess of Night, is the foundational mother of all of the various dark goddesses of the dark moon who reside as forces in the unconscious sphere of our psyches.

The ancient Dark Goddess who has been rejected has come, in modern psychology, to symbolize the feminine shadow. Because the daughters of Night inhabit the dark places in our psyche, they are difficult to access with the waking eye or conscious mind. Although we may not in a continuous sense be aware of their presence, or even acknowledge their existence, they live in us as foundations within our unconsciousness.[6]

If we acknowledge and pay respect to the dark forces in our unconscious, our inner dark goddesses will be well disposed toward us and provide insight, healing, and renewal. It is when we demean and exile the dark that her daughters (like the shadow self when rejected and denied) will, during our weakest moments, unexpectedly burst forth into our conscious reality. When the dark, feminine shadow deities take over with a vengeful autonomy of their own, they bring terror, destruction, and madness into our lives.

As the Dark Goddess archetype evolved through patriarchal culture, she became an object of fear and persecution. Over the course of his-story, the healing and prophetic wisdom of the Dark Goddess has been distorted as sorcery, and her image has been demonized into the ugly death-bringing hag or the witch, consort of the devil. As we have lost our knowledge of her gifts of renewal and ecstatic sexuality, our fear of her ways has diminished our capacity to regenerate ourselves and has poisoned our relationships with loved ones. In order to heal ourselves and our relationships, we must enter into the darkness of our unconscious and develop an honorable, respectful, and loving relationship with the dark goddesses in our midst.

Let us now begin the process of unraveling the mythological distortion of the many goddesses of the dark moon, and discover how the archetype of the dark feminine who exposed evil, shattered falsity, and demanded the truth was imbued with evil and became the secret fear of death and nonbeing. Our invocation and praise to the dark goddesses that have been banished to the neglected corners of our psyche begins with Nyx, primeval Mother Night, and her daughters, Nemesis, the Furies, the Hesperides, the Fates, and Hekate.

Notes

1. J. E. Cirlot, *Dictionary of Symbols* (New York: Philosophical Library, 1971), 214.
2. Adam McLean, *The Triple Goddess* (Edinburgh, Scotland: Hermetic Research Series, 1983), 9.
3. McLean, *The Triple Goddess*, 10.
4. Esther Harding, *Woman's Mysteries* (New York: Harper & Row, Colophon, 1976), 163.
5. Harding, *Woman's Mysteries*, 163.
6. McLean, *The Triple Goddess*, 13.

Nyx, Goddess of Night, and the Daughters of Night

✦

> . . . *Black-winged Night*
> *Into the bosom of Erebus dark and deep*
> *Laid a wind-born egg, and as the seasons rolled*
> *Forth sprang Love, the longed-for, shining, with*
> *wings of gold.*
> —*Aristophanes*[1]

$\mathcal{L}$ong before creation and the appearance of deities, humans, and nature, the ancients believed that there existed only the formless void of chaos—black, empty, silent, and endlessly yawning into infinity. According to the Orphic mysteries, out of this primeval chaos arose the first deity, Nyx, Mother Night, in the form of a great black-winged spirit hovering over a vast sea of darkness. Ancient Night conceived of the Wind and laid her silver Egg in the gigantic lap of Darkness.[2]

The upper section of this gigantic Egg formed the vault of the sky and the lower section was the earth. From the Egg sprang the son of the rushing Wind—a god with golden wings, named Eros, the spirit of love. The most beautiful of all the immortal gods emerged to create the earth. This firstborn of Mother Night is also known as Phanes, "the Revealer," related to the Greek word for light. An Orphic hymn praises him, "Ineffable, hidden brilliant scion, whose motion is whirring, you scattered the dark mist that lay before your eyes and, flapping your wings, you whirled about, and through this world you brought pure light. . . ."[3]

Nyx, whose name literally means night, was revered for her oracular powers. She could see beyond the night of the present, and her visions were made known from a cave that she shared with her son, Phanes. There Nyx displayed herself in a triple form as Night, Order, and Justice, and she ruled the universe until her power passed over to Uranus with the coming of the patriarchal gods.

Marija Gimbutas suggests that the beginnings of this myth lie in the Paleolithic era. From the early Aurignacian and on to the Magdalenian period, many engraved and sculpted images with silhouetted egg-shaped buttocks featuring bird's heads and long breasts have been found in western and central Europe.[4]

Nyx, invoked as nocturnal one, came from the earliest substratum of mythology, and by classical times she had little or no cult worship. Homer, who regarded Nyx as one of the greatest goddesses, of whom even Zeus stands in awe, tells in *Theogony* another version of the primal mother at the onset of creation. Broad-bosomed Earth; Eros, the spirit of love; Erebus, the personification of darkness; and Nyx, primordial night, were all fashioned out of the void. Then, from a union of Erebus and Nyx, were born Aether (Upper Air/Clear sky) and Hemera (Day).

The Goddess of Night was said to live in Tartarus (the underworld) jointly with Day. When her daughter Hemera entered the

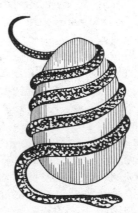

Fig. 4.1 The Orphic Egg of Creation

*Goddesses of the
Dark Moon:
Nyx, Goddess
of Night,
and the
Daughters
of Night*

palace, Nyx rode out in a chariot drawn by two black horses. Accompanied by the stars, she transversed the heavens until daybreak, when she returned to the palace. Nyx was portrayed as a black-winged goddess draped in a dark garment. On her head was a black-spangled veil, and she held an extinguished, inverted torch. She was sometimes shown carrying two children in her arms—one of them white to personify Sleep, the other black to symbolize Death.

Erebus (Darkness) and Nyx (Night) were soon deprived of the power by Aether (Light) and Hemera (Day), and the scepter then passed to Uranus (Sky) and Gaia (Earth) with the advent of the new gods.

In the earliest mythologies night was given precedence over day, and the moon over the sun. With the transition to the new solar gods, the sun gained prominence over the moon and day over night. In cult worship the mysterious Goddess of Night became diminished, neglected, and consequently feared. Later genealogies made Nyx the mother of a sinister brood of children, only some of which were deities. Everything that was inexplicable and frightful that befell humankind was personified and described as her offspring.

From Nyx were born some of the most powerful and portentous of the personified forces: Ker, Moros, and Thanatos as Death; Hypnos as Sleep and Dreams; Momos as Mockery; Oizys as Pain and Woe; Apate as Treachery; Geras as Grey Old Age; Eris as Strife; and Nemesis as Retribution. To the patriarchal solar consciousness of the ancient world, Night was a source of evil; while to the mystic consciousness of the Orphics, Night was a depth of love (Eros) and of light (Phanes).[5]

Nyx, the Goddess of Night, symbolizes the ground of the dark feminine principle that is the creative source of all that exists. According to Orphic tradition Nyx arose as a great, black-winged spirit from the primeval chaos. Her story contains the key elements of black, chaos, and void that describe the essential meaning of the dark. These elements have been distorted over the course of time, and now they have come to symbolize our fears of the dark. Let us look closer at this tale from the Orphic Mysteries, a metaphysical system influenced by a doctrine of love preserved in the sacred writings of Orpheus, and see if we can uncover the secret teachings of the Goddess of Night concerning the nature of our origin and the foundation of our being.

The Orphics taught that the first principle was Cronus, or Time. From this came Chaos, symbolizing the infinite, and Ether, symbolizing the finite. Chaos was surrounded by Night, which formed the enveloping cover under which, by the creative action of Ether, cosmic matter slowly organized. This finally assumed the shape of an egg, of which Night formed the shell.[6] Hesiod related that darkness came first, and from Darkness sprang Chaos; and that Night was born from a union between Darkness and Chaos.

Chaos and Night are represented by the ancient poets as exercising uncontrolled dominion from the beginning. Thus, in imitation of the ancients, Milton says:

> there eldest Night
> And Chaos, ancestors of nature, hold
> Eternal anarchy.
> —*Paradise Lost*, Book II, 894

and Spenser writes,

> O thou most ancient Grandmother of all,
> More old than Jove."
> —*Faery Queen*, Book I, canto 5, st 22

Creation myths the world over begin with chaos, but the original meaning of the word "chaos" did not imply confusion and turmoil. Rather it simply meant the infinite void. And void, which we now think of as black, empty nothingness, referred to the nature of the primal matter that existed before creation. Modern physics tells us that matter cannot be created or destroyed, but simply changed in form, moving back and forth between a solid state and an energy state. In Buddhist philosophy this principle is expressed as the doctrine of form and emptiness. The primal material of the void, embodied as Mother Night, refers to the condition of unity and the unlimited potentiality of all that exists before differentiation and actualization begin the process of formation.

In Eastern philosophy black is understood to represent the formless state of matter, as pure energy, which is called emptiness. Devotions to the Black Mother in Eastern traditions involve meditations that cut away the delusion of dualism, which is the root cause of all suffering—the mistaken belief that sees an independently arising self as separate from others. Wisdom lies in the realization that all that exists is unified as part of the same primal matter, and there is no difference between self and others. Life is in a constant state of flux, arising out of itself as infinite numbers of forms and falling back into itself as emptiness, the formless energy. The black, empty void is the primordial foundation of all manifested forms, the ground of potentiality for everything that exists.

This truth was conveyed by the ancient Greeks in the tale of Mother Night, who arose from chaos and gave birth to Eros/Phanes, LoveLight, who coordinated the elements and caused beings to come together in order to set the universe in motion. The Greek Nyx is related to the Egyptian Nut, Nuit, Neith, Goddess of the Black Night, who existed before heaven and earth were differentiated. Out of her watery womb arose the sun for the first time at creation, and back into her fathomless depths all things returned.

The wisdom of Black Mother Night, spanning Greek, Eastern, and Egyptian traditions, is that the preexisting nature of all life is a universally connected matrix of living energy whose first expression is as love. When we are ignorant of her truth, we experience a fear of the void and become involved in outer activity to escape the emptiness that terrifies us. We see this fear in those who cannot bear to have empty time or space in their lives or who have a fear of being alone.

And so, first of all, we call forth Nyx to reclaim our awareness that our original essential nature arises out of formless potentiality embodied by the night.

Journal Questions

1. In what ways do I link the words black to empty, chaos to confusion, and void to nothingness? How have these associations shaped my concepts of the dark?
2. Do I recognize the positive value of being alone, of having open unscheduled time in my life, or of having a spacious uncluttered environment? Can I utilize these situations to be open, receptive, and still; or do I perceive them as feeling lonely, bored, or impoverished?

The Daughters of Night

The description that Nyx laid a silver egg is another way of saying that Mother Night gave birth to the moon, silver being the lunar metal. From primal Mother Night there also emerged three sets of daughters, each of whom was a manifestation of the triple nature of the moon—the Moirai, the Erinyes, the Hesperides; and a fourth, single daughter, Nemesis. The daughters of Nyx arose from the earliest stratum of deities at the beginning of creation, and they were representatives of the Triple Moon Goddess in her death aspect.[7] Each of these daughters of Night reflects aspects of the dark side of the goddess.

In her triple aspect Nyx displayed herself as Night, Order, and Justice. Her daughters' tasks were to ensure that the natural laws of the universe were carried out and maintained. These sisters also saw to the punishment of those who transgressed these boundaries.

Nemesis was the Goddess of Retribution, who maintained the equilibrium of the human condition. The Erinyes (the Furies) protected the continuity of the maternal bloodline by avenging murders of family members. The Moirai (the Fates) spoke to the issue of fate, destiny, and the karmic patterning of the soul. And the Hesperides were the guardians of immortality and knowledge of the past. In our souls these dark sisters represent the primal elements in the dark, unconscious side of our beings who protest the violation of natural law.

The early Greek concept of justice and natural law evolved from the vision of an orderly, interconnected universe. Nature proceeded according to patterns that were not careless or random, and this implied the existence of some kind of foundational intelligence in the intricate complexity of the workings of the universe. Human beings also partook of the organic patterning of the universe; but when they acted in ways that were not in accordance with or harmed this natural order, the universe reacted. The daughters of Night were charged with balancing or avenging the transgressions of individuals when they overstepped the laws of natural development or the limits set by necessity.

Nemesis

Nemesis, daughter of primordial Mother Night, was most widely known as the Goddess of Retribution. While the patriarchy perceived her as a monstrous figure of revenge and anger, her earlier nature was more as an abstract force of justice rather than that of retaliation. She was a personification of the reverence for law, and she sought to restore balance when order was upset. Her endeavors to preserve an equilibrium in people's attitudes toward one another were recognized as springing from a deep-seated love.

Nemesis was depicted as a thoughtful, queenly figure, radiant with some of Aphrodite's beauty. She wore a silver crown adorned with staghorns, carried a wheel of fortune in one hand and an apple bough in the other, with a scourge hanging at her girdle. The wheel indicates that she may be derived from Kala-Nemi, the Mother of

Karma and of the wheel of time.[8] The apple bough shows her relationship to her sisters the Hesperides, who guarded the golden apples of immortality.

Nemesis's primary sanctuary was in Rhamnus in Attica. There, winged and draped in white, she was worshiped along with Adios (Shame) as attendants to Themis, the Goddess of Law. It was said that should Themis be disregarded, then Nemesis is there. When individuals broke the social rules that Themis represented, then Nemesis, powerful in her righteous anger, tormented those who violated this order, especially nature's law and norm.

Nemesis was said to be a check on Tyche, Goddess of Fortune, who indiscriminately heaped gifts upon some people, deprived others of all they had, and in doing so exemplified the uncertainty of chance. But if a person who had been bestowed with abundant good fortune did not offer a portion to the gods or to charity, then the ancient goddess Nemesis stepped in to humiliate him or her.[9] She was also known as Adastria, the Inescapable One, who embodied the anger of the gods toward those who committed the crime of hubris, pride, and insolence before the gods. Ovid called her the "goddess who abhors boastful words," because she brought all kings and heroes down to destruction in the end, no matter how arrogant they might have become.

Fig. 4.2 Nemesis

Nemesis, through the course of patriarchal culture, grew to become a philosophic concept of divine vengeance on overweening mortals.[10] As an impersonal moral force Nemesis appeared to overtake every act of wrong. She was held in awe and fear as a mysterious power who shaped the behavior of individuals in their time of prosperity, punishing crime and evil deeds, taking luck away from the unworthy, tracking every wrong to its doer, and keeping society in equipoise.[11] Nemesis also personified the resentment aroused in people when others who committed crimes were not punished, or toward those who had inordinate or undeserved good fortune.

According to the lost epic *Cypria* and several later works, Zeus fell in love with Nemesis; but she did not want to couple with the King of Gods and fled from his advances. Twice she changed her shape in order to evade him. The third time she transformed herself into a goose. Zeus, taking the form of a swan, raped her. Nemesis in due course laid the awaited egg, which was taken either by a shepherd or by Hermes to Leda, wife of King Tyndareos of Sparta. Leda cared for the egg, from which sprang Helen—the most beautiful of women, who precipitated the Trojan War.

Robert Graves points out that the Nemesis Zeus chased was not the philosophic concept of divine vengeance, but rather the original Nymph goddess in the earliest form of the love-chase myth. Nemesis's wheel represented the solar year, and she ensured the "due enactment" of the annual death drama. In pre-Hellenic myth the goddess chases the sacred king; and as he goes through his seasonal transformations as various animals, she counters each of them in turn, and devours him at the summer solstice. With the victory of the patriarchal system, the chase is reversed and the goddess now flees from Zeus.[12]

Nemesis, daughter of Night, existed as one of the first forces to ensure that humanity respected the natural laws that maintained the order of the universe. When we pay honor to this goddess and live in harmony with these laws, then Nemesis resides within us as a wise, kindly influence, ever-guiding us toward right action. Zeus's rape of Nemesis is an allegorical statement that he took the law into his own hands, deciding what was right and wrong. When the power passed over to the patriarchal gods, Nemesis was banished, and the new order ignored her jurisdiction over the codes of right conduct. Then, like the shadow who flourishes in exile and assumes the demonic form of our negative views and actions, Nemesis came to be personified by the patriarchy as divine vengeance and retribution, angrily claiming her due.

As we continue to deny this goddess her position of honor, she operates in our unconscious psyche, via projection, as the wrathful forces in our world that will not allow us to get away with wrongdoing. When we try to get away with wrong action and avoid our responsibilities, we live in terror that the fury of Nemesis will eventually catch up with us and inflict her punishment, a punishment that uncannily fits the crime.

Nyx, Goddess of Night, teaches us that we are, at our most fundamental level, all part of the same whole. Her daughter Nemesis then guides us toward respecting others as extensions of ourselves through right action with the natural laws of an orderly universe.

Journal Questions

1. Do I have a concept of right and wrong, and do I have a value system to determine the difference? Is there some force within me that advises me against following a course of wrong action? Do I believe in a wrathful, punishing divine force that operates outside of my control? Or do I have a sense that it might be my own actions and attitudes that eventually lead to my punishment?

2. Do I try to "get away" with things? Am I dishonest when it is to my advantage? If I have good luck, do I share my bounty with others? When I am wrong, do I admit it? Do I see the law and authority figures as hostile powerful forces who are out to get me?

The Erinyes

The Erinyes, known as the Furies to the Romans, were female spirits of anger and revenge, and their functions overlapped those of Nemesis. All the daughters of Nyx stood for the rightness of things within an established order, and they punished those who transgressed natural laws. While Nemesis appeared when Themis (Law) was in any way offended, the Erinyes had a more limited function. They took vengeance whenever family blood was shed, especially a mother's blood, and against those who broke oaths.[13]

The Erinyes were said to be among the most ancient goddesses, predating Zeus and all the other Olympians. Their antiquity is demonstrated by the fact that originally they were invoked primarily against those who killed kinsfolk (family members) related through the maternal line. As such they represented a force that held the

matriarchal world together, a time when all genealogies were reck-
oned through women. Protectors of the rights of matriarchal bloodlines, the Erinyes wrought vengeance against anyone who, by murder,
stopped the continuity of the female lineage of generations.

They were called the Children of Night by Aeschylus, and the
Daughters of Earth and Darkness by Sophocles. Hesiod assimilated
them into the later cosmologies by saying that the Erinyes were born
when the blood of castrated Uranus fell upon the Mother Earth,
Gaia. And when this same blood dropped upon the ocean, the resulting foam took shape as their sister Aphrodite, which is why Aphrodite is sometimes referred to as the oldest of the Erinyes. Robert
Graves comments that the three Erinyes who sprang from Uranus's
blood are the Triple Goddess herself; that is to say, during the king's
sacrifice, designed to fructify the cornfields and orchards.[14]

In their triple form the Erinyes appeared as Alekto, "the Never-
ending"; Megaira, which means envious anger; and Tisiphone, containing the word *tisis*, retaliation. They were portrayed as three
immortal black maidens, sometimes winged, with serpents wreathed
in their hair and bearing torches and scourges. They were depicted as
stern-faced but beautiful, and upon occasion they were shown with
poisonous blood dripping from their eyes. Aeschylus portrays the
Erinyes as frightening and hideous, and they came to represent a
man's hidden fear of woman as the Scolding Mother.

Fig. 4.3 The Erinyes

Ovid has described the attributes of Tisiphone in the following lines:

Then fell Tisiphone with Rage was stung,
And from her Mouth th' untwisted serpents hung.
Girt in a bloody Gown a Torch she shakes,
And round her Neck twines speckled Wreathes of Snakes.
Part of her Tresses loudly hiss, and part
Spread Poison as their forky Tongues they dart,
Then from her middle Locks two snakes she drew,
Whose Merit from superior Mischief grew.
    —*Metamorphoses*, Book IV

Whenever a mother was insulted, harmed, or murdered, the Erinyes would rise out of Hades; and emulating the dog-headed form of their sister Hekate, their approach was heralded by the sound of barking. When enraged, they were consumed with anger lodged deep inside their hearts. In a noxious swarm they would descend upon the criminal, stinging like bees and biting like horseflies. They would pursue the offender from land to land with relentless fury, driving him frantic and hounding him to madness, and then causing him to die in torment. The Erinyes, intractable to any argument, were not interested in retribution, only in vengeance. Their punishment was madness and death.

Sacrifices to the Erinyes most often occurred at night in a place that was wild in character, and the animals offered to them were black. In Greece several temples and solemn groves were dedicated to the Erinyes, such as Colonus near Athens, the site of Oedipus's death. The shrines of these goddesses were surrounded by stands of funeral trees—the alder, the black poplar, and the yew. They were worshiped in the sanctuary at the foot of the Areopagus Hill in Athens.

With the passage of time the Erinyes, as goddesses of the dead, were also called upon to avenge crimes committed against either parent and any violation of blood kinship. Their duties extended to punishing filial disobedience, irreverence to old age, treachery to guests, unkindness toward beggars, perjury, and all murder. Also called the Dirae, they were the executors of curses invoked by a person who had been wronged by another.

However, the dreaded Erinyes, the furious ones, were not regarded, at least in earlier times, as unjust or even malign. Their punishments were impartial and impersonal. Their work of avenging crimes protected those who were injured by members of their own family and satisfied the souls of the dead whom they represented. This function was essential to the orderly operation of society. With the advance of the patriarchal culture and the violent destruction of the matriarchy, the Erinyes were perceived by the new order as cruel and bloodthirsty as they furiously pursued their vengeance against the increasing number of offenders.

In *The Eumenides*, the third play in *The Oresteia*, Aeschylus brought this situation to a head. Here the Erinyes were pursuing and torment-ing Orestes for the crime of slaughtering his mother, Clytemnestra, which he did in revenge for her killing his father, Agamemnon. Apollo's defense of Orestes held that matricide, the murder of a mother by her son, was no crime because the mother is not the true parent of the child. Athena, born from the head of her father, Zeus, intervened to acquit Orestes, and thus effected the final transition from the law of mother-right to that of father-right, and the victory of the Olympians over the chthonic world of the matriarchy.

The Erinyes bitterly protested the trial and the verdict: If a con-fessed mother killer was to go free, they would lose all authority as avenging deities. Convulsed with anger at the derision of the old laws by the gods of the younger generation, they threatened to retaliate by ravaging the land, causing famine and barrenness in humanity. Athena consoled them with offers of honor and sacrifices. The final subjugation of their ancient powers by the new order occurred when the Erinyes, the Furies, become renamed as the Eumenides, the Kindly Ones.

For the ancient Greeks the Erinyes were the force that protected the sanctity of the maternal bloodline, and they defended the con-tinuity of what can be passed on through the generations. The ulti-mate taboo was the murder of one's mother, and then of any other blood kin. However, this injunction left the Greeks in a difficult predica-ment. If it was forbidden to kill a person to whom you are related through your mother's blood, and if a kinsfolk violated or murdered a member of your family, then what recourse did you have for justice, if by avenging the crime you committed the same transgression?

Nyx and her daughters represented the natural laws of the uni-verse, which maintained the orderly workings of the world. When humanity caused an upset by violating these laws, the universe would react to restore the balance. This belief in the divine mechanism of retributive justice was personified as the daughters of night. The

Erinyes represented a cosmic force that ensured the punishment of offenders of blood crime. If a person tried to avenge such a crime committed by a clan member, he or she would then be guilty of the same crime. The Erinyes relieved members of the clan from having to take direct responsibility for retributive justice.

When the law of the patriarchy triumphed over the jurisdiction held by the Erinyes as avenging deities, these goddesses were banished from their honored position in society. Fearful stories circulated that it was unwise to even mention them by name in conversation; instead, to be on the safe side, one should refer to them euphemistically as the "kindly ones" or the "lovely ladies."

The Erinyes, as ancient spirits of anger and revenge, reside in us today as psychological forces operating in our unconscious. To the extent the Erinyes are an emanation of the Dark Goddess, their energies constitute a part of the shadow in individuals and the collective. The Erinyes, as the shadow, represent the primal rage within us that hungers after vengeance. If this primal aspect of ourselves is activated, then we can become so one-pointed in focusing our energies in pursuit of vengeance that we may be shocked by the extremes to which we might go.[15]

When we banish the Erinyes and do not allow them to exercise their power in protecting the code of right relationship to our family members, they will emerge in our shadow selves as our own worst enemies. When the shadow Erinyes take over our lives, we may discover the furious, raging personality within us, consumed with a desire for vengeance. Caught in the grip of this archetype, we may commit horrible and ugly deeds against our kinsfolk or other loved ones whom we think have wronged either us or a member of our family. The Erinyes will then take the form of our subsequent pangs of conscience. They will torment us relentlessly with remorse, guilt, and fear of retaliation or punishment. As we internalize the role of these avenging deities, our tortured conscience will cause us to go mad and, in some cases, even to kill ourselves. A classic example of this can be seen in the tormented main character of Edgar Allen Poe's "The Telltale Heart."

In our evocation of the forces of Night, after Nyx and Nemesis, we honor the Three Erinyes, who teach us that it is not necessary for us to commit crimes of vengeance in order to "get even." There exists a mechanism in the divine order of the universe that ensures the punishment of offenders and restores balance "'Vengeance is mine, I will repay' saith the Lord" (Rom. 12:19).

····· *Journal Questions* ·····

1. How often do I feel anger or even blind rage toward those whom I think have wronged me or toward those who have harmed or violated my family or loved ones? Have I ever felt driven to exact revenge, and then suffered from a tortured conscience?

2. Do I believe that if I don't personally take steps to ensure retribution, the offender will get away with his or her crime? Can I consider the possibility that the universe might have a built-in mechanism of justice that will eventually and inevitably occur without my willful, direct participation?

The Hesperides

The Hesperides, as children of Mother Night, were known as the daughters of Evening. They lived in a garden of paradise, where they guarded the golden apples of immortality. This garden was said to be beyond the river ocean at the extreme western limits of the world, which modern travelers have located on the coast of Africa between Tangier and Casablanca. These Nymphs of the West were identified with the sun setting over the western waves at the edge of night. In their triple form these goddesses were known as Hespere, the evening one, Aegle, the luminous one, and Erytheia, the crimson one.

In some genealogies the Hesperides are the children of Phorcys and Ceto; and later mythologies make them the daughters of the

Fig. 4.4 The Tree of the Hesperides

giant King Atlas, who stood upon the western edge of the world and supported the heavens on his shoulders. Other names that have been given to the Hesperides are Lipara, "of soft radiance," Chrysothemis, "golden law and order," and Asterope, "star-brilliant."

At the wedding of Zeus and Hera, Gaia, Mother Earth, presented Hera with a beautiful tree that bore golden apples. This tree was growing in an orchard, fabled to be the birthplace of Hera, at the foothills of Mt. Atlas. Hera placed the tree under the guardianship of the Three Hesperides, who were stewards of magical objects. The three sisters were assisted in this task by Ladon, a three-headed (or alternately hundred-headed) serpent, child of Typhon and Echidne. The apples are a symbol of eternal life growing in the Garden of Immortality, which is the temple of Hera's regenerative womb.[16]

The Hesperides were known for their sweet singing voices and their pleasure in bright songs. This was frequently mentioned in the tales along with the ability of the serpent Ladon, who was gifted with the power of human speech, to converse in many divers tongues. When one heard their soft music at dusk, it was said to be an enticement to secret rites. The secrets of these ceremonies could sometimes be terrifying to the uninitiated.

The West symbolized the gateway to death, and the Hesperides were an aspect of the Dark Moon Death Goddess. Robert Graves suggests that the garden was placed in the far west because the sacred king, as the sun's representative, met his death at sunset.[17] The Hesperides, with their sweet love songs, called the king to his death; and, as the sun set, Hespera, the Evening Star, appeared. It was said that Hera sometimes took the form of Hespera, the star sacred to Aphrodite. The golden apples were given to the king at the end of his reign as his passport to immortality.

This legend of the Hesperides, which contains the elements of the garden, the apple, and the serpent, is an early forerunner of the biblical story of the Garden of Eden. The golden apples of immortality are a symbol of the cycles of renewal. In the Jewish myth the serpent, who then represented the principle of evil, tempted humankind to partake of the forbidden fruit of the Tree of Knowledge. As such it represents the patriarchy's long persecution of learning concerning the death and renewal mysteries of the Dark Moon Goddess and her serpent.

The Twelve Labors of Hercules can be read on one level as the hero's conquest of the Goddess. In the eleventh labor Hercules must steal the golden apples of the Hesperides. After many journeys and inquiries trying to discover the whereabouts of the golden apples, Hercules was finally directed to King Atlas, who the Olympians made to be the father of the Hesperides. Atlas had built a wall around the garden to protect its treasures, because he had been warned by Themis that one day a son of Zeus would strip his tree of its gold. As the classical version of the story is told, King Atlas, after listening to all Hercules had to say, promised to fetch the apples if Hercules would relieve him of his burden for an hour's respite and hold up the heavens in his stead. However, Atlas feared Ladon, so Hercules killed the serpent with an arrow shot over the garden wall. Atlas then entered his daughters' garden and plucked the golden apples.

Relishing his sense of freedom, Atlas did not want to resume the weight of the world. When he returned to the place he had left Hercules, he offered to carry the golden apples himself to Eurystheus. Hercules pretended to acquiesce, but asked Atlas to first hold the heavens for only one moment while he placed a pad on his head. Atlas, easily deceived, laid the apples on the grass and took back the world again. Hercules then grabbed the apples and easily strode away. Other legends have it that Hercules himself entered the garden, killed the serpent who watched over the tree, and stole the golden fruit. The apples were later returned to the garden by Athena, because the sacred fruits were not to remain long anywhere else.

Shortly afterward the nymphs of the West were visited by Jason and the Argonauts. The Hesperides, frightened after Hercules' theft of their treasures, transformed themselves into trees—Hespere into a poplar, Erytheis into an elm, and Aegle into a willow. When they realized that the stranded Argonauts were not hostile, they showed them a spring that Hercules had created in the desert so that they could quench their thirst.

The Hesperides and the serpent Ladon are the guardians of the golden apples. The apple, along with the pomegranate, is the fruit of the underworld and, according to Alan Bleakly in *Fruits of the Moon Tree*, it represents the fruiting of the creative imagination. He goes on to say that when we meditate, engage in reverie, or experience spirit vision, this is often felt as a rushing up the spine, the rising of the *kundalini* energy, symbolized by the snake. The *kundalini* snake rises in creative vision, flowers in the garden of the mind, and matures as the fruits of the imagination.[18]

The golden apples are also the symbol of immortality, and, as such, they preserve our knowledge of cyclical renewal. In our unconscious the golden apples represent the essence of our past lives, our previous incarnations, and the collective essence of the eternal part of our humanity.[19] The Hesperides guard the knowledge of our past in order to protect our conscious awareness from becoming overwhelmed by information that we may not have the wisdom to understand nor the capacity to integrate.

In their sweet singing voices the Hesperides tell us there are some things that are better for us not to know unless we have been "initiated." We can use this information in positive and beneficial ways. When we do not honor the Hesperides, we experience the rejected shadow side of these goddesses at times when the revelation of the past destroys our peace of mind and disrupts our life as we have known it. Suddenly and unexpectedly, our past secrets may burst forth in disturbing nightmares, madness, schizophrenia, gossip, scandal. When we have the wisdom and compassion to assimilate this knowledge of the past, then the fruit of the Hesperides can be a source of inspiration, insight, and creativity.

The Hesperides teach us that we are immortal, and that we have an infinite past. They allow this material to be revealed only when we are able to use it wisely. Knowledge of the past and its impact upon the present and future are tied up with the questions of fate and destiny, the domain governed by the Moirai—the third set and the most powerful of the daughters of Night.

Journal Questions

1. Do I believe in rebirth or in reincarnation? If so, do I remember or have I tried to explore any of my past lives? Do I think that this kind of knowledge of the past is of interest and value, or do I think that this information is not necessary in order to live out well the present and future? Do I believe that there are some things that it is better not to know?
2. Do I think that somewhere in my mind resides a collective memory of all that has come before me? If so, do I believe that I can access this source of information? Have I ever had a feeling of déjà vu, a flashback, or the sudden awareness that I am remembering something from a long time ago? Have glimpses of the past allowed me to access a source of inspired wisdom or creativity?

The Moirai

The Moirai, the final triple set of Night's daughters, were held in awe as the goddesses of fate. To the ancient Greeks fate was the inescapable destiny that followed every human being and was personified by these three daughters of Nyx. In a singular form the Goddess of Fate was called Moira, and her triple form, the three sisters, were known as the Moirai—Klotho the Spinner, Lachesis the Measurer, and Atropos the Cutter.

The name Moira means "part," and this refers both to the three parts of the moon and to the concept of a person's allotted portion in life. As a lunar symbol the triple Moirai correspond to the three phases of the moon, the three seasons of the year (spring, summer, and winter), and the three stages of a person's life. As a person's lot in life, Moira, in the Mycenaean period, meant a landholding possessed by a female property owner according to the old matriarchal system. Hence Moira was "a lot," which later became "allotted Fate."[20]

As Spinners of Fate these three goddesses spun out the days of our lives as a yarn and wove it into a tapestry. The length of the yarn was decided entirely by them. Klotho spun the thread of life from her distaff and passed it on to Lachesis, the Disposer of Lots, who measured it against her rod and assigned each person's destiny. Atropos, the Inevitable—"she who cannot be turned"—then cut the thread with her shears at the appointed time of death. Once the destiny of an individual was woven, it was irrevocable and could not be altered. The length of life and time of death were part of the pattern designed by the Fates. Not even Zeus, supreme god of the Heavens, could go against their decree.

Fig. 4.5 The Moirai

The Fates were a trinity older than time. At Athens the archaic great Love Goddess Aphrodite was called the eldest of the Moirai. Robert Graves points out that Aphrodite Urania was the Nymph Goddess to whom the sacred king had in ancient times been sacrificed at summer solstice.[21] Greek funerary hymns consigned the dead to Aphrodite's care and were known as the *Moirologhia*, invocations to the fates.

In later poetry the Moirai were portrayed as stern, inexorable women, aged and hideous, clothed in dark attire, and sometimes seated near the footstool of Hades. However, earlier images described them as dwelling amidst celestial spheres where, clad in robes spangled with stars, and wearing crowns on their heads, they sat on thrones radiant with light. Orpheus sang of the Moirai in white raiment living in heaven beside a pool in a cave from which gushes white water. This clear image of moonlight indicates their lunar nature.

The function of the Fates was to see that the natural order of things was respected. They sat in the assemblies of the gods and possessed the gift of prophecy. They were worshiped seriously in Greece and Italy with sacrifices of honey and flowers, and sometimes ewes were offered to them. In Rome and Sparta the Fates had temples and altars.

The Fates were divine beings who determined the course of events in human lives. As the personification of the idea of implacable destiny, it was said that the whole of a person's life was overshadowed by the Moirai. Like the dark phase of the moon, which signifies the transition between death and birth, the great triad of the Moirai were associated with the three decisive moments of life—the beginning and the end, birth and death, along with marriage as the third great season. Accompanying Ililthyia, Goddess of Childbirth, they arrived at the cradle of every newborn to set the child's fate and apportion its share of good and evil. Folklore and fairy tales tell of the offerings made to the fairy godmothers on the child's behalf. When a person was married, the three Fates had to be invoked so that the union would be happy; and when the end of life approached, the Moirai hastened to cut the thread of life.

An individual who tried to challenge his or her fate was punished for trying to overstep the boundaries set by the Moirai. To scorn fate or commit hubris (excessive arrogance and pride before the gods) was to bring the righteous anger of Nemesis, whose punishment fit precisely the nature of the crime. One of the few exceptions was when

Apollo, a younger god, made the Moirai drunk in order to save the life of his friend Admetus. For the most part, it was said that even Zeus walked in awe of the Fates, who frequently functioned against his will. He was powerless to stop them and was bound by their decisions.

The power of the Moirai came down from a time before Zeus. It was derived from their ancient existence as part of the very order of the universe itself. Later poets called Zeus the Leader of the Fates when he assumed supreme sovereignty, and he took the prerogative of measuring a person's life, informing the Fates of his decision, and saving whom he pleased. In order for Zeus to assimilate the power of the Fates, the Moirai became his daughters from the union with Themis, who was the principle of law, order, and justice in the world. Other versions of the myths have the Moirai as bridal attendants who came to bless the wedding of Zeus and Themis.

Many different cultures shared the notion that life was a mystical thread that was spun by a trinity of goddesses who are the weavers of fate. In Anglo-Saxon literature, fate is woven. In Latin *destino* (destiny) means that which is woven and fixed with cords and threads; fate is "bound" to happen, just as the spells of fairy women were binding.[22] The trinity of fate reflected the triad of virgin, mother, and crone, who ruled the past, present, and future and symbolized the creator, preserver, and destroyer aspects of the Great Goddess.

The colors of the fates were white, red, and black. Indian mystics called the threads of life *gunas* or strands. The pure white of the Virgin was *sattva*, the Mother's royal red was *rajas*, and the Crone's funerary black was *tamas*. These colors symbolized the progress of life in nature from light to darkness.[23]

The Greek Moira was also known to the Romans as Fortuna, to the Scandinavians as the Norns, to the Anglo-Saxons as Wyrd, and to the Celts as Morrigan. In Rome the goddess Fortuna controlled the destiny of every human being, and her magic wheel of time determined the propitious days. This later degenerated into the carnival wheel of fortune, and she was invoked as Lady Luck by gamblers. In the Scandinavian religion three sisters known as the Norns (Urd, Verdandi, and Skuld) sat of the foot of the World Tree and were the fates that ruled each life. They were the most powerful of all the deities, and not even the gods could undo what they had done or do what they did not wish.

The Wyrd sisters are the three witches in Shakespeare's Macbeth chanting over the cauldron. They are direct descendants of the Anglo-Saxon Goddess of Fate Wyrd, whose word was immutable law.

Throughout the Dark Ages the Wyrd sisters or three fairies were invited to the house of a newborn to cast a good destiny for the child, and they were offered a feast with three knives laid out their service. In the tale of Sleeping Beauty, when the third fairy (or, in some versions, the thirteenth fairy) was not invited to the birth celebration, she put a curse on the young princess that she would prick herself on a spinning wheel (of the Fates) and the kingdom would fall into a deep sleep. The Celtic Morrigan (Ana, Babd, and Macha) was known as Mother Death, and her derivative Morgan Le Fay or Fata Morgana cast a destroying curse on every man.

Fate, the Unconscious, and *Karma*   During the dark moon times in our lives, when it seems as if our known security is being destroyed, we are often overcome with feelings of helplessness. We are unable to understand why such terrible things are happening to us. We worry that our life might be marked by a tragic fate.

This idea of fate—that each person's life is preordained and determined by forces beyond his or her control—is as old as humanity itself. And right behind this eternal question arises the issue of free will. Do we have any influence over our destiny? The resolution to this query is not an either/or answer, but the synthetic realization that at each moment we are simultaneously subject to fate and offered free will.

The Moirai, as determiners of fate, are not an external force separate and more powerful than us; but these three sisters, who spin our fate and embody our destiny, live within us in the dark unconscious realms of our psyche. Like the shadow self when rejected and denied, the Moirai, when dismissed and disregarded, can suddenly manifest as the circumstances of our tragic misfortune.

It is important to remember that, in the myths, the three sisters apportioned both good and evil for the newborn child. If we have a sense of positive currents working in our soul, then our inner Moirai will be well disposed toward us. This can release great forces of positivity, and resources of life energy become available to us. But if we come to feel our Moirai have woven a tragic or empty future for us, then we will be depressed and feel drained of life energy.[24]

At these times the dark aspects of our personality are called up as rage and despair over what we perceive to be the injustice, without any apparent reason or cause, of our situation. Yet the pattern of our fate is not imposed upon us by some external power but comes from the depths of our own souls.

Liz Greene equates the three Fates to the Wheel of Fortune key in the Tarot. "On an inner level, the three Moirai who hold the Wheel of Fortune present an image of a deep and mysterious law at work within the individual, which is unknown and unseen yet which seems to precipitate sudden changes of fortune that overturn the established pattern of life."[25]

What is this mysterious law, older than time itself, that the Fates are entrusted with carrying out and preserving? Today most of us reject a fatalistic model of the universe, because the idea that our lives are totally predetermined by an unseen, impersonal, and random force is a terrifying thought. It nullifies any possibility that we can dream, aspire, and use our will to shape the course of our lives. This popular conception of fate renders us powerless and impotent.

Yet the Fates, born at the onset of creation, wove the strands that maintained humanity's connection to the natural order of the universe itself. To the Greek poet Hesiod, Fate was the guardian of justice and natural law. The Moirai, who were present at both the birth and death of an individual, turned the wheel of fortune, which is also the wheel of time. In cyclical process the end of the old cycle is both the foundation and precursor of the beginning of the new cycle. The seed sprouts, flowers, and returns back to seed, only to germinate once again. The seed from which the new plant arises contains the essence of its predecessor.

At some time in the succession of our human lives, we reap the harvest of all the seeds that we have previously planted. This is the basis for the law of *karma*, which postulates a cause-and-effect relationship between our prior actions and present circumstances. *Karma* is the fruit of our seeds, or the results of our actions, in both a positive and negative sense. *Karma* is often linked with the concept of reincarnation, which proposes that we have not one but many lives, one right after the other, here on earth. These two principles working together imply that throughout countless lifetimes, we reap the results of all our actions. Biblical scripture sums up the Eastern doctrine of *karma* in the verse, "As ye sow, so shall ye reap" (Gal. 6:7).

From this point of view fate is the inevitable ripening of our *karma*. Up to the ever-present now, everything that occurs to us has been preordained by our own personal or groups' former actions and thoughts. This is our fate. It has not been imposed upon us from the outside, but is a product of our own inner creation. Where the possibility of free will exists is in how we respond to our fate. The intentions and motivations that underlie the choices we make and the actions we take in the present determine our destiny. Our free will exists as the choice and opportunity to create the future according to our level of wisdom and compassion.

The Moirai operate from the unconscious level of our beings. Because of our limited vision we are often unable to see the full implications of how or even when our beginnings initiate a process that leads to an inescapable conclusion. By our prior actions we spin the threads of our fate. By the nature of our response and actions to the inevitability of our present circumstances, we weave the pattern of our future destiny.

The Moirai within us are the "minions of justice" who preside over the unseen mysterious orderly workings of the cosmos. They guide us through our pain and suffering toward change and renewal, and toward attunement to living in harmony with the soul of the world. By honoring and respecting the daughters of the Night as our own dark, unconscious forces, we can make our peace with the Fates.

In the procession of the goddesses of the Night, Nyx, Nemesis, the Erinyes, the Hesperides are the Moirai. These sisters teach us that it is none other than our own previous actions that are the foundational cause of our bad fate or misfortune as well as our good luck. Furthermore, by our present actions and attitudes, we are the ones who control and create our future destiny.

Journal Questions

1. Do I think that everything is fated or predetermined? Do I feel helpless to change anything? Do I feel that the course my life has taken is the result of the actions of others upon me, or simply good or bad luck? Do I think that I have free will to shape my future?

2. Do I assume any personal responsibility for my misfortune? Do I believe that victims are innocent, helpless bystanders who have been willfully abused by oppressors? Do I see any relationship between my own actions and the circumstances of my life?

Hekate, Queen of the Night

Queen of the Night, triple-faced Hekate is one of the most ancient images from a pre-Greek stratum of mythology and an original embodiment of the great Triple Goddess. She is most often linked with the dark of the moon and presides over magic, ritual, prophetic vision, childbirth, death, the underworld, and the secrets of regeneration. Mistress of the crossroads, this lunar goddess dwells in caves, walks the highways at night, makes love on the vast seas, and is the force that moves the moon.

Genealogy   Hekate is a primordial figure in the oldest stratum of our unconscious. Her genealogy leads us back to her birth at the beginning of time as a daughter of Nyx, Ancient Night. On an inner level Hekate is a guardian figure of the mysterious depths of our unconscious that accesses the collective memory of the primal void and whirling forces at the onset of creation.

Hekate may have been originally derived from the Egyptian midwife goddess Heket, who in turn evolved into Heq or the tribal matriarch of predynastic Egypt. In Greece Hekate was a pre-Olympic goddess, whose geographical origins place her as a native of Thrace, in the northeast part of the country, which links her to goddess worship of old Middle Europe and Asia Minor in the third and fourth millennia. Unlike many other primordial deities, Hekate was absorbed into the classical Greek pantheon.

Hesiod, in *Theogony*, gives us the following account of her parentage. The Titan couple Phoibe and Koios had two daughters: Leto, the mother of Apollo and Artemis, and Asteria, a star goddess. Asteria mated with Perses, both symbols of shining light, and she gave birth to Hekate, "most lovely one," a title of the moon. Hekate is therefore a cousin to Artemis, with whom she is often associated,

Fig. 4.6   Hekate

and a reappearance of the great goddess Phoibe, whose name poets give to the moon. Hekate is portrayed as a torch-bearing Moon Goddess who wears a gleaming headdress of stars lighting the way into the darkness of the vast past of our origins and the depths of our inner being.

The Olympian Greeks had a difficult time fitting her into the scheme of their gods. The Titans, with whom Hekate was associated, were the pre-Olympic deities whom Zeus had ousted and degraded. However, the new conquerors bowed to Hekate's antiquity by granting to her alone a power shared with Zeus—that of granting or withholding from humanity anything she wished. While she never joined the Olympian company, Zeus honored her above all other deities by giving her a special place and granting her dominion over heaven, earth, and the underworld. According to Hesiod she became a bestower of wealth and all blessings of everyday life, and in the human sphere she ruled over the three great mysteries of birth, life, and death.

Later traditions make Hekate the daughter of Zeus and Hera and reduce her power to only that of the underworld and the waning dark moon. The following tale was told to explain her descent to the underworld. Hekate incurred the wrath of her mother, Hera, by stealing a pot of rouge to give to Europa, a lover of Zeus's. She then fled to earth and hid in the house of a woman who had just given birth. Although Hekate was a patron of midwives, by these times contact with childbirth rendered a person impure. To wash away her stain the Cabiri plunged her into the Acheron, a river of the underworld, where she then remained.

As Prytania, Invincible Queen of the Dead, Hekate became a wardress and conveyor of souls through the underworld. As Goddess of Magic and enchantments, she sent prophetic or demonic dreams to humankind. Her presence was felt at tombs and scenes of murders, where she presided over purifications and expiations. Like her namesake Kali, in India, Hekate, as a funerary priestess, conducted her rites in charnel or burial grounds, assisting in liberating the souls of the newly dead.

Because her nature was originally that of a mysterious deity, more prominence was given later to her gloomy and appalling features. The Hellenes emphasized Hekate's destructive powers at the expense of her creative ones, until at last she was invoked only as a goddess of the netherworld in clandestine rites of black magic, especially at places where three roads met in the darkness of night.

Hekate's prophetic character survived in Norway and Sweden as the old, hooded, wise "conversation women," who traveled about the farmlands and countryside foretelling the future. They were welcomed, fed, and given gifts. But with the coming of patriarchal dominion the goddesses diminished in influence and grandeur. The medial powers of the wise crone were repressed and later emerged as the patriarchy's twisted and tortured projections, now perceived as dangerous witchcraft and sorcery.[26]

By medieval times, when the patriarchal dualistic worldview saw the human soul as the battleground for the warring forces of good and evil, Hekate became particularly diabolized by Catholic authorities. The church projected onto her their own inner fears and spiritual insecurities, and distorted her figure into the ugly hag Queen of the Witches. It was Hekate who was now responsible for inciting the pagan country people—who were simply practicing their ancient fertility and folk customs—to supposed acts of uncanny evil, unspeakable horror, and abominable rites. The people who were most dangerous to the church were precisely those whom Hekate patronized: midwives, healers, and seers. And 9 million women were burned as witches, accused of being inhabited by evil spirits such as Hekate.

Hekate's Triple Nature   Hekate is one of the oldest embodiments of the Great Triple Goddess, known as Hekate Triformis, who expressed her threefold dominion over many realms. Porphory wrote, "The moon is Hekate . . . her power appears in three forms." Statues of this goddess often depict her as three female figures, or crowned with a triple-turretted headdress, or with three heads. Her three faces reflect the triple extension of her powers over heaven, earth, and underworld. Here in the realm of nature she was honored as Selene, the moon, in heaven; Artemis, the huntress, on earth; and Hekate, the destroyer, in the underworld. In this triad form she had control over birth, life, and death.

As the essence of the moon, Hekate also presided over the three lunar phases in the raiment of Artemis, the crescent new moon, Selene, the luminous full moon, and Hekate, the waning moon. Artemis/Diana represented the moonlit splendor of the night, while Hekate represented its darkness and terror reigning over the power of the dark moon.

The new, full, and dark phases of the Triple Moon Goddess also reflected the three stages of a woman's life as Artemis the virgin, Persephone the nymph, and Hekate the crone, and alternately as Persephone the daughter, Demeter the mother, and Hekate the grandmother. She was also a part of the Queen of Heaven trinity and, as the three phases of a woman's mating relationship, consisted of Hebe the maiden, Hera the wife, and Hekate the widow.

Hekate was worshiped as a goddess of fertility, whose torch was carried over freshly sown fields to symbolize the fertilizing power of moonlight. In women's agricultural mysteries her trinity took form as Core the green corn, Persephone the ripe ear, and Hekate the harvested corn.

Hekate was also a key figure in reuniting the mother and daughter in the story of Persephone's abduction into the underworld by Hades, and her periodic return to her mother, Demeter. This myth was the basis for the Eleusinian initiation rites of birth, death, and rebirth, which were derived from the mysteries of the vegetative cycle. Demeter was an expression of the force that sustains the vegetative growth above the ground; while Hekate, as female keeper of the underworld, pushes the vital force of the plants from below to above, sending the wealth of the earth, the crops, to the living. Persephone here mediates between the light-filled upper world and the dark underworld.

All wild animals were sacred to Hekate, and she was sometimes shown with three animal heads—the dog, snake, and lion, or alternately the dog, horse, and bear. This aspect refers to her rulership over the ancient tripartite year of spring, summer, and winter. However, her primary animal form and familiar was the dog. She was associated with the three-headed dog, Cerberus, who derived from the Dog Star Sirius, whose helical rising foretold the annual flooding of the Nile.

In later times the Triple Hekate took on the form of a pillar called a Hecterion. One such statue depicts her with three heads and six arms, bearing three torches and three sacred emblems—the Key, Rope, and Dagger. With her key to the underworld, Hekate unlocks the secrets of the occult mysteries and knowledge of the afterlife. The rope, which is also a scourge or cord, symbolizes the umbilical cord of rebirth and renewal. The Dagger, later the Athame of the witches, is related to the curved knife that cuts delusion and is a symbol of ritual power.

Hekate, invoked as the "Distant One," was the protectress of remote places, roads, and byways. At night, particularly at the dark moon, Hekate could be seen walking the roads of ancient Greece accompanied by her howling dogs and blazing torches. As Triple Hekate of the Crossways, her nature was especially present where three roads converged at one of the entrances to the underworld.

In Greece the Gorgon, as Artemis-Hekate, was also the mistress of the night road, of fate, and of the world of the dead.[27]

Her devotees kept the places of her worship sacred by erecting the triple-figured Hectarea at these sites. At dead of night or on the eves of full moons, they would leave offerings of ritual foods known as "Hekate's suppers." They would also call upon her in this way on her festival days or in rites of divination, magic, or consultation with the dead. Thus was the threefold goddess honored at places where one could look three ways at once.

Hekate's Companions Among Hekate's companions were the dogs, the Erinyes, Hermes, and her priestesses, Circe and Medea.

Hekate was intimately connected with the dog, her sacred animal, which was offered to her as sacrifice. Sometimes she was addressed as a "black she-dog," the black color connected with her chthonic character. She was often accompanied by a pack of black, baying hounds, or with the three-headed dog, Cerberus. Cerberus, guardian of the underworld gates, was related to the Egyptian dog-headed god, Annubis, who conducted souls to the underworld. The appearance of black, howling dogs at night signified the presence of Hekate, and their barking announced her approach.

Virgil writes,

> Then earth began to bellow, trees to dance
> And howling dogs in glimmering light advance
> Ere Hekate came.
> —*Aeneid*, Book VL [Dryden]

In ages past Hekate herself was the dog of the moon. At Colophon and Samothrace, where it was said that this goddess could turn herself into a dog, dogs were sacrificed to Hekate. The dog represents the Death Goddess because the dog has long been associated with transporting the dead to the underworld. Since ghosts and apparitions of the astral plane appear to be visible to dogs, the dog howling at the moon is believed to be a harbinger of death. Hekate and her dogs are described as journeying over the graves of the dead to search for souls of the departed and carry them to refuge in the underworld.

Hekate was also accompanied at times by her sisters from Mother Night, the Erinyes, spirits of avenging justice. Known also as the Furies, these three goddesses hounded and punished offenders who broke the taboo of insult, disobedience, or violence to a mother.

The herms, or stone pillars, which were dedicated to the god Hermes, stood at main crossroads alongside the Hecteria pillars engraved with images of Hekate. These two, Hermes and Hekate, were linked as companions, and in some traditions as lovers, who bore Circe as their daughter. Hermes, as psychopomp, leader of souls to the underworld, was credited with transmitting Hekate's art of foretelling during the later Hellenic periods.

Both Circe and Medea in some genealogies are daughters of Hekate, and some say that Circe is the aunt of Medea. Hekate taught both Circe and Medea the arts of magic and divination. As priestesses of Hekate, Circe and Medea were held in awe and fear as potent sorceresses well versed in the properties of magical herbs, enchantments, witch's lore, and shape-shifting, which they used for good and for destruction. Jason made his promise to marry Medea standing before the altar of Hekate and called the goddess to witness his oath. The vengeance that Medea later leashed upon Jason for his betrayal came from the lineage of Hekate and the Erinyes.

Gifts of Hekate: Vision, Magic, and Regeneration   Hekate is every woman's potential as a witch, seer, medium, healer, which might be linked directly with the locked energies of menstruation, and every man's contact with this energy, reflected as his anima.[28] Hekate is the archetypal shaman as she moves between worlds in a fluid and facile way. She bridges the visible and invisible realities delving for insight into the magical realms for the ultimate purpose of effecting a healing and regeneration.

Vision   Hekate was skilled in the arts of divining and foretelling the future. As she looks three ways at once, Hekate gives us an expanded vision whereby we can stand illuminated in the present and simultaneously see warning or promise of the future from the Great Above or call back the past from the Great Below. She gives us dreams and prophetic visions, whispers secrets to our inner ears, and enables us to converse with the spirits of the dead and unborn. Hekate bestows the power of ancestral communication with the psychic world.

An instrument called "Hekate's circle" was used for divination. A golden sphere with a sapphire concealed in its center was twirled with a thong of oxhide as a means to procure revelation of the future.

Hekate was both the giver of visions and the sender of madness. Called Antea, Sender of Nocturnal Visions, she had a son Museus— the Muse-man. The kind of understanding that this Dark Moon

Goddess brings is not rational thinking, but it is more like the radiant suffused light upon which are borne the inspired visions of artists, dreamers, and seers. However, her light may bring more insight than a person can bear and result in chaos, shattering the illusions of the human mind. It was said that Hekate could send demons to earth who tormented men through their dreams. Like hallucinogens to the underdeveloped mind, Hekate can poison as well as intoxicate and turn ecstatic inspiration into madness.

Hekate is also responsible for a condition called lunacy, which is usually regarded as a particular effect of the moon. While today the term lunatic has a negative connotation that implies a wild, crazed person, this was not always the case. When one was moonstruck, a condition sent by Hekate, the shroud of confusion that enveloped a person often carried a clear stream of divine madness. In the initiatory traditions of many primitive cultures, a quality that in modern times appears to be mental derangement was specifically cultivated by aspirants. This temporary state of insanity was believed to facilitate the descent of the vision, the prophetic insight, or magical work to be performed.

Magic Queen of the Ghosts, Mother of Witches, Mistress of Magic, Hekate was invoked during many midnight rituals. Her worshipers gathered inside their homes to eat Hekate's suppers. They then placed the leftovers outdoors as offerings to this goddess and her hounds. This ceremony was a form of ritual purification.

For those who worshiped her honorably, Hekate would bestow upon them her magical knowledge that was connected with "love, metamorphosis, and *pharmaka*." She held the secrets to the workings of magical spells, charms, enchantments, and the medicinal use of potent healing and destructive substances. It was felt that contact with the dark side of the Moon Goddess was the sole reliable instrument for the workings of magic, and her priestesses claimed to be able to draw down the moon by singing magical incantations.

Hekate's name was a feminine form of a title of her cousin Apollo, "the far-darter." The essence of magic is operating at a distance. Another of Hekate's appellations was the "Distant One," and her magic was known for its far-ranging airborne movement and its capacity to strike far from home.

Greek women called upon Hekate to protect their families from her hosts of dead. It was felt that this goddess could hold back the spectral hordes from the living if she chose, and so an image of her was set outside of homes to avert evil. This was to tell wandering spirits that inside this house lived friends of their queen, and the inhabitants must not be bothered with eerie noises or apparitions.

On August 13 each year a great festival was held in Hekate's honor as the Goddess of Storms and Fertility. She was invoked to avert storms that might injure the coming harvest. Mystery rites in her behalf were also held each year on the island of Aegina in the Saronic Gulf. Another holy day in the Celtic tradition dedicated to Hekate was Hallowmas on October 31, when the veil between the world of the living and dead was said to be most transparent. And in lower Italy, beside the lake of Avernus, was a dark, sacred grove of Hekate, which was near the entrance of a deep cavern of Hades' kingdom. In private worship to this goddess, her devotees offered Hekate's suppers. However, in public festivals, honey, black female lambs, and dogs were sacrificed to the Queen of the Night.

Regeneration As Prytania, the Invincible Queen of the Dead, Hekate dwelt in the underworld alongside Hades, Persephone, and other children of ancient Night—Thanatos (Death), Hypnos (Sleep), and Morpheus (Dreams). As Guardian of the Western Gate that marked the road into the mythical darkness of the underworld, Hekate was a wardress and conveyor of souls. She ruled the spirits of those who had been returned to the dark earth. This nocturnal Goddess of the Moon knew her way in the realm of spirits, and stood at the triple crossroads in the underworld. Holding a lighted torch she directed the souls on their way to the realm of their judgment—the Aphodil Meadows, Tatarus, or the Orchards of Elysium.

Because Hekate dwelt in the world below, she was the only one to hear the cries of Persephone's abduction. In the Eleusinian mythos it was Hekate who, after nine days, told Demeter the whereabouts of Persephone. At the conclusion of the tale she lit the way for Persephone's return to the world of the living and was the guardian for Persephone's stay in the world of the dead. As Queen of Death Hekate ruled over the powers of regeneration. Both Hekate and Persephone stood for the pre-Hellenic hope of regeneration, while Hades was a Hellenic concept of the ineluctability of death.[29] It was to Hekate that the ancients prayed for protection, long life, and fortunate rebirth, since it was she who controlled both birth and death.

In the legends Hekate has been described as a "phosphorescent angel" that shines in the darkness of the underworld. This phosphorescence is the glow of death and decay. This is the hypnotic light of transformation (trance-formation), where the intrinsic nature of things is revealed through decomposition and renewal.[30] Hekate symbolizes a kind of underworld consciousness of disassembly and assembly, which allows us to foretell certain kinds of catastrophic events because we are familiar with the signs and stages that precede the breakdown of form.

The sacred groves dedicated to the goddesses of the underworld, many of which later became the sites of churchyard cemeteries, were planted with stands of funeral trees—the alder, poplar, and yew. The black poplar and yew trees were sacred to Hekate. As Hekate stood at the gateway between shadow and light, the underworld and the upper world, the bicolored leaves of the black poplar reflect her borderland qualities. The shadowed, dark green upper side of the leaves that face heaven make a striking contrast with the light, pale green underside of the leaves that face the earth.

The yew is considered the central tree of death, and is associated with immortality because it takes longer than any other tree except the oak to come to maturity. Hekate's cauldron contains "slips of yew," and her sacred tree is said to root into the mouths of the dead and release their souls. It also absorbs the odors of putrefaction and phosphorescence of the bodies.[31]

Hekate is the goddess of all composting materials as her gift of fertility from the underworld. From death and decomposition come the fertile substance that ensures and vitalizes new life. In her emanation as age, change, deterioration, decay, and death, she finds the seeds for new life in the composting heap of decomposing forms.

Guardian of the Unconscious   Triple-faced Hekate stands at the crossroads of our unconscious. As she watches us approach she can see both backward and forward into our lives. When Hekate is honored she bestows the gifts of inspiration, vision, magic, and regeneration. However, when we reject and deny Hekate, her shadow side manifests as madness, stupor, and stagnation. Her creative activity takes place in the inner world. As Dark Moon Goddess of the dead, she not only represents the destructive side of life, but also the necessary forces that make creativity, growth, and healing possible.[32] The paradoxical function of this goddess of the moonlit crossroads is to pierce the darkness.

As the Queen of the Underworld Hekate is a guardian figure of the unconscious. She enables us to converse with the spirits and thus is mistress of all that lives in the hidden parts of the psyche. This Goddess of the Dark Moon holds the key that unlocks the door to the way down, and she bears the torch that illuminates both the treasures and terrors of the unconscious. Hekate guides us through this dark spirit world wherein we can receive a revelation of meaning. She then shows us that the way out is to ride on a surge of renewal.

Hekate may inspire us with a vision, insight, or prophetic fore-telling, but the way to her wisdom most often involves a descent into the underworld of our unconscious. When Hekate comes upon us we can experience her as a plunge into darkness. She is often present in our nightly sleep and casts her glow to illumine our dreams. She is also hovering over us when we are immobilized in long, sleeplike stupors of addiction, depression, or blocked creative energy. During times of drastic change, when we face the loss and death of that which gave our life structure and purpose, Hekate is there. And when we encounter her through the vast transpersonal realms of the collec-tive unconscious, her light can show us God/dess or the Devil as she fills us with divine inspiration or deluded madness. Hekate guides us whenever we do our inner work through both spiritual and psycho-logical processes.

Shakespeare offers the dream to "the mysteries of Hekate and the night" (Footnote, *King Lear*, Act 1, Scene 1), as this goddess has long been associated with dream interpretation. Jungian psychologist James Hillman points out that both the magical view that considers dreams to be foretellings, and the nineteenth-century view that attributes them to waste products of physiological sensations (garbage as Hekate's suppers), show Hekate's influence.[33] The symbolic images found in our dreams are messages from Hekate. They show us in visual form the drama of our internal personalities and the issues that live in the unconscious, as well as the shape of the future and the delusions of our minds. It was here that she was feared in ancient times as the Nightmare Hag who sent demons to torture men's minds.

As the howling of the black dogs announced her approach as an emissary from the underworld, we may also meet up with Hekate at times of drastic change that upset our known and predictably secure way of life. As the Goddess of the Dead hovering over the souls of the newly departed, she snatches us at those unexpected moments when an old life structure, relationship, or physical body come to closure.

Hekate, a primary Goddess of the Dark Moon, embodies the cycle of death and renewal. Death always brings us face-to-face with our fears of the unknown, which surface during these critical crises of our lives. The process of renewal necessitates change and the sacrifice or letting go of the old. As our life forms begin to deteri-orate, the phosphorescent light of decay begins to glow and illumines the landscape of our inner darkness.

If we are not familiar with the terrain of our unconscious, Hekate's sudden intrusion into our light-filled world may plunge us into the swirling dark waters and overwhelm us with confusion. Because Hekate's origins place her near to the onset of creation, she moves us beyond our personal unconscious into the deeper strata of the primal forces moving in the sea of the collective unconscious with their memories of all time.

This vast transpersonal dimension contains both positive and negative energies, which are constantly changing and shifting back and forth into one another; and here we can easily lose our sense of individual self who has an identity, purpose, and direction. Because the shape of things keeps changing in these more fluid realms and we do not understand what is happening to us, we can be filled with fear, anxiety, and feel as if we are going mad. There is a sense that we are out of control, this can't really be happening to us, everything seems unreal. She can come through the nightmares of sleeping dreams or the hallucinations and paranoid fantasies of waking dreams. A descent into what appears like madness may often be involved in the coming to terms with this ancient Triple Goddess.

Hekate also suggests the motif of incubation as we go down deeper still into the darkness of unconscious sleep as a necessary step in the cycle of transformation and renewal. The silence, stillness, and solitude that descends and envelops us in a cocoon of what seems like nonbeing. This is a space of inactivity and unknowing when nothing seems to be happening. Because Western culture emphasizes action and productivity and devalues those times of lying fallow and waiting for what one knows not, we sometimes label Hekate's incubation periods as being immobilized, getting stuck, being in limbo, spacing out, depression, despair, feeling numb, blank, or frozen.

This time encompasses the formless void in the transformation cycle when what was is no longer and what is to be has not yet appeared. Like the ebb tide, which is the still pause between the tidal waters going out and those coming in, this extreme stage generally occurs prior to the creative freeing of bound-up energy.[34] The still pause of nonactivity is Hekate's contribution to the journey of becoming.

Contemporary recovery theories propose that addiction to drugs and alcohol is a misguided search for spirituality and a state of oneness. In ancient times drugs and intoxicants were consciously used in religious rituals to induce the required sleep and descent in order to work the magic, healing, or prophetic vision. The poppy, sacred to both Hekate and Demeter, is a flower that brings this deep sleep. When its purpose is forgotten and qualities misused, Hekate is also present in the blackness and stupor of chemical addictions.

Patriarchy has taught us to fear this goddess, envisioned as a twisted old hag who, like the dark of the moon, was considered to be negative and even hostile to men. It was said that she stalked the crossroads at night with her vicious hounds of hell, waiting to snatch unsuspecting wayfarers to her land of the dead. They portrayed her as Moon Goddess of ghosts and dead surrounded by a swarm of female demons. And as Queen of Ghosts she swept through the night, followed by a dreadful train of questing spirits and baying hounds.

Feared as the Goddess of Storms, destruction, and terrors of night, it was said that she demanded her worshipers to perform their rites of placation at the dead of the night in order to turn aside the wrath and evil she so often wrought. Associated with sorcery and black magic, this dread goddess was later credited with being the mother of man-eating empusae and lamias, which suck the blood of young men and devour their flesh. She gave her priestesses the power to enchant, to turn men into animals, and to smite them with madness.

It is important to recognize that these shocking, hideous images associated with this torch-bearing goddess who illumines the dark passageways are but the historical record, accumulated over millennia, of the patriarchy's unconscious fears of the dark feminine. While this is not the original nature of Hekate, these twisted and distorted beliefs about her are nevertheless part of the unconscious collective conditioning to which each one of us is heir.

To the extent that our own internal images of her are encrusted with layers of repression and misperception, our experience of this Dark Moon Goddess may well be as the frightening apparitions of her spectral hordes of demons and ghosts who threaten our sanity. Our fears come from the toxic by-products issuing from our conditioning of the Dark Goddess as an embodiment of feminine evil. When we project these aspects of our inner Hekate outward upon our external world, we may create a paranoid reality in which we are pursued by the furies of injustice, hatred, and persecution, which subliminally recall our fears of medieval witch-burning times.

In order to redeem the illuminative and regenerative qualities that Hekate represents within us, we must realize that these images have no inherent existence of their own. In the process of stripping away our erroneous beliefs, we can gradually begin to see the true face of Hekate and move through her luminosity to perceive the visions of the transpersonal archetypal realms. These motifs, also contained within the fluid images of the collective unconscious, are the sources of creative inspiration that essentialize the moving force behind great works of art, literature, philosophy, and scientific invention.

And in this domain we can also receive an insight of understanding or an image of a future direction and purpose. With this inspired vision comes the release of blocked, immobilized energy lying in wait. We are then thrust into the labor pangs of a birth of meaning and renewal.

Hekate teaches us that the way to the vision that inspires renewal is to be found in moving through the darkness. As we enter into Hekate's realm, we must confront and come to terms with the dark, unconscious side of our inner nature. If we are to receive her gift of vision and renewal, we must face this Dark Goddess within ourselves, honor, praise, and make our peace with her. By giving her our trust as guardian of our unconscious and surrendering to her process, we can allow ourselves to grow into an awareness of the rich realm of our personal underworld.[35]

Nor Hall advises, "One has to give something to the death dealing mother, acknowledge her presence, leave a candle at her crossroads, admit your shadow side to view. If you give a part of yourself to lunacy, she will permit you to pass to and from the realm of the moon's dark phase. Otherwise she will detain you and stupor and blackness will possess you."[36]

Journal Questions

1. Do I ever have foretellings through dreams, visions, voices, or sudden insights? Can I honor my extrasensory wisdom, or am I frightened when these prophecies come true? If they are bad, do I fear that I caused them to happen because I thought of them?

2. What comes up for me at those times when I feel as if I am "going crazy"—seeing things, imagining voices? Can I follow these inner promptings, or am I afraid and do not know why?

3. Have there been times when I've felt as if I was plunged into darkness—feeling lost, confused, depressed, despondent, inactive, or unproductive? Have I ever felt as if I didn't know who I was or where I was supposed to be going? Was I vulnerable at those times to my addictions, which helped to numb and block my awareness of reality? In retrospect can I see some of these "dark" times as preceding creative bursts or new beginnings?

Notes

1. Aristophanes, *The Birds*.
2. Karl Kerenyi, *The Gods of the Greeks*, translated by Norman Cameron (New York: Thames & Hudson, 1982), 16.
3. *The Orphic Hymns*, translated by Apostoios Athanassakis (Atlanta: Scholars Press, n.d.).
4. Marija Gimbutas, *Goddesses and Gods of Old Europe: Myth and Cult Images* (Berkeley: University of California Press, 1982), 102.
5. James Hillman, *The Dream and the Underworld* (New York: Harper & Row, 1979), 34.
6. Pierre Grimal, ed., *Larousse World Mythology* (New York: G. P. Putnam's Sons, 1965), 90
7. Robert Graves, *The Greek Myths*, vol. 1 (New York: Viking Penguin, 1985), 34.
8. Barbara G. Walker, *The Woman's Encyclopedia of Myths & Secrets* (San Francisco: Harper & Row, 1983), 721.
9. Graves, *The Greek Myths*, 125.
10. Graves, *The Greek Myths*, 126.
11. Alexander S. Murray, *Manual of Mythology* (New York: Tudor Publishing Co., 1895), 213.
12. Graves, *The Greek Myths*, 126.
13. Kerenyi, *The Gods of the Greeks*, 106.
14. Graves, *The Greek Myths*, 38.
15. Adam McLean, *The Triple Goddess* (Edinburgh, Scotland: Hermetic Research Series, 1983), 13.
16. Barbara G. Walker, *The Woman's Encyclopedia of Myths & Secrets*, 400.
17. Graves, *The Greek Myths*, 151.
18. Alan Bleakley, *Fruits of the Moon Tree* (Bath, England: Gateway Books, 1988), 44.
19. McLean, *The Triple Goddess*, 13.
20. Barbara G. Walker, *The Woman's Encyclopedia of Myths & Secrets*, 302.
21. Graves, *The Greek Myths*, 49.
22. Barbara G. Walker, *The Woman's Encyclopedia of Myths & Secrets*, 302.
23. Barbara G. Walker, *The Secrets of the Tarot* (San Francisco: Harper & Row, 1984), 167.
24. McLean, *The Triple Goddess*, 13.
25. Juliet Sharman-Burke and Liz Greene, *The Mythic Tarot* (New York: Simon & Schuster, 1986), 55.
26. Nor Hall, *The Moon and the Virgin* (New York: Harper & Row, 1980), 203.
27. Erich Neumann, *The Great Mother*, translated by Ralph Manheim (Princeton, NJ: Princeton University Press, 1974), 30.
28. Bleakly, *Fruits of the Moon Tree*, 60.
29. Graves, *The Greek Myths*, 123.
30. Bleakly, *Fruits of the Moon Tree*, 61.
31. Bleakly, *Fruits of the Moon Tree*, 111.
32. Fred Gustafson, *The Black Madonna* (Boston: Sigo Press, 1990), 96.
33. Hillman, *The Dream and the Underworld*, 39.
34. Hall, *The Moon and the Virgin*, 254.
35. McLean, *The Triple Goddess*, 42–43.
36. Hall, *The Moon and the Virgin*, 65.

5

The Serpent-Haired Queen Medusa

✦

Still not satisfied, one lord asks, why, alone of
sisters, is Medusa's hair snaked?
—Ovid[1]

The Dark Goddess, in her guise as Medusa, was best known as the third Gorgon sister, whose beautiful, abundant hair became a crown of hissing serpents and the gaze from her evil eye turned men into stone. Yet Medusa was once known for her beauty. She was depicted with graceful golden wings arched above her shoulders, and she took the Sea God as her lover.

The Orphics called the moon's face the Gorgon's Head. According to Robert Graves, during the earlier matriarchal times the Gorgon sisters were representatives of the Triple Moon Goddess. They were masked guardians, the protectors of her mysteries.[2] The fact that Medusa was the only one of the three sisters who was mortal and could die suggests her association as a dark goddess connected to the dark closure aspect of the lunar cycle.

The patriarchy's fear of the Dark Goddess led them to perceive Medusa as a demonic mythical monster, who was then fortunately decapitated by the hero Perseus. Mythographers have called her a nightmare vision—"a face so horrible that the dreamer is reduced to stony terror."[3] According to Freud Medusa's head represents the terrifying toothed genitals of the Great Mother. Erich Neumann writes that "the petrifying gaze of Medusa belongs to the province of the Terrible Great Goddess, for to be rigid is to be dead," and that she is the devouring aspect of the mother.[4]

The Tale of Medusa

How did the Sea Goddess with the most beautiful of tresses become transformed into a hideous, lethal demon? The story of Medusa is intertwined with that of the cold, detached virgin Athena, Olympian goddess of wisdom and war, who flaunts the Gorgon's Head in the center of her breastplate. Medusa may in fact be Athena's dark sister, who personifies the shadow side of her powerful instinctive femininity.[5] The historical origins of these two goddesses take us back to North Africa and to the Egyptian goddess Neith, who was known as Anatha in Libya and as Athena to the Greeks.

Neith emerged from the primeval floodwaters, and her name means "I have come from myself." The inscription on her temple at

Fig. 5.1 Medusa

Sais reads, "I am all that has been, that will be, and no mortal has yet been able to lift the veil that covers me." Neith represented Mother Death, and to see her face behind the veil was to have died.[6]

In Libya Neith, known as Anatha, was said to have arisen out of Lake Tritonis, the Lake of the Triple Queens. She displayed her triple nature as Athena, Metis, and Medusa, who corresponded to the new, full, and dark phases of the moon. Athena was the new moon warrior maiden who inspired the Amazon tribes of women to courage, strength, and valor. The Sea Goddess Metis, whose name means "wise counsel," was the full moon mother aspect of this trinity who, in later mythical tales, conceived Athena from Zeus. Medusa embodied the third, dark aspect as destroyer/crone, and she was revered as the Queen of the Libyan Amazons, the Serpent Goddess of female wisdom.

Originally Athena and Medusa were two aspects of the same goddess, Anatha; and as such they are part of the same archetype associated with a feminine-defined strength and wisdom. We will now see how, in the classical Greek tales, these two goddesses were split off from one another and set up as deadly rivals.

In *Theogony* Hesiod gives the following account of Medusa's origins. Medusa was one of the three Gorgon sisters, who were born from the ancient sea deities Phorcys and Keto. Two sisters were both immortal and ageless: Stheno, "Mighty One," and Euryale, "Wandering One." Medusa, "Cunning One" or "Queen," was the only mortal. They lived on the road to the golden apple trees of the Hesperides at the far western edge of the world on the ocean's edge near the borders of night and death.

According to the classical texts the three Gorgon sisters were originally beautiful golden sea goddesses. The lovely maiden Medusa was pursued by many suitors, but she would have none of them until she lay with the dark-haired Sea God Poseidon, earlier known as Hippios the horse deity, in the soft grass under the spring blossoms. Poseidon, in the shape of a horse, seduced Medusa. After Medusa made love with Poseidon in one of Athena's sanctuaries and became pregnant with twins, she incurred the wrath of Athena. Some say that Athena's anger was due to Medusa daring to compare her beauty to that of Athena. Athena may have resented Medusa's sexual encounter because she had renounced her own sexuality in order to maintain her exalted position on Olympus. Furthermore, Poseidon was Athena's longtime bitter rival, who contested her rulership of Athens.

Whether Athena's rage came from the desecration of her temple, sexual jealousy, or competition for supremacy in Libya, she transformed Medusa and her sisters into ugly hags. They became winged monsters with glaring eyes, huge teeth, protruding tongues, brazen claws, and serpent locks. Medusa was singled out as the most terrifying of the three, and her face was made so hideous that a glimpse of it would turn men to stone. Tales, embellished with danger, spread far and wide, telling how the lands and cavern of these fearsome sea monsters abounded with the rigid shapes of petrified men and animals. The Gorgons were feared for their deadly power. Hence the death of Medusa became a worthy heroic quest for the patriarchal solar heroes.

The tale of Perseus's slaying of Medusa is one of the most ancient of all the Greek myths. The classical version may actually be based on a far older myth, preserved by local folk tradition, which extends back to the Mycenaean Period of the second millennium BCE. It was later overlaid with the heroic elements that were so popular among the Greeks of the Historic age. Graves feels that this story portrayed actual events during the reign of the historical King Perseus (ca. 1290 BCE), founder of the new dynasty in Mycenae. During this period the powers of the early moon goddesses in North Africa were usurped by patriarchal-dominated invaders of mainland Greece. The legend of Perseus beheading Medusa means that the Hellenes overran the Goddess's chief shrines, stripped her priestesses of their Gorgon masks, and took possession of the sacred horse.[7] This historical rupture and sociological trauma registered itself in the following myth.[8]

Perseus, a son of Zeus, was conceived in a shower of golden rain that descended upon his mother Danae, princess of Argos. The king, warned by an oracle that the only child of his daughter would kill him, had Danae and her infant placed in a great chest and cast adrift in the sea. Zeus saw that they floated safely to the island of Seriphus and were rescued by a kindly fisherman, Dictys. Perseus grew to manhood there, following the fisherman's humble trade. In due time Polydectes, cruel and ruthless leader of the land, lusted after Danae and sought a way to rid himself of her protective and troublesome son.

Polydectes' plan was to raise a tax of horses from the islanders (according to another version these horses were intended as a bride gift he meant to offer for the hand of Hippodameia). Because Perseus was poor, there was no way for him to obtain a horse; and he was tricked into pledging that he would bring the king the head of the Gorgon with its deadly power. The oldest narratives of the myth of

Medusa relate that she was a mare whom Poseidon had mated while in the form of a stallion. Thus Perseus was promising the king the head of a most terrifying horse.

Perseus was assisted in this task with the help of Hermes and Athena. Hermes, messenger of the gods, gave him a curved magic sword, the only weapon capable of slaying the Gorgon. Pallas Athena, protectress of heroes, lent Perseus her brightly polished great shield to use as a mirror against Medusa, thereby avoiding direct contact with her deadly face, which could turn him to stone. They then appeared in a vision and led Perseus to the cave of the Graiae, who were the only ones who knew the exact whereabouts of Medusa.

The Graiae were three old women, a fateful trio of swan maidens, living at the foot of Mt. Atlas in Africa. Between them they shared one eye, with which they could see everything, and one tooth. Perseus tricked them into revealing Medusa's whereabouts by grabbing their one eye and refusing to return it until they divulged the information he sought. He also forced them to tell him where to find the Stygian Nymphs, from whom he received a magic pouch to contain the severed head of Medusa; the dark helmet of Hades, which would render him invisible; and a pair of winged sandals, which would enable him to fly with the speed of a bird to the desolate island lair of the Gorgon sisters.

Perseus then flew over the stream of Ocean to the extremities of the western shores and found the three Gorgons asleep in their great cavern. They were creatures with great golden wings, their bodies covered with golden scales and crowned with wreaths of serpents, evoking the regalia of the royal Egyptian sea priestesses. He kept clear of Stheno and Euryale, who were immortal and could not be killed, and advanced toward Medusa, watching her reflection in his mirrored shield. His arm guided by Athena, Perseus, with one stroke of Hermes' blade, slashed off Medusa's head and hid it in his pouch. He then donned Hades' cap of invisibility, in order to escape the wrathful pursuit of the remaining Gorgons, and flew off the island.

From Medusa's severed neck sprang her twin sons by Poseidon— Pegasus, the winged moon horse, who became a symbol of poetry; and Cryasor, the hero of the golden sword and father of King Geryon of Spain. As Perseus flew away, drops of Medusa's blood trickled onto the hot African sands, causing oases to grow in the desert. In an alternate version these droplets of blood gave birth to a race of poisonous serpents destined to infest the regions with plagues in future ages.

Athena later gave two phials of Medusa's blood to Asklepius, the God of Healing. It was said that blood from her right vein could cure and restore life, and that the blood from her left vein could slay and kill instantly. Others say that Athena and Asklepius divided the blood between them; he used it to save lives, but she to destroy and instigate wars. In some traditions it was Athena's serpent son Erichthonius to whom she gave the blood to either kill or cure, and she fastened the phials to his body with golden bands. Athena's dispensation of the Gorgon blood to Asklepius and Erichthonius suggests the curative rites used in this cult were a secret guarded by priestesses, which it was death to investigate. The Gorgon's Head was a formal warning to pryers to stay away.

Among Perseus's adventures on his way back to Seriphus were the turning of Atlas into stone and the rescue of Andromeda. In order to escape from Africa, Perseus had to defeat the huge King Atlas, father of the Hesperides, who were the guardians of the apples of immortality. Atlas, warned by an ancient prophecy that a son of Zeus would rob him of his golden fruits, refused Perseus hospitality and attempted to thrust him away. In anger Perseus held up the Gorgon's Head and turned the giant into stone, which then formed the Atlas Mountains, upon which rest the sky and all the stars.

Perseus's story continues with the rescue of the Ethiopian princess Andromeda, who was bound to a rock on the seashore as a victim to a great sea monster, Cetus. He then takes her for his bride and they return to Seriphus to free his mother from the clutches of Polydectes. Perseus presents his promised gift and thereby turns the king and his court to stone. Perseus's daughter with Andromeda is named Gorgophone.

Perseus gives the Gorgon's Head to Athena, who affixes it to her breastplate. Some say that her aegis was Medusa's own skin, flayed from her by Athena. Other legends tell of the head being buried in the *agora* before the goddess Hera's temple in Argos.

Medusa and Athena

In order to penetrate the mystery that stands behind the Gorgon's Head, we must first untangle the threads that weave and bind Medusa and Athena. Medusa and Athena are aspects of the same goddess who emerged from Lake Tritonis in Libya. They are both associated with female wisdom, which is depicted in the serpent symbolism that surrounds them—Medusa with her serpent locks and Athena with her serpent-fringed aegis. Medusa, as wise crone, holds the secrets of sex, divination, magic, death, and renewal. Athena, the eternal maiden, is linked with the new moon and presides over the female qualities of courage, strength, and valor. This African triple goddess, who was born out of the sea and reigned in the desert, displayed herself as both the armored chaste virgin warrior Athena and the serpent-crowned Queen Medusa, protector of the dark moon mysteries, who celebrated the sexual rites with the lineage of sea gods.

The warrior form of this Libyan triple goddess was clothed in the original legendary aegis—a goatskin chastity tunic. She also wore a Gorgon mask and carried around her waist a leather pouch containing sacred serpents. This outfit was duplicated in the dress of the Amazon women, and later worn by the classical Athena in her Olympian reign. Any man who removed one of these tunics without the owner's consent would be killed for violating the potent maidenhood of these young women.

The infamous Gorgon masks were called *gorgoneions*. They portrayed a face with glaring eyes, bared fanged teeth, and protruding tongue, similar to many images of Kali. They were worn by priestesses in moon-worshiping rituals, both to frighten away strangers and to evoke the Goddess herself. The purpose of the mask was to protect the secrecy required for the magical work associated with the third or dark triad of the Triple Moon Goddess. It served to warn people against intruding upon the divine mysteries hidden behind it.

These ceremonies included divination, healing, magic, and the sexual serpent mysteries associated with death and rebirth. The female face, represented by Medusa, surrounded by serpent hair was a widely recognized symbol of divine female wisdom. The Ephasus Gorgons with four wings each almost duplicate the flying Gorgons at Delphi, the temple of the world's greatest oracular priestesses. The venom from the bite of certain snakes induced the hallucinatory state in which the oracular vision was revealed.

The Gorgon face, often red in color, held the secrets of the menstrual wise blood that gave women their divine healing powers. Certain primitive tribes believed that the look of a menstruating woman could turn a man to stone, which links Medusa with the menstrual mysteries.[9] The blood that Perseus took from Medusa could both heal and kill; it may originally have been her menstrual blood rather than blood from the wound in her neck.

The mask was also worn by the priestesses in the sacred sexual rites to symbolize that they were acting not as individuals, but as representatives of the Goddess, whom she empowered to transmit her blessings of healing and regeneration through ritual intercourse. The prophylactic mask was also donned by the funerary priestesses, who initiated people into the mysteries of death. In later times to possess a replica of a Gorgon's Head was to be protected with a charm against ills that repelled the attack of harmful forces. It was believed to be a protection against the evil eye, and was often depicted in shields, ovens, town walls, and buildings to frighten enemies and ward off malicious spirits.

With the passage of time, Libyan refugees emigrated to Crete. They had brought with them their Serpent Goddess, Anatha, and by 4000 BCE she had become known as Athena, the protectress of the palace. Her worship was adopted and then passed on to mainland Greece and Thrace in the Minoan/Mycenaean period. From this era there arose a new genealogy of the birth of Athena. She now was said to have sprung forth from the head of her father, Zeus. Earlier versions reveal that Athena was conceived in a union between Zeus and a mother goddess named Metis/Medusa, who came from the sea.

The tales that come from the transition period between the matriarchy and patriarchy tell how the wise Metis helped Zeus achieve victory over his father, Cronus, by giving him an emetic that forced him to cough up his swallowed children. In honor of her great service Zeus decided to make Metis the first consort of the new supreme ruler of the heavens. Although Metis changed into many shapes to avoid Zeus's lustful advances, she was finally ravished and got with child. Zeus was warned by an oracle that Metis would bear him a second child, who would become king of gods and men. To maintain his sovereignty Zeus consumed Metis whole while she was pregnant with Athena. The blinding headache that resulted when Zeus walked the shores of Lake Tritonis in Libya could only be relieved through having his head cleft with a double-edged axe (a matriarchal symbol of the lunar crescent). Amidst the rumbling of the earth and raging of the sea, out sprang Athena in armor of gleaming gold. She immediately became her father's favorite.

Later versions cut out the transitional story of Metis and claim that Athena was conceived and birthed solely from Zeus himself. From a sociological perspective this myth marks the ingestion of the feminine warrior wisdom principle to the needs of the new patriarchal order. The patriarchy championed Athena as benevolent, suppressed Metis altogether, and denounced Medusa as evil. Athena and Medusa were then cast as opponents.

As Athena was absorbed into the classical Greek pantheon, she was the only one of the old goddesses who was elevated and respected, and she became part of the new ruling trinity along with Zeus and Apollo. She had to pay a steep price for her supremacy in the new order. First she was forced to deny her femininity and to sacrifice her sexuality, becoming a perpetually chaste virgin. She was cut off from her cyclical nature, which included renewal through sexual rites. She then promised to become champion of the patriarchy by using her warrior potency to denounce, slaughter, and conquer her matriarchal ancestors from Africa.

Graves says that Athena was a traitor to the old religion by affiliating with the solar gods and assisting the solar heroes to slay all the resisting matriarchal factions, who were now feared as the Terrible Mother. As she joined Zeus and his son Perseus to kill her own mother Metis/Medusa and supplant her in the hierarchy, Athena was then most appropriately chosen to preside over and pardon Orestes in his trial for matricide.

During this time Athena's prime rival for the rulership of Athens was Poseidon; and it was through the union of her two sworn enemies, Poseidon and Medusa, that she began to wage her war. Historical evidence points to the fact that Medusa was a high priestess of Africa who presided over Libyan tribes of Amazon warrior women. Dating from at least 6000 BCE, these fierce and noble African Amazons populated not only North Africa, but also Spain and Italy.[10] The Greek legends of Poseidon mating with Medusa, and Perseus slaying the Gorgon, derive from actual battles waged by the patriarchal Greek soldiers against these warrior women from North Africa. The tribe against whom Perseus fought was a race called the Gorgons.

Medusa, Athena, and Poseidon   In the oldest tales there are references to the beautiful third Gorgon sister, Medusa, who willingly takes the Sea God as her lover in the celebration of the sexual mysteries of the Goddess and her Consort. At a certain point after 2000 BCE the legends tell of the "marriage" or alternately "rape" of Queen Medusa to the oceanic King Poseidon, one of the original Olympians, who had been known in his earlier form as Hippios the horse deity as well as lord of the sea. Poseidon in the form of a stallion mounted Medusa as a mare and fathered Pegasus, a winged moon horse.

An early representation of Medusa, dating from the seventh century BCE in Boeotia, shows her as a small, slender mare-woman who, although masked with a Gorgon's Head, shows none of the frightful aspects of the classical Gorgon. By associating the Gorgon mask with the slender equine form, this artist permits us to catch a brief glimpse of a far more ancient tradition, in which the dark sister was not an isolated object of fear. The Gorgon mask, as the face of the moon, suggests that Medusa was one of the three aspects of the pre-Hellenic Moon Goddess, and the small native horses of these indigenous peoples were sacred to the early moon cults in rainmaking ceremonies. Poseidon's rape of Medusa in the form of a stallion tells the story of how the first wave of invading Hellenes from Greece, who rode large, vigorous horses, forcibly married the Amazon moon priestesses and took over the rainmaking rites of the sacred horse cult through the birth of Pegasus.[11]

This is one variation of many similar stories that appear all over the Mediterranean Crescent around this time, describing the transition from the reign of the goddesses to that of the gods. The supremacy of the Great Goddess who took the young God as her Consort/lover was overturned as the God matures and then usurps her power by forcibly raping, marrying, and subjugating her and by suppressing her worship. Poseidon's soldiers likewise raped the Amazon priestesses, and they ignored the injunction of the aegis and Gorgon mask to stay away unless invited. The Gorgon mask then turned into the portrait of horror, fear, and rage frozen on the faces of these warrior women resulting from their forceful violation.

It was only after Medusa's union with Poseidon that Athena transformed the beautiful Libyan Amazon Queen into the deadly monster whose horrible face would turn men into stone. In Athena's rivalry with Poseidon she may have been enraged that Poseidon laid claim to the country of her birth. She saw Medusa's submission to him in one of her own temples as an act of betrayal from the peoples of her native land. Thus Medusa represented a rival matriarchal religion that needed to be suppressed.

In retaliation against Medusa, Athena, who had already sacrificed her own sexuality, ensured that Medusa would never again participate in the Goddess's sexual mysteries, because one look at her face would petrify any approaching man. And Freud concluded that the Gorgon's Head represented the terrifying genitalia of the Great Mother, which threatens to castrate men. An alternate interpretation suggests that in Athena's compassion for her lost sisters, she imbued the Gorgon mask with a new, deadly power, one which could kill the attackers. This was to protect the Queen and her priestesses from continuing to be defiled, degraded, and destroyed through the sexual assault of the invaders.

Medusa, Athena, and Perseus According to the Olympian Greeks Athena finally succeeded in destroying and conquering Queen Medusa during the reign of King Perseus, around 1200 BCE. Perseus, whose name also means destroyer, acted on Athena's behalf. At her request and with her help, Perseus overthrew the principle shrine of the Old African religion in Libya and slayed the high priestess, thus furthering the suppression of the matriarchal consciousness. Perseus then delivered the Gorgon's Head to Athena, who wore it over her heart as a continuing token of her underlying connection to Medusa. She displayed the Gorgon's Head both to strike terror in her enemies and to affirm her supremacy in having denounced and demolished her matriarchal ancestors.

While the earliest representations depicted the Gorgon as a protector of the dark moon mysteries, the patriarchy later conceived her as a demon. Then, in later artistic portrayals, the Gorgon became a beautiful angel. She passed through phases of becoming sinister, sad, and increasingly pathetic, and finally metamorphosed into a calm, dignified death mask.[12]

Serpent-Haired Medusa

I saw you once, Medusa; we were alone.
I looked you straight in the cold eye, cold.
I was not punished, was not turned to stone.
How to believe the legends I am told? . . .
I turned your face around! It is my face.
That frozen rage is what I must explore—
Oh secret, self-enclosed and ravaged place!
That is the gift I thank Medusa for.
—May Sarton, "The Muse as Medusa"[13]

Serpent-haired Medusa was once a queen of the awesome powers of the dark moon. She ruled over the regenerative mysteries of sex and death, and protected these magical rites from being discovered and abused by the uninitiated. As the third, crone/destroyer aspect of the lunar triad, Medusa's message was one of wisdom, and it concerned the inevitability of death. The West is the gateway to death, and Medusa's oceanic cavern situated at the far western edge of the world lies at the entrance to the underworld. The patriarchy, in their fear of the wise woman, of death, and of the magical sexual power of the menstruating feminine, demonized Medusa (as they did the other dark goddesses) into a monstrous figure of the devouring, castrating mother.

Medusa continues to haunt generations of men with her deadly power to turn them into stone with a glance from her evil eye. The ancients projected this fear on the star of Agol in the constellation of Perseus. Perseus is holding up the head of Medusa as a trophy of his conquest, and Agol, known as the demon star, represents the eye in the Gorgon's Head. Agol is an eclipsing binary and is made up of two stars revolving around each other. Approximately every sixty hours, when the fainter star passes in front of the brighter and hides or eclipses it, Agol gives a long, gradual "wink." The ancients explained this phenomenon as the winking of the demon's eye still blinking after her body had been decapitated.[14]

On an outer level the myths of the solar heroes slaying the monsters, like that of Perseus and Medusa, are the patriarchal stories telling the tale of their conquest of the old matriarchy. On an inner level these myths depict the maturation of the masculine principle. They relate the struggle of the young god who is the son and lover of the Goddess to transform himself into the mighty hero who conquers and then dominates the feminine. Interpreting the myth of Medusa has been a subject of fascination for both Freudian and Jungian psychoanalyst writers. Examining the ways in which men have tried to intellectualize and distance themselves from the instinctual powers of the dark feminine can give us clues as to how Medusa currently appears in the male psyche. Men then project this anima image upon actual women who evoke some of qualities of the serpent-haired queen.

The Gorgon Medusa, like other of the dark goddesses, became greatly feared by the patriarchy when humanity forgot the cyclical nature of death-becoming-life. Commentaries about Medusa as written by modern male psychoanalytic theorists emphasize her demonic and destructive qualities. Wolfgang Lederer, in The Fear of Women, states that "nothing but terror emanates from Medusa's head."[15] The terror of Medusa that turns men into stone is their terror of death and castration.

Erich Neumann writes that the winged Gorgon's " . . . are uro-boric symbols of the primordial power of the Archetypal Feminine, images of the great pre-Hellenic mother goddess in her devouring aspect as earth, night, and underworld."[16] Sigmund Freud's interpretation, "Medusa's Head" (1922), suggests that Medusa's head, surmounted by snakes, is the symbol of the maternal genitalia—the hairy maternal vulva as seen by the son. He says that to decapitate is synonymous with to castrate. However frightening the snakes may be in themselves, they serve as a mitigation of the horror, for they replace the penis, the absence of which is the cause of horror. Freud felt that being turned to stone implied erection as a defense to the threat of castration.[17]

Philip Slater agrees with Freud that Medusa's head is a symbol of maternal genitalia, but he disagrees with Freud's interpretation of turning to stone as a symbolic erection as a defense against the fear of castration. Slater argues that "while the idea of erection may be present in the stiff with terror response, the immobility is much more suggestive of impotence, and this interpretation fits better the many examples of paralysis and turning to stone. . . . The purpose of Athena's aegis was to render potential ravishers impotent rather than to provide reassuring erections."[18]

For the Greeks the vulva had the magical power not merely to neutralize, but also as an apotropaic device to frighten away evil spirits such as the Devil. It was used by women against men and against bogies. From a masculine perspective the alarming hypnotic, staring eyes of Medusa within the maternal genitalia, which turn men into stone, produces immobility, impotence, and anesthesia. Slater cites clinical studies that show how frequently these outcomes are associated with early incestuous arousal.[19] Incest with the mother calls up a terrifying chain of psychological associations for the young man. These fears could be partly associated with certain traditions and rituals practiced in the matriarchy.

For example, in the rites of the year king, the young god, after participating in the sacred marriage, was ritually killed. His dismembered bodily parts were then plowed under the earth in order to assure fertility and abundance for the coming harvest. Held in the unconscious psyche of the masculine is the image that deep sex with the mother results in death. It brings one to a loss of manhood, sexual potency, and life itself. And when death is separated from the cycle of rebirth, this event signifies the final termination of the life force.

Perseus is a hero to the patriarchy because he attacked and killed a representative of the Terrible Mother, who was reputed to seduce and then devour men. In beheading the Gorgon he castrated her and thus deprived the maternal genitalia of its power to render men impotent. Once protected from the deadly power of the Medusa's sexuality, the turning-into-stone motif becomes, as Freud surmised, the stiff erection. The male phallus is now bent on violent rape as an expression of destructive rage toward the threatening sexuality of the maternal principle. This trend to separate sexuality from motherhood culminated in the Christian tradition, with the idealized mother of the young god, the Virgin Mary, who immaculately conceived her child.

When the distorted shadow image of Medusa is active in the male psyche, the situation arises as a young boy desires to be held in the nurturing bosom of his mother. But at the same time, he resists the urge, fearing that he may become engulfed and smothered. He also struggles to be freed from feeling the intensity of his mother's unconscious sexual needs and his subsequent sense of his inability to gratify them. Or, if he succeeds in doing so, the result would be, like the year king, the inevitability of his own death. The infant boy's primal image of the feminine arises from his perception of his mother as possessive and sexually devouring. He fears being swallowed by the womb itself, the hairy vulva reminiscent of the Gorgon's Head, which is imaged as *vagina dentata*, a vagina with teeth. A young boy, who is in the shadow domain of Medusa, may inherit his mother's unconscious rage and bitterness, which taints his own inner soul so that he carries her hatred for her.[20]

When a man's anima consists of such a Medusa-like figure shaped on his relationship to his mother, he later projects it onto his mates. His partners take on the form of the wrathful, deadly female who threatens his sexual potency. She dares him to approach her, only to then reveal a face like the terrifying Gorgon, which is frozen in rage. Medusa's face reflects her anger over the ways in which the patriarchal mentality has violated, castrated, desexualized, and disempowered her as the queen of the serpent mysteries. When men cease to honor the sexuality of the dark feminine, the contortions of the Gorgon's grimace show her bloodthirst for revenge. When men evoke this response from the women in their lives, they are overcome with the raw terror of the offender who fears that this vengeance will petrify and render them impotent.

167

*Goddesses of the
Dark Moon:
The Serpent-
Haired Queen
Medusa*

When Medusa is a primary archetype in a man's life, he will be attracted to a woman who will respond to his unconscious attempts to set her up to act out his worst fears of the terrible feminine. His partner will come to hate him, belittle him, reject him sexually and criticize his performance, call him repulsive, and repel his advances. His Medusa-like mates will fulfill his shadow projections of women as ball-busting castrators who reinforce his insecurities concerning his sexual potency and "maleness." His pain, humiliation, sense of diminishment, and ineffectuality, whose source lies in the sexual arena, gradually overtakes his entire self-image and reduces his capacity to function strongly in the rest of his life affairs. He may overcompensate for his inner sense of impotence by becoming increasingly rigid in his negative attitudes and violent actions toward women.

The Romantics of the nineteenth century found in Medusa a vision that Lederer writes encompassed the full circle from her beauty, to the love of woman as pain, as corruption, as the undoing of men, as death.[21] Shelley, upon seeing a painting of Medusa in the Uffizi Gallery, wrote,

> It lieth, gazing on the midnight sky,
>
>   Upon the cloudy mountain peak supine;
> Below, far lands are seen tremblingly;
>   Its horror and its beauty are divine.
> Upon its lips and eyelids seem to lie
>   Loveliness like a shadow, from which shine,
> Fiery and lurid, struggling underneath,
>   The agonies of anguish and of death . . .
> "Tis the tempestuous loveliness of terror. . . ."

This glassy-eyed severed female head, this horrible, fascinating Medusa, was to be the object of the dark loves of the Romantics and the Decadents throughout the whole of the century.[22] Lederer continues that the evil and sin that obsessed the imagination of the Romantic poets and artists was always incest with the mother; not the Oedipal incest that would make them into men who replaced their fathers, but the uroboric incest that dissolves them back into the amniotic fluid.[23]

From a Jungian perspective the myth of the hero symbolizes the archetypal stages in the development of consciousness. Initially the ego, which is defined in the West as the organized faculty of the masculine psyche, is born out of the soul, which is the feminine uroboric unity of the Great Goddess, that is, the young god as the son/lover of the Great Mother. The development of consciousness involves the ego's growth in learning the qualities of reason, intellect, and logic with which to first recognize and discriminate itself as a distinct individual entity, and then to separate itself from the mother. "The stronger the masculine ego consciousness becomes, the more it is aware of the emasculating, bewitching, deadly and stupefying nature of the Great Goddess."[24]

According to this point of view Medusa, as a devouring female monster, represents the dread of the irrational and fear of annihilation by unconscious forces. While the masculine may desire to sink back and dissolve into the pleasure of the womb, this is seen as a regressive trend to the development of the male ego. The hero needs to slay the monster in order to prevent his return to the feminine uroboric unity and to free himself from the power of the mother in the unconscious. The violence to the feminine is a reaction to the pull of the mother. The hero's path of individuation necessitates a movement away from the soul, represented by the dark instinctual feminine. He is aided in this quest by the impetus of the spirit embodied by the light, rational masculine, or the Great Father archetype.

Men who have not made peace with Medusa in themselves will see feminine sexuality as something that fascinates them, but also as the source of their self-undoing. As they try to protect themselves against its frightening power by destroying the monster, they will unconsciously incite the Medusa woman in their lives to retaliate by castrating them physically and psychologically. For many of us direct confrontation with this aspect of our being, often unknown and unnamed as it hides in the dark caverns of our psyche, can overwhelm and immobilize us with its raw intensity.

And yet a man who desires a positive relationship to women's dark moon sexuality must make the descent into his unconscious, listen to the wailing agony of his decapitated Medusa, reach out in sympathy to her pain, heal the wounds of her rejection, and return whole-within-himself to the upper world. After the hero has proved his separation from his mother, he must reestablish a loving relationship to his inner dark feminine. Until he can do this he will remain trapped in the web of destructive sexual relationships.

Let us now look at the psychology of the feminine who wears the Gorgon's Head over the center of her breastplate. In what ways have women been conditioned through patriarchal culture to deny and reject the power of the serpent-haired queen within them, and how has this affected their relationship to themselves and to others?

Medusa, in her association with the serpent and with the menstrual blood that could both heal and destroy, embodies the dark moon mysteries of the Goddess. In her red-faced Gorgon mask surmounted by a crown of snakes, Medusa in women signifies a source of feminine wisdom that is connected to their sexuality. She points to the source of women's powers of divination, creation, destruction, and regeneration.

Buffie Johnson explains that hair stands for energy and fertility. On the head hair signifies higher spiritual forces, and below the waist it indicates the fertilizing forces. When snakes replace the hair as they replace the Gorgon's tresses, they represent the higher forces of creation.[25]

The serpent symbolizes the *kundalini* force coiled like a snake at the base of the spine that stands behind our sexual procreative energy. When *kundalini* is activated, it rises up through the central spinal column, activating each *chakra* in turn, and eventually comes out of the top of the head as cosmic enlightenment. When Medusa's hair is transformed into snakes, this symbolizes the rising of the *kundalini* and our ability to utilize this force for regenerative healing, mental creativity, oracular wisdom, and spiritual power.

To the extent that we have culturally repressed and feared the powers of this Dark Goddess and have accepted the patriarchal view of her as a monster to be destroyed, we have cut ourselves off from our ability to access our sexual power to create, regenerate, and know the truth from within ourselves. In fact we have been taught to shirk from and reject the kind of menstrual, ecstatic, and nonreproductive sexuality that activates these powers. Medusa in us carries the patriarchy's projection of women's dark sexuality as evil.

The pure form of Medusa symbolizes the source of our instinctual bodily wisdom and power. However, in our fear and denial of her, she has come to represent the ways in which we feel the most ignorant and incapable. She signifies a place of deep insecurity in us; and when we are challenged in her domain we become stiff with terror and immobilized from taking action. We are rendered powerless, and our inner Medusa remains vulnerable and unprotected.

In our fear we erect a defense to hold back the forces of those who might take advantage of our weakness and violate us. By donning the Gorgon's mask we create a hideous face that we hope will frighten and repel others. It is a portrait of feminine anger and hatred, and her effect upon anyone who looks at her is paralysis.[26] Medusa's mask is ugly, yet underneath her hard and unattractive exterior she is soft, beautiful, and sensitive. And she usually has been deeply wounded by a man at some point in her life.

Jean Bolen comments on the woman who is wearing Athena's armor with Medusa's aegis on her breastplate. If the Athena side of the archetype is more active, her well-armored (usually intellectual) defenses are up and her authority and critical gaze keep others at an emotional distance.[27] Lederer, commenting on Athena's stance, says, "As she displays the genitalia of the Mother (i.e., the Gorgon's Head), she proclaims herself as a castrated woman, and her terrible sight cannot fail to repel all enemies. She becomes the Unapproachable, who fends off all sexual lust, numbs her enemies with terror, and repels desire."[28]

But for those of us who are severed from Medusa's serpent power and cannot access our wisdom and strength, we continue to experience failure and humiliation in her sphere. As our fear of inadequacy increases, so do the protective barriers of our defenses. Our frustration and rage serve to crystallize the grimacing mask of frozen rage upon our face. While we are powerless behind the mask, others feel intimidated. We give looks that will turn a person to stone. The mask, now inseparable from our true face, acts to keep others away. Often we do not fully realize the effect of our glare, and so we experience an increasing sense of being ostracized, rejected, and hated by others. These negative and destructive attitudes reflect back upon ourselves, and we become bitter, blaming, and judgmental. If the mask turns inward, we are repulsed by our impotence, which grows into a pervasive self-hatred; and this self-rejection is added to our other problems.

In order to transform the mask, we must first recognize and acknowledge the wrathful face that we present to others. Our next task is to recall Medusa from her banishment and once again reclaim the serpent-haired queen by honoring the dark moon wisdom that arises from our sexuality. Medusa is the source of our deep, regenerative healing power. The menstrual blood of the Serpent Goddess that could heal, kill, and even raise the dead is reflected in the twin serpents of Life and Death twining about the winged staff that is today the emblem of the medical profession.[29] Her blood was given by Athena to the God of Healing, Asklepius, whose daughter Hygeia,

171

*Goddesses of the
Dark Moon:
The Serpent-
Haired Queen
Medusa*

Goddess of Health, was in classical times the guardian of the sacred serpents in the healing temples.

In order to claim the spiritual power of the ancient Libyan Serpent Goddess of wisdom, we must develop our talents and inner resources that will give us a new sense of our value and self-worth. We will then see her blessings in our lives as our increasing confidence in our ability to be creative and assertive in all our life endeavors. We will remember how to use her ancient wisdom in recognizing truth, healing and regenerating ourselves and others. And we will recover the magic of our dark sexuality.

Remembering that intelligence, strength, and creativity were once rooted in the feminine tradition, we can call upon the lineage of the Triple Goddess Neith/Anatha. From Athena we can receive valor, strength, and courage; from Metis the intuitive wisdom of wise counsel and creative self-expression; and from Medusa our psychic sexual abilities to heal and regenerate. The power that comes from the core of our being, which is grounded in the stability of our inner wisdom and strength, is what can truly ward off the threat of violation. We no longer need the frightening mask as a weapon of defense to conceal our insecurity.

Journal Questions

1. How do I feel about snakes?
2. How do I respond to the sight of hair on a woman's vulva? Do I find it beautiful? Am I somewhat fascinated but repulsed at the same time? Can I remember my childhood reactions when I first saw pubic hairs on my mother or some other woman?
3. If I am a man, have I ever felt that a woman's sexuality and power were something potentially threatening to me? Have I had experiences where I felt sexually manipulated or psychologically castrated by a woman? If I have had sexually devastating relationships, have I considered that the kinds of difficult experiences that I seem to attract may reflect my unconscious inner images of the dark feminine?
4. If I am a woman, do I feel insecure and inadequate in my ability to express my sexuality, wisdom, and power in my life? Have I ever put on a wrathful face or given a "look that could kill" in order to protect myself from being exposed? Have I ever felt shunned and rejected by others because of my appearance or personality? Can I acknowledge and honor my female serpent power as my inner source of creativity, actualization, and strength in my life?

Notes

1. Ovid, *Metamorphoses, Book IV,* translated by Charles Boer (Dallas, Texas: Spring Publications, 1989).
2. Robert Graves, *The Greek Myths,* vol. 1 (New York: Viking Penguin, 1985), 129.
3. H. J. Rose, *A Handbook of Greek Mythology* (New York: Dutton & Co., 1959), 29.
4. Erich Neumann, *The Great Mother,* translated by Ralph Manheim (Princeton, NJ: Princeton University Press, 1974), 166.
5. Christine Downing, *The Goddess: Mythological Images of the Feminine* (New York: Crossroad, 1981), 124.
6. Barbara G. Walker, *The Woman's Encyclopedia of Myths and Secrets* (San Francisco: Harper & Row, 1983), 629.
7. Graves, *The Greek Myths,* 17.
8. Joseph Campbell, *The Masks of God: Occidental Mythology* (New York: Penguin Books, 1981), 152.
9. Sir James George Frazier, *The Golden Bough* (New York: The MacMillan Company, 1960), 699–700.
10. Norma L. Goodrich, *Priestesses* (New York: Franklin Watts, 1989), 364.
11. Graves, *The Greek Myths,* 129.
12. Tobin Siebers, *The Mirror of Medusa* (Berkeley and Los Angeles: University of California Press, 1983), 24.
13. May Sarton, *Collected Poems* (New York: W. W. Norton, 1974), 332.
14. Julius Staal, *The New Patterns in the Sky* (Blacksburg, VA: The McDonald and Woodward Publishing Co., 1988), 25.
15. Wolfgang Lederer, *The Fear of Women* (New York: Harcourt Brace Jovanovich, 1968), 3.
16. Neumann, *The Great Mother,* 169.
17. Sigmund Freud, "Medusa's Head" (1922), in *Collected Papers,* vol. 5 (London: Hogarth, 1953), 105–6).
18. Philip Slater, *The Glory of Hera* (Boston: Beacon Press, 1968), 321–22.
19. Slater, *The Glory of Hera,* 322.
20. Liz Greene, *The Astrology of Fate* (York Beach, ME: Samuel Weiser, 1986), 229.
21. Lederer, *The Fear of Women,* 256.
22. Mario Praz, *The Romantic Agony* (London: Oxford University Press, 1951), 9.
23. Lederer, *The Fear of Women,* 257.
24. Erich Neumann, *The Origins and History of Consciousness,* translated by R. F. C. Hull (Princeton, NJ: Princeton University Press, 1973), 63.
25. Buffie Johnson, *Lady of the Beasts* (San Francisco: Harper & Row, 1988), 150.
26. Greene, *The Astrology of Fate,* 229.
27. Jean Shinoda Bolen, *Goddesses in Everywoman* (San Francisco: Harper & Row, 1984), 103.
28. Lederer, *The Fear of Women,* 3.
29. Genia Pauli Haddon, *Body Metaphors: Releasing God-Feminine in Us All* (New York: Crossroad, 1988), 154.

6

The Dark Maid Lilith

✦

You gotta give it to Lilith,
she was a hell of a woman.

Said she'd rather
fuck demons on the beach
than lie under the belly
of that whiner Adam
& flew from Paradise . . .

Jonelle Maison[1]

Lilith was known by patriarchal cultures as a winged and wild-haired she-demon who flew through the night. They said that her powers were "greatest at the time of the waning moon when the dogs of night are loosed from their chains to roam about till morning."[2] As a Goddess of the Dark Moon, Lilith carries the patriarchy's shadow projection of the defiant woman as seductress and child-killer. She has come to embody men's fear of the feminine as dark and evil.

The *Zohar*'s account of creation tells the following version of Lilith's origin. God made two great lights, the Sun and Moon, which shone with equal splendor. At first the Moon wanted to merge with the Sun and bask in his light, but when a dispute arose, God took the side of the Sun. He sent the Moon down to follow in the footsteps of humankind as his shadow.[3] When the light of the Moon was diminished, it was said that Holiness became surrounded by a husk of Evil (*qehpah*), from which Lilith was born. She arose out of primal darkness, flaming forth with all of its assertive power.

We find accounts of Lilith throughout the lands of the ancient Near East, and she makes appearances in the Sumerian, Babylonian, Assyrian, Hebraic, and Arabic mythology. Legends tell of her as the first wife of Adam in the Garden of Eden, the paramour of lascivious spirits in the Red Sea, as the bride of Samael the Devil, as the Queen of Sheba and Zemargrad, and as the Consort of God himself in fifteenth-century Cabbalism.

During the last five millennia Lilith, as an aspect of the Dark Goddess, has been cast out into the desolate wilderness and banned from the boundaries of community. Denied and rejected, Lilith was vilified as Torturous Serpent, Blood Sucker, Harlot, Impure Female, Alien Woman, Witch, Hag, and Enchantress. Over the ages fragments of her history have surfaced from the dark and unfathomable depths of her exile. But first of all, in the beginning of her time, Lilith's epithet was "the beautiful maiden."

Lilith's Story

We will now unravel Lilith's mythical biography from the time she first emerges in ancient Sumaria as a handmaiden to the great goddess Inanna. The threads of her story lead us through the Hebraic

Fig. 6.1 Lilith

mythology where she is the first wife of Adam and later the consort of God in the Cabbalistic tradition. To the Romantic poets of the nineteenth century, Lilith came to embody the image of woman as femme fatale—alluring, irresistible, and deadly. Now, at the close of the twentieth century, Lilith reasserts herself as the liberated feminine, exalting ecstatic sexuality, upholding integrity, and refusing submission.

Lilith in Sumeria and Babylonia

Lilith is preeminently an emanation of the great winged Bird Goddess. She is a wind spirit, and her earliest associations are with the Sumerian Goddess of the Grain, Ninlil, Lady of the Air, who birthed the moon in the darkness of the netherworld and bestowed the divine right to rule.

Lilith's recorded story begins with Innana, granddaughter of Ninlil, who was the "Queen of Heaven" in early Sumeria. The legend of Innana and Enki told of the sacred sexual customs that were one of Innana's gifts to civilize the people of Erech. Here, the holy women of the temple were known as the *nu-gig*, the pure and spotless virgin priestesses. They took as their lovers the members of the community who came to the temple to worship the Goddess and to receive a healing. At this time Lilith's name is recorded as a young maiden, the "hand of Innana," who gathers the men from the street and brings them to the temple at Erech for the holy rites.[4]

Between 3000 BCE and 2500 BCE the ancient Sumerian culture began to interface with the coming of the patriarchy. As the patriarchy moved to overtake the reign of the Goddess, they first needed to sever the people from the Goddess's vast power, which was centered in her inner temple of sacred sexual love. In order to accomplish this task the patriarchy rejected and suppressed the sexual rites of the Goddess religion. Like the denied shadow when projected, women's sexual power became demonized as a force of evil. Over the centuries the young maid Lilith, who first approached the men to take them to Innana's holy temple, became in patriarchal culture the embodiment of everything that was evil and dangerous in the sexual realm. She especially catalyzed men's worst fears concerning the sexual power of the feminine.

By 2400 BCE Lilith, Spirit of the Air, was distorted into a demon of the night who personified natural disasters such as storms and winds. She was imaged as a beautiful maiden who would not release her lovers or ever give them real satisfaction. There existed four classes of demons: the Lillu demons, who were vampires; the Lilitu or she-demons; the Ardat Lili and the Irdu Lili, who were female and male counterparts, dwelling in waste places, preying upon men and women by night and conceiving ghostly children. These demons haunted desolate places in stormy weather and were dangerous to pregnant women and children.

Lilith's flower was the *lilu*, or lily, or "lotus" of her genital magic, which represented the virgin aspect of the Triple Goddess. A Sumerian king list dating from this time states that Lugalbanda, father of the great hero Gilgamesh, was a Lillu-demon.[5] This statement can also be read as a veiled reference pointing to Gilgamesh, who was reputed to be two-thirds divine and one-third human, to have the sacred blood lineage descending from the sexual rites of the Goddess.

A Babylonian terracotta plaque from 2300 BCE depicts Lilith as a Bird Woman and Lady of the Beasts. She is beautiful, with a slender nude body, wings that fall behind her like an open veil, and powerfully clawed owl feet. Her head is adorned with a crown of multiple horns worn by all great deities, and she holds the ring and rod symbols of power. Surrounded by lions as her protectors, and owls depicting her nocturnal wisdom, she is the animal soul of the world, who is associated with every living creature that creepeth and all the beasts of the field. The literal meaning of Lilith's name is "screech." She was associated with the screech owl of the night, and later as a demon of screeching.

The story of how Lilith was cast out of the Sumerian cosmology was told in the epic tale of *Gilgamesh and the Netherworld* (dating ca. 2000 BCE).[6] Innana saved a sacred huluppu tree on the banks of the Euphrates that had been uprooted by a great windstorm. She then planted this willow in her holy garden, planning to use its wood for her throne and bed. As the years passed the tree matured, but it bore no branches or leaves for three reasons: the snake who could not be charmed made its nest in the roots of the tree; the fierce Anzu bird set its young in the crown; and, in the middle, the dark maid Lilith built her home. And so Innana, who loved to laugh, wept because the snake, bird, and Lilith would not leave her tree. She turned to Gilgamesh for help. He slayed the serpent. His men cut down the tree and presented it to Innana for her throne and bed. The Anzu bird escaped with its young to the mountains, and Lilith smashed her home and flew to the wild and uninhabited places. Innana rewarded

177

*Goddesses of the
Dark Moon:
The Dark
Maid
Lilith*

Gilgamesh with a drum and drumstick from the base and crown of the tree, which enabled him to talk with the gods and to descend to the netherworld.

From a feminist perspective, this story raises several disturbing questions. Why would Innana weep at the presence of her handmaid Lilith in her tree? Why did she wish for the symbols of the ancient Bird and Snake Goddess to be gone from her life? And why did Innana reward Gilgamesh for destroying the sacred serpent and banishing Lilith and the Anzu bird?

The *Epic of Gilgamesh*, as inscribed upon the clay tablets dating from 2000 BCE, was the later Babylonian version of an earlier Sumerian tale that had occurred over the preceding one thousand years. It is known only in fragments today. From the patriarchal perspective Innana must sacrifice her virginity, that is, her new moon maiden nature as a goddess who is free and autonomous. She must also submit to the new solar gods and allow Gilgamesh to destroy the key symbols of her power: the bird, the snake, and the tree.

It now becomes clear why Innana wept at the continued presence of Lilith, the serpent, and the Anzu bird, who all resided in her sacred tree. The ancient Bird and Snake Goddess who made her home at the crown and base of the tree of life united heaven and earth. This image contained the power and knowledge inherent in the eagle-winged, lion-faced bird and the wisdom of sexual renewal embodied by the serpent. Innana had to give up these symbols of her power if the new patriarchy was to grant her throne and bed, her new symbols signifying co-rulership in the new reign. If she could not let go of them voluntarily, they would be taken away from her in any case by the coming patriarchal onslaught. The home of her handmaiden Lilith was destroyed, and Lilith had to flee to the desolate wilderness.

Lilith's banishment continued into the following centuries as the Babylonian, Hittite, and Semitic civilizations superseded the Sumerian culture in the ancient Near East. The wild, free, and virgin (belonging to no man) aspect of feminine sexuality that Lilith symbolized became distorted into the irresistible, lascivious, insatiable, unmarried she-demons who seduced men in their sleep against their will and excited their nightly emission. An ancient Babylonian cylinder seal shows a man copulating with a vampire whose head has been cut off in order to keep away the nocturnal visits of Lilith and her sisters. Another charm has the reference,

The Lilu, the Lilit, the night Lili,
Enchantments, disasters, spells,
Illnesses, evil charms,
In the name of heaven
And in the name of earth
Let them be exorcised.

In a seventh-century BCE Syrian tablet Lilith was portrayed as a winged sphinx with the following inscription, part of an incantation used to help women in childbirth:

O, Flyer in a dark chamber,
Go away at once, O Lili.

Lilith was feared as a female demon who endangered women in childbirth and strangled infants. This terror may be linked to her attempt to defend Ninlil's right to bestow rulership by preventing the survival of the conquering tribes' heirs. Many of these incantation texts warding Lilith off have been found in Ninlil's city of Nippur in Babylonia.

Lilith in Hebraic Tradition

The next layer of Lilith's imagery as a demoness comes from the Hebrews, where she was assigned a central place in Jewish demonology. In the early part of the first millennium BCE the Hebrews invaded Canaan and later went into exile in Babylonia, where they had to assimilate the local mythology and customs. In Lilith's Canaanite queendom the priests could not dissuade their females from praying to the Fertility Goddess, Anath, whose worshipers were permitted prenuptial promiscuity. The prophets denounced the Israelite women for following these practices, and defamed Lilith as an evil and unnatural spirit in an attempt to suppress their women's demands for sexual freedom.

Most of the Hebrew legends about Lilith were developed after the Babylonian exile (586 BCE) and the Roman deportation of the Jews into captivity (70 CE). They brought back from Babylonia the names of various demons, among them that of Lilith. The only appearance of Lilith in the Bible is in the Old Testament when Isaiah, describing Yahweh's day of vengeance when the land will be turned into a desolate wilderness, says, "The wild beasts shall meet with the jackals and the satyr shall cry to his fellow; and Lilith shall repose there and find her a place of rest" (Isa. 34:14).

Exile was a threat to Jewish survival; and in their powerless condition Hebrew men needed to ensure their manhood. It was therefore necessary that their women be programmed to be submissive and to enable the interests of men, family, and society, not their own. Proving one's maleness was also defined as the ability to father children, which in Exile was essential to the continuity of the race; so any threat to a man's potency or his offspring was tantamount to extinction. The concept that Lilith signified, that of a sexually independent female who had control over pregnancy and infancy, was antithetical to the survival of the race. It needed to be addressed.[7]

In establishing their genealogy the Jewish patriarchs had to contend with the two different versions in Genesis concerning the creation of man and woman. Genesis 1, which embodies the earlier belief that the universe was created from the union of the Father Sky and Mother Earth, relates that God created the first man and woman at the same time. The later version, Genesis 2, states that woman was an afterthought and appendage of man. The new monotheistic religion, which worshiped only one God, the Father, had to remove the vestiges of the female deities and repress the goddess cults. Lilith is that part of the Great Goddess that has been rejected and cast out in postbiblical times.[8] Female worship went underground and survived only in the distorted projections of men's worst fears concerning their manhood and potency.

Lilith and Adam   This then is the background for the development of Lilith's next phase as the first wife of Adam, before he mated with Eve. Lilith left him and then became transformed into an evil seductress, a mother of demons and a killer of children in the Hebrew mythology. This story was developed in the Babylonian Talmud, the *Zohar,* and the *Alphabet of Ben Sira,* all of which were written or compiled outside of Eretz Israel, presumably after 70 CE, although they draw upon earlier oral and written tales.

The earliest biblical account of Creation relates that God created the first man and woman at the same time. "And God created the human species in His own image . . . male and female created He them" (Gen. 1:27). Jewish legends tell us that this woman was Lilith. The *Alphabet of Ben Sira,* an early Jewish commentary on the Bible written around 1000 CE, weaves together the various earlier versions of creation and the subversive concept of woman's equality.

After the Holy One created the first human being, Adam, he said: "It is not good for Adam to be alone." He created a woman, also from the earth, and called her Lilith. They quarreled immediately. She said: "I will not lie below you." He said, "I will not lie below you, but above you. For you are fit to be below me and I above you." She responded: "We are both equal because we both come from the earth." Neither listened to the other. When Lilith realized what was happening, she pronounced the Ineffable Name of God and flew off into the air.

Adam rose in prayer before the Creator, saying, "The woman you gave me has fled from me." Immediately the Holy One sent three angels after her.

The Holy One said to Adam: "If she wants to return, all the better. If not, she will have to accept that one hundred of her children will die every day." The angels went after her, finally locating her in the sea, in the powerful waters in which the Egyptians were destined to perish. They told her what God said, and she did not want to return. . . . [9]

Originally he and she, Adam and Lilith, were created equal and together and set in the Garden of Eden to give things their names and thereby bring the world into manifestation. They had a very difficult time because Lilith insisted upon full equality, which Adam refused, and they could not agree upon anything. Adam would have sex with Lilith only if he was on the top and she was on the bottom because he was superior, having been created from the pure dust, and she was inferior, having come from filth and sediment. After some time Lilith realized that Adam was never going to accept as valid and worthwhile anything she had to offer, so she uttered the secret name of God, flew off, and vanished into the air.

Adam complained to God that the wife he had been given had deserted him. God then sent three angels, Senoy, Sansenoy, and Semangelof, to capture Lilith. They found her beside the Red Sea, a place of ill repute abounding in lascivious demons, with whom Lilith engaged in unbridled promiscuity and bore scores of demonic children. The angels relayed God's warning that if she did not return she would have to see to the death of one hundred of her children every day. When she refused to go they threatened to drown her in the sea. She protested, claiming that she was expressly created to harm newborn infants: boys until their eighth day of life (after circumcision) and girls until their twentieth day. However, she swore an oath that whenever she saw the image of those angels in an amulet she would lose her power over the infant. And if she could not destroy a human infant because of the amulet, she would have to kill her own.[10]

Lilith did not return to her husband. She chose a lifetime of exile in a desert cave on the shores of the Red Sea rather than one of subjugation and domination to Adam's will. Lilith went through a great period of grief. Not only had she voluntarily removed herself as the feminine aspect of wisdom from the process of a new creation of the world, but daily one hundred of her children were dying for her defiance. After her mourning was done she made love with the water elementals, and many beings arose from this union—namely the sea of the unconscious, from which the feminine aspect of our wisdom arises from the depths of our psyche.

Meanwhile, in the Garden of Eden, God took a rib from Adam's side and turned it into Eve, Adam's second wife and helpmate. Adam was pleased to be rid of Lilith, who only gave him trouble, and to now have Eve, who was submissive and dutiful in all ways. However, the fact that he never gave up resenting Lilith for having made the choice to leave him addresses man's (or the man within each woman's) primal anger toward any woman who has ever left or rejected him, even though he may be very happy that she is out of his life.

The legend concerning the wife of Adam who preceded the creation of Eve merged with the earlier legend of Lilith as a demon who killed infants and endangered women in childbirth. When the story of creation was being written down, mention of Lilith was wholly exorcised from scripture, with the one exception of Isaiah. The biblical patriarchs did not want to give the world a model of a wife who demanded equality and defied and left her husband; instead they extolled the virtues of Eve, who had no such ideas but instead would be subservient, enabling her husband in all ways.

Lilith was punished for her defiance by being exiled from legitimate society and cast out into the wilderness. What remained of Lilith's story was then distorted, and the image of her that abounded in the Hebraic literature and folklore of the next several millennia was one of feminine evil. She was known as the harlot, the wicked, the false, and the black. The first woman on earth who was equal to man and a free spirit was condemned to survive for eternity as a she-devil, mating with demons and devils and bearing monsters instead of human children.[11] This image was to serve as a threat and warning to any woman who might consider leaving her husband or defying male authority.

Lilith in the Dark and Middle Ages

During the next period in Lilith's mythical biography society perceived her as a crazed madwoman who was obsessed with wanton, perverted sexual desire. She spent her time seducing men, breeding demons, and murdering small babies.

Lilith as a Seductress   Adam's idyll with Eve did not last long. Legends tell that it was Lilith, crowned and winged with a serpent's tail entwined around the Tree of Knowledge (reminiscent of the ancient Bird and Snake Goddess), who persuaded Eve to offer the forbidden apple to Adam and initiate him into the sexual mysteries of the coiled *kundalini* serpent. The *Zohar* myth relates that Lilith was "the Serpent, the Woman of Harlotry who incited and induced Eve . . . causing Eve to seduce Adam while she was in her menstrual impurity."[12] Peter Redgrove believes that Lilith carries the qualities of an "initiatrix of the male magician who would be sensitive to the woman's dark body of data and rhythm through his black senses and closely associated with her wise blood."[13]

After Adam's fall and expulsion from the Garden of Eden he repented by fasting, mortifying his flesh, and taking a vow of celibacy for one hundred and thirty years. Lilith took her revenge by visiting him at night and tempting him with erotic dreams. She mounted him and captured his nocturnal emissions, from which she bore demon babies. At the same time similar male spirits impregnated Eve, and from these unions originated the plagues of humankind.

Lilith's seduction of Adam served as the mythical prototype to validate men's fears of the sexual power of women as succubi. Rabbinical literature warns that "Lilith is a Harlot who fornicates with men . . . who sleep below in the impurity of spontaneous emission and from them are born demons and spirits and Lilin." "She is the Alien Woman . . . the sweetness of sin and the evil tongue. And from the lips of the Alien Woman honey flows." "Lilith is the Torturous Serpent who seduces men to go in torturous ways." "She is the Impure Female."[14]

Lilith was the secret fear of men who slept alone; she would attack their bodies in lascivious ways. A passage in the *Zohar* states,

> She [Lilith] roams at night and goes all about the world and makes sport with men and causes them to emit seed. In every place where a man sleeps alone in a house, she visits him and

grabs him and attaches herself to him and has her desire from him, and bears from him. And she also afflicts him with sickness, and he knows it not, and all this takes place when the moon is on the wane.[15]

She lurks under doorways, in wells, and in latrines, where she continues to lead men astray until the last judgment. The offspring of Lilith's nocturnal rapes are the demons that plague the world.

Once her daughters, the lilin, attached themselves to a human, they acquired the rights of cohabitation, and had to be given a *get*, a letter of divorce, in order to be expelled. It was said that if a pious man had a wet dream, Lilith laughed. Her enchanting, unearthly beauty was especially dangerous to young men who lusted after her; once visited, they could never be aroused again by a mortal woman. The lilin haunted men for thousands of years, and generations of celibate monks clutched their crucifixes and malas over their genitals at night to protect themselves from the evil Lilith.

Lilith as a Child-Killer Lilith's exploits as a child-killer are documented in the incantation texts inscribed on bowls and amulets found throughout the Near East from the fifth to seventeenth centuries. It was believed that Lilith's power could be trapped under an inverted bowl on which magical formulas had been written. As a personification of the destructive life force Lilith was a threat to pregnant woman, causing miscarriage and birth complications. Favoring the children born out of wedlock, the lilin hated those born of ordinary human marriage and would attack them, plague them, suck their blood, and strangle them. To protect a newborn child from Lilith, especially males until they were safeguarded by circumcision, a ring was drawn with charcoal on the wall of the birth room and inside it was written, "Adam and Eve. Out, Lilith!" The names Senoy, Sansenoy, and Semangelof—the three angels with whom Lilith bargained at the Red Sea—were written over the doorway of houses and on amulets hung around a child's neck to ward off Lilith's vengeance.

Many amulets include the story of the prophet Elijah meeting Lilith on her way to the house of a woman in childbirth "to give her the sleep of death, to take her son, and drink her blood, to suck the marrow of his bones, and to eat his flesh." Elijah excommunicated her, whereupon she undertook not to harm women in childbirth whenever she saw or heard her name. If a male child smiled in his sleep, people said that Lilith was fondling him. To avert danger one should strike the child's lips with one finger three times and cry out, "Away Lilith, you have no place here."[16]

The Greeks adopted the lilin and called them the Lamiae. They tell the story of an African queen, Lamia, who lived only for her beauty. She incurred the jealousy of Hera, who killed her children by Zeus. Lamia was driven mad, became ugly, and sought to destroy other women's children. She was also supposed to be able to change her shape. Lamia later became the "nursery bogey" who stole children, seduced sleeping men, and sucked their blood. They were also known as the Empusae ("forcers-in," *Mormolyceia)*, frightening wolves, and Children of Hekate.

Lilith and Her Consorts   During Lilith's stay in the desert by the Red Sea, a fiery, furious, seductive energy emerged from her. Cabbalistic tradition says that the Blind Dragon arranged the marriage between Lilith the Elder and Samael, King of the Demons, and she reigned as queen in the realm of the forces of evil. Lilith the Younger became the bride of Ashmodai, also a King of Demons. The *Zohar* says that from her union with Samael and Ashmodai, Lilith bore alien and evil cohorts who were destroyers of the world of Above and Below. There was jealousy between the two kings, and Lilith commanded legions of demons to arouse war and all kinds of destruction.[17] It was also said that Lilith was the Queen of Zemargad, who traveled with her army of demons for three years from her home in the desert to attack the sons of Job.[18]

The double nature of Lilith appears again in her association with a sister demoness called Naamah. Naamah means "the charmer," whose extraordinary, irresistible beauty and sweet cymbal music seduced both angels and men. Some writings identify Lilith and Naamah as the two harlots who tested King Solomon's wisdom in asking for his judgment in their quarrel over the surviving child. Barbara Koltuv feels that Lilith the Younger is Naamah as maiden and seductress, while Lilith the Elder or Ancient One is the child-killer, hag, and snatcher.[19] This corresponds to the new and dark phases of the Triple Moon Goddess as virgin and crone.

In Arabic lore there exists a widespread identification of Lilith with the Queen of Sheba. A Jewish and Arab myth from the third century told that the Queen of Sheba was a *jinn*—half woman and half demon. She had cloven feet and hairy legs, a kind of sphinx who posed riddles. It was said that King Solomon had dominion over demons, spirits, and lilin and knew the language of each. Preparing for the visit of the Queen of Sheba, he ordered the Djinns to build a throne room with a floor of glass. When the Queen of Sheba entered, she thought that his throne sat upon water and she lifted her garments in order to cross the water and approach him. Thus her hairy legs, showing her natural bestial origin, were revealed.

The evidence that she was Lilith was that the riddles the Queen of Sheba posed to King Solomon are a repetition of the words of seduction that Lilith spoke to Adam. "What is water that is neither in the air nor in the river nor in the ocean nor in the rain?" The answer to this is supposed to be "the sweat of a horse in its mane," but it is also a double riddle for "woman's love" or the wetness between the thighs of the Queen of Sheba's animal pubic mane.[20] Solomon accepted her instinctual feminine sexuality and they had a child, from whom the Abyssinian rulers claim lineage descent.

During the fifteenth-century Kabbalistic age, Lilith rose to triumph as the queenly consort at God's side. When the Temple of Jerusalem was destroyed, the Matronit, mother of the House of Israel, had to leave her husband and go with their children into exile until the time of their redemption. God, Israel's father, took the slave woman (that is, Lilith) in the Matronit's place and she became the Mistress of his House.[21] From this union Lilith became the mother of the unholy folk who constituted the "mixed multitude."

This sinful connubium between God and Lilith will continue until the coming of the Messiah, who will put an end to it by casting Lilith out and restoring the Matronit to her rightful place beside God. The messianic days will also mark the end of Lilith's existence. For while she has existed since the sixth or even fifth day of creation, she is not immortal. In the Days to Come, when Israel will take revenge on Edom, both she and the Blind Dragon, who arranged the match between her and Samael, will be killed.[22]

Lilith in the Nineteenth Century

Lilith achieved considerable vogue in the nineteenth century, when the artistic mind was obsessed with the figure of the *femme fatale*. R. F. McGillis writes that to the Romantic writers, Lilith represents a source of evil, a siren who destroys those who fall under her spell. She is the unknown and mysterious, and to turn away from her enchantment is to preserve humanity. Men fear her and love her, both terrorized and fascinated by her power. She either destroys her lover or prompts him to a new awareness and a new life.[23]

In the Talmud Lilith was portrayed as a long-haired demon of the night. A woman's hair is considered to be one of her seductive adornments, and this is the reason why the hair of monastic women, such as the Brides of Christ and the Vestal Virgins, has traditionally been cut, bound, and covered. Men's fascination with Lilith's long, seductive hair is a theme in several nineteenth-century literary works.

Lilith appears in Goethe's *Faust*, Part 1. In the midst of the revelry atop the Broken in the Walpurgis Night scene, Lilith appears, the supreme temptress who even frightens Mephistopheles. He warns Faust:

> Beware of her fair hair, for she excels
> All women in the magic of her locks;
> And when she winds them around a young man's neck,
> She will not ever set him free again.[24]

And in the Pre-Raphaelite artistic movement Dante Gabriell Rossetti portrays Lilith in the following poem.

> Of Adam's first wife, Lilith, it is told
> (The witch he loved before the gift of Eve,)
> That, ere the snake's, her sweet tongue could deceive,
> And her enchanted hair was the first gold.
> And still she sits, young while the earth is old,
>   And, subtly of herself contemplative,
>   Draws men to watch the bright web she can weave,
> Till heart and body and life are in its hold.
>
> The rose and the poppy are her flower; for where
> Is he not found, O Lilith, whom shed scent
> And soft-shed kisses and soft sleep shall snare?
> Lo! as that youth's eyes burned at thine, so went
> Thy spell through him, and left his straight neck bent
> And round his heart one strangling golden hair.[25]

Lilith as the Shadow of Feminine Sexuality and Freedom

Lilith, in the matriarchal world, was once an image of all that was the finest of a woman's sexual nature, especially in her fiery, dark aspect, which relates to the menstrual mysteries. After the patriarchy repressed women's sexuality and the old Goddess religion disappeared,

187

Goddesses of the
Dark Moon:
The Dark
Maid
Lilith

Lilith came to embody mankind's projection of the feminine shadow, which Barbara Koltuv sees as representing the assertive and rebellious woman. As a demonic dark goddess she was then feared and hated rather than revered.

To enter into the figure of Lilith is to remember a time in the ancient past when women were honored and praised for initiating and fully expressing their personal freedom and sexual passion. If we then recall a time in the more recent past when women tried to reenact that ecstasy, only to be abused, suppressed, and rejected, we will understand how Lilith has been transformed by patriarchal culture. In the following discussion we will ask, What does it mean to reclaim the qualities she once bestowed upon the feminine as her birthright?

Reclaiming Lilith within Us

In the mythical literature there exist three Liliths. They reflect the new, full, and dark lunar phases of the Triple Goddess. Lilith the Younger was Naamah, the maiden and seductress. Lilith as the Consort of God was the mother of the "mixed multitude." And Lilith the Ancient One was the child-killer, hag, and snatcher. In the night skies there also exist three astronomical bodies that all bear the name of Lilith. There is an asteroid named Lilith; a controversial dark moon Lilith (another satellite of the earth); and a black moon Lilith, which is defined as the empty focal point in the moon's orbit around the earth.[26] In mythic-astrology the positions of these bodies in a person's birth chart point to the psychological process that unfolds in a person's life when Lilith is a prominent archetype.

Images of humiliation, diminishment, flight, and desolation, followed by fiery rage, and revenge as seductress and child-killer, abound throughout Lilith's mythology.[27] This is her pattern. For both women and men, in our quest to find and redeem Lilith within us, she takes us through a threefold process. In the first phase we must confront all the ways in which we have been repressed and take a stand to uphold our integrity. The second phase of her archetypal journey leads us into exile of despair over our rejection, where our shadow plots and executes its revenge. And in the final phase of her process, Lilith cuts away the layers that obscure and distort her true nature, whereby we are released from captivity and are redeemed.

Rebellion against Subservience In her earliest days Lilith, as handmaiden to Innana, was a symbol of the temple priestesses. These holy women brought the Goddess's blessings of sexual love and fertility into the lives of humanity and the earth. They also transmitted the blood lineage of divine rulership through their children conceived in sacred rituals. At the beginning of a new spiritual and political era ruled by solar gods, it was this Lilith who came to Adam to offer her wisdom and her commitment to an equal partnership. She was the first woman on earth, equal to man and a free spirit.

But Adam rejected her sexually and intellectually, and tried to force her into subservience. She refused subjugation, and, as a wind spirit, flew away and resumed her ancient sexual practices in the Red Sea. Lilith was then envisioned as a jealous avenger who personified the destructive life force. This image arose from Adam's refusal to accept her as an equal, and has become the prototype for men's unwillingness to accept women's equality and instinctive sexuality.

Lilith lives within each man and woman, and she represents our primal, instinctive feminine sexuality. Over the millennia the masculine part of each person both longs for and fears the power of this wild woman. She is free and unrestrained in her animating, pulsating, transforming sexuality that remembers and evokes the original orgiastic aspect of the Great Goddess.

When this Lilith speaks through us, she is the voice who demands absolute equality in whatever situation we find ourselves (relationship, job, family, group, and so on). She will not settle for anything less, and is unwilling to compromise if that means denying her essential values, beliefs, or ideals. Lilith radiates strength, courage, and passion, and she takes a stand for independence and freedom from tyranny. She is that quality in us that refuses to be bound in a relationship, . . . but wants equal freedom to move, change, and be herself.[28] She will not cooperate in her own victimization, and will opt for no relationship as opposed to a bad one. Rather than be dominated and suppressed, Lilith accepts the loss of physical security, loneliness, and exclusion from society. In her voluntary exile from relatedness, she has the capacity to nurture and sustain herself.

With the coming of the patriarchy it became unacceptable for women (and the woman in each man) to experience Lilith's original essence as a sexually vital free spirit who was equal to man. She appears in our daily lives when we find ourselves in those situations where we are not free to express ourselves nor valued for our wisdom. We are prevented from acting, moving, choosing, and determining our life circumstances. We may feel forced to obey others against our better judgment, and pressured to suppress the qualities that others find unacceptable and threatening, especially the sexual, independent, and rebellious parts of our personality. Experiences of humiliation and denial also contribute to a buildup of smoldering resentment.

The inner pressure that accumulates when any energy is confined and constricted eventually precipitates a violent explosion. In the forceful outburst of our repressed anger, we have the capacity to see and speak our truth. However, this clarity can also destroy the false pretensions that give form to our self-defeating relationships with our partners, parents, bosses, spiritual and academic teachers, or groups. In the face of what has been exposed, we cannot go back to the old patterns of self-denial and resume our relationship as if nothing happened.

Flight into Exile By standing up for ourselves, we may be denounced and humiliated. Like Lilith, who after her rebellion was forced into exile, the fate of many female rebels is to suffer ostracism, excommunication, or some form of banishment because of their assertive and defiant behavior.[29] We are then filled with a fiery rage, feeling forced to flee and losing our "homes" in order to preserve our integrity. While we are the ones doing the actual leaving, we feel rejected, wounded, and betrayed. In those cases where we are not able to leave because of children, other familial obligations, or financial consideration, and we fear for our safety, we may deny and banish Lilith's voice inciting us to action so that we can survive and go on. But we know that the shadow in exile, whether its flight into the desolate wilderness occurs externally or internally, does not meekly resign itself to passively accepting its rejection.

Like a caged and wounded animal fleeing from its captor, desperately trying to find a hiding place in which to heal itself, Lilith flies off into the desert to seek refuge. We may leave our relationship in an actual physical way; or if we cannot escape on an outer level, we may withdraw on an inner level by severing ourselves emotionally and psychologically from our oppressor. In either case the second phase of Lilith's mythical journey is a flight into desolation, which can often be experienced as a period of madness. Feeling alone, betrayed, rejected, and wounded, we writhe in the pain of our anguish. In the process of saving ourselves, we have destroyed our connection to another. In addition we are often ostracized by the social group in which our relationship existed. A woman who leaves her relationship, and especially because of a sexual liaison with another, is often deprived of her home, possessions, and financial resources from the marriage. She is humiliated, and it is not uncommon for women to have a less secure and lower standard of living after divorce or separation.

To the extent that we have difficulty in moving through our suffering to reclaim our dignity, we may internalize our rage and thus turn it against ourselves. In our rejection we feel lonely and unwanted. We interpret this to mean that there is something about us that is unacceptable and undesirable. Filled with bitterness and blame, we become men who hate women and women who hate ourselves.

In Lilith's mythical drama there comes a time when there are no more tears or futile hopes for acceptance and reconciliation left inside of us. Then another emotion starts to build, that of outrage and a desire for revenge against the person or situation that has caused us so much suffering.

While Lilith is off in the desert of her voluntary exile, wounded and suffering, she is attempting to find her inner source of strength and to reclaim her integrity. However, the world she has left punished her for the act of leaving. Her vital female qualities of independence and passion intimidated male dominance. She was slandered as demoness, seductress, and child-killer, much as many women today leave abusive relationships only to be called bitches and whores or to have their children taken from them. Lilith became a hated, and perhaps secretly envied, female symbol who served as a threat to straying or rebellious women, warning them how society would treat them if they were to leave their husbands or defy male authority.

Cabbalistically Lilith's name corresponds to the screech owl, the night owl who remains in the shadows. When an aspect of the wholeness of the self is denied, it develops into the shadow. When we repress Lilith's essence, the rejected shadow self becomes distorted by the pressure of suppression and the anguish of the pain. As the shadow self festers in exile, it releases poisons into our mindstream that distort our perception of reality.

With the patriarchal denouncement of feminine sexuality and freedom, we have collectively transformed Lilith into a fatal, seductive demoness who becomes the Bride of the Devil. She became a scapegoat for men and women's fears of their instinctual desires and sexual urges, and she grew to embody men's worst fears concerning their sexual potency and performance. Lilith's mythical imagery carries our dark projections of the feminine shadow who has been banished to the darkest crevices of our psyche. As an emissary of the ancient Bird and Snake Goddess, Lilith is powerful.

Rather than withering away in exile, the Lilith shadow grows and flourishes in the same way that she was prolific in breeding demonic offspring on the shores of the Red Sea. When this aspect of Lilith's shadow is active in our lives, our psyche becomes overwhelmed with images of revenge and retaliation. When the shadow inevitably erupts and violently breaks through our boundaries of constraint, she unleashes the terror of her vengeance.

Lilith's mythos contains the patriarchy's associations of the rebellious woman with that of the she-devil. When women step outside the boundaries of acceptable submissive feminine behavior and actualize their ability to say no, they trigger men's fears and fantasies that their rebellion will lead to an out-of-control, unstoppable rampage, like that of mythical Lilith.

Lilith, by being true to herself, actively threatened the survival of Adam's patriarchal dominion. In her shadow aspect as the jealous avenger, humanity projected onto her the image of the Dark Goddess who destroys life. Desirable and dangerous, she became the embodiment of men's sexual longing and their fear of women's sexual power over them. Try as they might, they could not totally eradicate her alluring, forbidden beauty, which evoked her original orgiastic nature. She became the symbol of fatal enchantment, deadly in her seduction. She had the power to destroy men by exciting and coupling with them at night against their will. She undermined their vitality by sucking their blood, and drained their potency by causing the nocturnal emission in order to breed demons who would multiply her revenge. Succubus and vampire, Lilith was shunned by those who feared, and thus negated, all erotic experiences except those that led to the conception of children.

When shadow Lilith is active in a man's life, and he is projecting his own inner demonic images of Lilith onto women, he will be intrigued and irresistibly drawn to the dark, enchanting, forbidden female, whom he then attempts to ravish and destroy because of his fear of her deadly sexual power over him. He experiences a woman's passion as a voracious and demanding sexuality that causes his manhood and erection to diminish. He blames the Lilith woman for making him feel impotent and maligns her as a castrating ball-buster. Lilith's rejection of Adam and her flight to the sensual Red Sea also triggers men's fears of abandonment and the loss of woman's companionship and emotional support. Women like Lilith, who refuse to nurture men, threaten their sense of survival.

When shadow Lilith is active in a woman's life, hatred of her own sexuality can lead to barrenness, frigidity, emotional coldness, and excessive detachment. Lilith women cannot have their needs met in relationships that restrict and devalue them. Trapped in this kind of abuse, in covert retaliation, they use their sexuality like a weapon with which to control, manipulate, and punish others. Taken to extremes this kind of indiscriminate, destructive sexual activity can backfire, making one vulnerable to contracting sexually transmitted diseases. Even if a woman is still a child or an innocent, she may unconsciously magnetize society's images onto her as the vamp, whore, or nympho-maniac "who is asking for it" and therefore "deserves what she gets." Lilith's shadow material is often an underlying theme in a woman's predisposition to repeated patterns of sexual abuse.

Women who deny Lilith—suppress their instinctive sexuality and instead fulfill patriarchal expectations for male approval—will know her in their hatred and secret jealousy of attractive, independent females who might seduce their own mates. These threatening projections challenge their own decisions to accept obedience and submission for the security of marriage and societal acceptance. Lilith is feared as the "other woman," divorcée, prostitute, office wife, and vamp.

Shadow Lilith claims not only the lives of men, but as child-killer she takes her revenge on their offspring and threatens the survival of the race of Adam's children by other women. Her crimes included killing or harming pregnant and birthing women and new-born infants. When shadow Lilith in us is operative, she may emerge as the murderous rage we sometimes feel toward our children when we feel tied down and restricted by our responsibilities to them and have no time and space for ourselves. She appears in those individuals who hate children and who harm them through sexual or physical abuse. Distorted images of Lilith in our unconscious can contribute to miscarriage, patterns of repeated abortions, births of deformed children, and crib deaths. For all of us who carry the pain of our wounded child whose infantile needs were strangled, Lilith is present.

The deeper significance of Lilith as child-killer lies in her relationship to the ebb and flow of a woman's menstrual cycle. As we will more fully discuss in chapter 7, the Dark Goddess is the muse of menstruation. Mythical Lilith was seen as the child-killing witch of the menstrual period, when the womb fills with blood instead of off-spring, which denies men their heirs.[30] The menstrual period is also a time when women instinctively want to flee from the demands of others and withdraw into themselves. If they are not allowed to do so, Lilith protests as the PMS witch, the raging bitch. In her menstrual aspect, Lilith was hated for refusing to service men or conceive their children.

From the perspective of women's mysteries, Lilith, who engaged in unbridled promiscuity on the shores of the Red Sea, the ocean of red blood, is a goddess of woman's menstrual blood. Menstruation is the source of a woman's psychic power, and it was used as a time to engage in ritual tantric sexual practices. It was Lilith who persuaded Eve to have intercourse with Adam during her bleeding time and initiate him into the mysteries of the garden.

Because the sexuality of menstruation does not lead to conception in a physical sense, it "is the gateway to magic and extrasensory perception."[31] The Cabbala states that Lilith is the ladder on which one can ascend to the rungs of prophecy.[32] The patriarchy rejected Lilith's menstrual sexuality because it did not result in the birth of children. They also feared the psychic power of a woman's red time. In defaming Lilith, menstruation was simultaneously tabooed to prevent women from discovering the power of their wise blood.

In this second stage of Lilith's exile, we are caught in the grip of the shadow. As the Lilith archetype continues to be repressed over generations, the ways in which she operates in us become ever more distorted and perverted. These hidden images of Lilith as seductress and child-killer lie buried in our unconscious psyche. They incite and sustain the war between the sexes. The original wound comes from our conditioned fear of woman's instinctive sexuality and its power over men. The more this aspect of the self is rejected and unintegrated, the more we are predisposed to experience sexuality as a destructive act of violence.

And in our silent rage of being denied our experience of sexuality as a blessing of the creative life principle, Lilith's shadow passes her time in exile by plotting our revenge and executing our retaliation. We then become trapped in the web of patriarchy's distorted projections, and in fact actualize their worst fears of the demonic feminine furiously trying to claim her due. However, the seeds of these thoughts and actions yield a crop whereby we continue to create new patterns of suppression and rejection in our future.

Release and Redemption When Lilith is active in our lives, we may find ourselves caught in the dilemma of maintaining our integrity, the right to express and act upon our truth, at the cost of separation from relatedness and exclusion from society. The secret of Lilith's alchemical transformation lies in the darkness of the final stage of her threefold process. This Dark Goddess who shares a name with the astronomical black moon is related to the Black Mother of Eastern mythological traditions. Many old amulets for protection against Lilith are in the form of knives, which represent Lilith's quality to instinctively cut to the essential nature of things. The Hebrew Lilith, the "Flame of the Revolving Sword," is an ally of the Hindu Kali and the Tibetan Black Dakini, the destroyer aspect of the Triple Goddess. Emanating fiery sparks, she brandishes her curved knife in one hand and in the other holds up a severed head. This symbolizes cutting the attachments in the ego's belief in a separate self.

The spiritual practice of the Black Mother cuts away at the ways in which we perpetuate our mistaken beliefs concerning our true nature. In the process she leads us to an awareness of the fundamental unity of all life. We come to understand that all life is an ever-changing, undifferentiated, universally connected matrix of living energy that is not separated by its containment in physical forms and mental concepts.

With her curved knife she severs all our false images and pretensions that have accumulated in our individual and collective repressed past. She does not tolerate any attempt to falsify ourselves from either a good or bad motivation; when we try to do so it ends in disaster. She ruthlessly destroys all that is not our true individuality or appropriate life path. She will not lead us to our goal by revealing what it is but rather by eliminating everything that it is not. The black aspect of Lilith closes all the wrong doors that face us.

The enforced clarity of black Lilith enables us to penetrate the delusion of our false needs, which force us into roles not in accordance with our true individuality. Her compassionate wrath allows us to see who we really are and forces us to be true to ourselves. The black Lilith in us will accept nothing less than our true individuality, not in the sense of its separateness, but in the sense of who we intrinsically are. When we are secure in acknowledging and expressing our true self, we do not falsify ourselves in order to be accepted by others. We are then not as vulnerable to becoming entrapped in situations that deny and disempower us, which is where Lilith's self-destructive cycle begins.

For many of us, however, Lilith presents a dilemma of how to be true to our integrity when the patriarchal value system that permeates our society continues to reject this aspect of the feminine nature. The issue is compounded by our conditioned Lilith reaction to flee from problematical confrontations. When we are caught in Lilith's shadow, we do not stay around long enough to develop the necessary tools for resolving conflict. This pattern reinforces the alienation, bitterness, and separation from relationship and family that is often found in the Lilith experience.

To the extent that we inhabit a dualistic reality where there exists a strong demarcation between oppressor and victim, our Lilith's anguished cry of hurt and rage cannot be healed. Throughout lifetimes we will alternate between these two roles, giving and receiving power ultimatums that insist on the exclusion of the other view. This stance moves us ever farther away from the state of wholeness.

Many philosophic traditions eventually come to the realization that it is through the reconciliation of opposites that the path opens toward balance, integration, and wholeness. Lilith seeks reconciliation between the male and female sexes, between individuals who are violently opposed to one another, and between the various warring aspects within our own psyche. In Lilith's realm consensus is one skill that we can learn to heal our separation from the wholeness of ourselves and from the rest of life.

The view of consensus encompasses the qualities of integration and synthesis. It is the creative third solution that is the both/and resolution to any problem that is being seen in as a black/white or either/or alternative. Consensus does not require the kind of compromise that pressures us to give up our essential values while mediating with another person. If we believe that such a solution theoretically exists, then Lilith's process is the willingness to search for this solution. If one possibility does not work out, to let it go and not reject or belittle the other person; and try another one until we can experientially arrive at a solution that we believe exists.

By practicing consensus we can begin to move out of a dualistic reality whose inherent nature is polarization, separation, and struggle for power, with one side inevitably losing and being rejected—in this case the qualities of the feminine nature as represented by Lilith. Consensus in Lilith's realm can lead us to the state of grace, called "oneness" by the ancients, whose qualities are inclusion and acceptance. In this way we can heal the rift that perpetuates our experiences of being cast out and fleeing into the exile of our separations.

After going to the root and cutting away all of the hidden and distorted aspects of Lilith's shadow self, who perpetuates the cycle of conflict and separation, the black Lilith places all of our ego attachments (ego in the sense of belief in a separately existing self) into her cauldron of transformation. She then transmutes the poisonous accumulations into the wisdom nectar of lucid perception and conscious participation in unification. The peacock is viewed as a bird of doom and associated with moonlight, owls, and infectious disease, all related to Lilith's mythical imagery. However, the peacock can eat poisonous plants; and instead of dying it is able to transmute the deadly poison into the brilliant colors of its plumage.

The Jerusalem Bible states that Lilith returns evermore as seductress and child-killer and will continue to do so until the Messiah comes and drives the unclean spirits from the land (Zech. 13:2). From the perspective of black Lilith this verse can be interpreted as the healing qualities of the Dark Goddess, who will continue to destroy and cleanse her distorted images from our mindstream. We can then reclaim the pure form of these rejected parts of ourselves. Healing entails moving toward a state of wholeness within ourselves, and this awareness precipitates a realization of our connection with all of life. As we accept Lilith within our psyche, the quality of our life will move from a state of alienation in exile to conscious expression of our individuality and purpose within the larger whole.

In Lilith's archetypal threefold process, she first shows us how and where we experience the themes of suppression, resentment, explosive anger, taking a stand for our dignity, only to be rejected and forced to flee. In the second phase she brings us to the exile of desolation where we feel our anguish, alienation, fear, and hatred of our sexuality. She exacts revenge by fulfilling the patriarchy's worst fears and enacting their monstrous shadow projections. In the final phase we can discover her transmuting and healing activities, as she cuts away our pretensions, false roles, and delusions and helps us fully to actualize our true, essential selves. Maxine Harris says that only recently have feminist writers championed the cause of Lilith, and proclaimed her to be the first liberated woman, a woman who was unwilling to accept a position of subservience to her husband.[33]

Journal Questions

1. Where in my life do I feel repressed and unacknowledged by others? Do I find myself in situations where others are forcing me to do

197

*Goddesses of the
Dark Moon:
The Dark
Maid
Lilith*

things that I don't want to do, and therefore I act in ways that are not like my true self? Does my repressed anger sometimes break through my facade and explode in tears, accusations, fury, rage, or flight as I reveal my dissatisfaction? To what extent am I then rejected, dismissed, hated, or ostracized by others when I am trying to be myself, speak my truth, and act upon my beliefs?

2. How do I feel about my sexuality? What is my relationship with the wild woman within me whose sexuality is instinctual, uninhibited, unrestrained, and animating? Do I think that erotic experiences are sacred or dirty? Do I allow the wild woman, or do my partner(s) allow her expression? If I deny, fear, or disapprove of this aspect in myself, how do I react to others who openly express it?

3. If I am a man, am I secretly attracted to and then overtly denounce erotic women? Do I think they are sexually manipulative and basically evil or dangerous so that I need to protect myself against their sexual power? If I am a woman, do I hate sex? Do I find it degrading and humiliating? Am I unable to receive pleasure or sexually cold, or emotionally detached? Am I indiscriminately promiscuous?

4. Have I been a victim of rape or other forms of sexual or emotional abuse? Have I ever been blamed for it afterward and told that I "was asking for it"? To what extent am I attracted to dark, intriguing, forbidden lovers whose sexual power over me I fear? Do I refer to my lovers as bewitching or beguiling? Like the spider who makes love with her mate and then kills it, have I ever had sex with someone and tried to hurt or destroy him or her? Have I ever been a victim of this activity? Might it have anything to do with my fear of their sexual power?

Notes

1. Jonelle Maison. From the poem "A Hell of a Woman."

2. *The Zohar*, 5 vols., translated by Harry Sperling and Maurice Simon (New York: Rebecca Bennet Publishers, and London: Socino Press, 1985), *Zohar* 2, 163 b.

3. Barbara Black Koltuv, *The Book of Lilith* (York Beach, ME: Nicholas Hayes, 1986), 22.

4. Merlin Stone, *When God Was a Woman* (New York: Harcourt Brace Jovanovich, 1976), 158.

5. Raphael Patai, *The Hebrew Goddess* (New York: Avon Books, 1978), 180.

6. Noah Kramer, *The Sumerians: Their History, Culture and Character* (Chicago: University of Chicago Press, 1963), 199–205.

7. Avina Cantor Zuckoff, "The Lilith Question," *Lilith* 1 (June 1976).

8. Koltuv, *The Book of Lilith*, 121.

9. *Alfa Beta di Ben Sira*, OM, 47, as found in Raphael Patai, *Gates to the Old City* (New York: Avon Books, 1980), 407–8.

10. Patai, *Gates to the Old City*, 407—8.

11. Maxine Harris, *Sisters of the Shadow* (Norman, OK, and London: University of Oklahoma Press, 1991), 172.

12. Patai, *Gates to the Old City*, 456.

13. Peter Redgrove, *The Black Goddess and the Unseen Real* (New York: Grove Press, 1987), 168.

14. Patai, *Gates to the Old City*, 463–64.

15. The *Zohar* as found in Patai, *The Hebrew Goddess*, 196.

16. Naphtali Herz ben Jacob Elhanan, *Emeq Hamelekh* (in Hebrew) (Amsterdam: 1648), 84d, as found in Patai, *Gates to the Old City*, 467.

17. Moses Cordovero, *Pardes Rimmonim* (in Hebrew) (Cracow: 1592, and Koretz: 1780), as found in Patai, *Gates to the Old City*, 458, 465.

18. Targum, Job 1:15, as found in Patai, *Gates to the Old City*, 465.

19. Koltuv, *The Book of Lilith*, 121.

20. Redgrove, *The Black Goddess*, 69.

21. *Zohar* 3: 69a, as found in Patai, *Gates to the Old City*, 468.

22. *Emeq Hamelekh*, as found in Patai, *The Hebrew Goddess*, 221.

23. R. F. McGillis, "George MacDonald and the Lilith Legend in the XIXth Century," *Mythlore* (Winter, 1979).

24. P. B. Shelley, *Poems of Shelley*, edited by Thomas Hutchinson (London: 1965), 759.

25. Dante Gabriel Rossetti, *Collected Poems*, edited by W. M. Rossetti (London: 1906), vol. 1, 308.

26. For more information on the three astrological Liliths, see Demetra George, *Asteroid Goddesses* (San Diego: ACS Publications, 1986); Delphine Jay, *Interpreting Lilith* (Tempe, AZ: American Federation of Astrologers, 1981); and Marc Beriault, "The Dark Moon," *Considerations* (1987).

27. Koltuv, *The Book of Lilith*, 19.

28. Koltuv, *The Book of Lilith*, 22.

29. Harris, *Sisters of the Shadow*, 171.

30. Redgrove, *The Black Goddess*, 117.

31. Redgrove, *The Black Goddess*, 167.

32. Patai, *The Hebrew Goddess*, 215.

33. Harris, *Sisters of the Shadow*, 172.

✦ PART III ✦

Rites of Rebirth

Why fear ye the Dark Queen, oh men?
She is your renewer.
—Dion Fortune

7

The Dark Goddess as the Muse of Menstruation and Menopause

✦

You imagine yourself standing reverently before your vagina. . . .
You find that you can slip easily into the soft opening . . .
through the red gate into your body . . . you move
easily into the silky fluids around you . . . the soft,
rosy walls surrounding you sparkle and
shine. . . . See how lovely they are. . . .
—Jean Mountaingrove[1]

The mythical Dark Goddess continues to live on in each one of us today. We can find her presence in our physical bodies and in the forces of our personality that guide us into the darkness wherein we can find the seeds for our renewal. How can we recognize her in our midst? Hidden behind her dark veil, she is mysterious and elusive. However, when she parts her veil, she reveals a face that is fiery, fearless, and powerful. Over the course of the days, months, and years of our lives, she periodically appears for us as surely as the moon cycles through her phases. The most direct route to discovering the nature and workings of the Dark Goddess is through exploring the female sexual cycle, which is regulated by the Goddess's lunar cycle.

There exist two major feminine cycles in the physiology of women's bodies. Both cycles are physically and symbolically related to that of the moon. The first one is a monthly cycle, marked by ovulation and menstruation, that reflects the twofold alternation of the light and dark phases of the moon. The second is a lifelong developmental cycle, whose threefold stages of (1) menarche, (2) pregnancy, birth, and nursing, and (3) menopause correspond to the new, full, and dark phases of the moon.

The Dark Goddess is to be found in menstruation and in menopause, the dark moon phases of each of their respective cycles. The patriarchy's rejection of the Dark Goddess has included maligning the gifts of her blood mysteries, which have been repressed in the dark, exiled realm of the collective unconscious. These dark moon phases of a woman's life were considered blessings before they became known as the "curse." Our word "blessing" comes from the Old English *bloedsen,* or "bleeding." Vicki Noble writes in *Shakti Woman* that Western women have forgotten the spiritual significance of the menstrual cycle and need to reconnect in order to empower themselves. The blood mysteries of birthing, menstruation, and menopause are the core of female shamanism.[2] As we revision the dark, we need to reclaim the positive, healing, and regenerative qualities that are to be found in the dark moon phases of women's monthly and lifelong sexual cycles.

The Dark Goddess and Menstruation

The principle of polarity, which operates in our world as sets of complementary opposite forces (masculine/feminine, *yang/yin*, light/dark), is expressed within the female sexual cycle as the two poles of ovulation and menstruation. The average menstrual cycle is twenty-nine

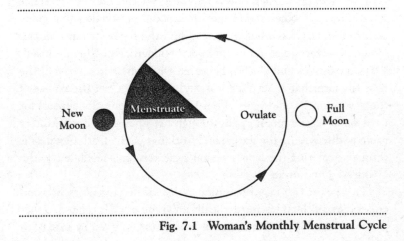

Fig. 7.1 Woman's Monthly Menstrual Cycle

and one-half days, which is exactly the length of the moon's cycle. As we have seen, the words for moon, month, and menses are all derived from the root *mens*. When we overlay the lunar cycle on a woman's monthly sexual cycle, the light phase of the full moon corresponds to ovulation and the dark/new moon is analogous to menstruation.

When women work and live closely together, they all tend to ovulate and bleed at the same time. In early societies people spent much of their time outdoors, under natural sunlight and moonlight, attuned to natural and vegetative cycles. Under these circumstances women were more likely to ovulate at the full moon and bleed at the dark moon. Today, when we spend much of our time indoors under artificial light, this is no longer the case. It is important to note that if a woman does not bleed at the dark of the moon, it is neither an aberration nor cause for alarm. However, it has been demonstrated that a woman can regulate her cycle by exposing herself to varying amounts of light each night that duplicate the rhythms of increase and decrease of the moon's phases.[3] We will now briefly discuss the physiological stages of a woman's menstrual cycle as it relates to the symbolism of the lunar phases.

Various hormones rise and fall in a woman's bloodstream each month and affect changes in her uterus. These monthly fluctuations flow according to the same rhythm of increase and decrease as the

Rites of Rebirth: The Dark Goddess as the Muse of Menstruation and Menopause

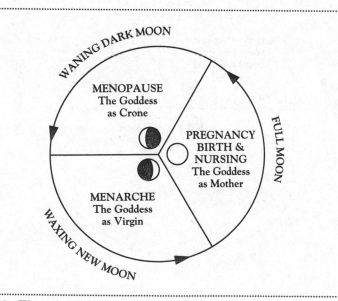

Fig. 7.2 **Woman's Lifelong Blood Cycle**

moon's cycle. Estrogen rises in the bloodstream during the waxing half of the cycle, when the moon's light is increasing; while progesterone predominates during the waning half, when the light is decreasing.

The hormonal cycle begins with the waxing crescent moon. At this time the pituitary gland secretes follicle stimulating hormone (FSH) into the bloodstream. This stimulates the eggs to ripen in the ovaries and gives the signal for the production of estrogen. Rising levels of estrogen prompt a buildup of tissue in the womb and an increased blood supply to the uterus. The body uses food in a building and assimilating way during this time; thus women feel more energetic, optimistic, and emotionally expansive. This is a powerful time; women can use this energy high by taking risks and initiating action to make things happen.

With the approach of the full moon, the estrogen level begins to peak. This blocks further production of FSH, and instead the pituitary gland manufactures leutening hormone (LH), which causes only

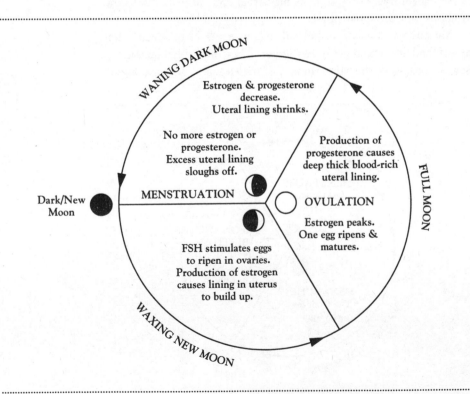

Fig. 7.3 **The Menstrual Cycle and the Lunar Phases**

Rites of Rebirth:
The Dark
Goddess as the
Muse of
Menstruation
and
Menopause

one of the eggs to ripen and mature. The vaginal mucous prepares for the sperm to enter the body. The sex drive increases, the body needs less sleep, and the night vision becomes sharper. These changes are linked to the instinctual nocturnal mating urge. A woman's receptivity and openness also peak at this time, as her body and emotions are prepared for conception and fertilization. A woman can utilize the energy that comes with the moon's maximum illumination to fulfill her wishes and to accomplish what she initiated at the new moon. At the full moon, ovulation occurs and the egg is released.

Several days after the full moon the estrogen level rapidly drops; but another hormone, progesterone, is then manufactured in the ovaries and begins to predominate. The combined effects of these two hormones produce an even greater growth of deep, spongy, blood-rich lining in the uterus that can nourish a fertile egg. Emotionally a woman's energy moves into a holding pattern when she wants to settle in and feel more stable.

With the waning phase of the cycle, if conception has occurred, the egg will implant itself into the uteral lining, and pregnancy begins. Otherwise the progesterone and estrogen levels abruptly decrease, causing the uteral lining to shrink and decompose. A woman may likewise feel an emotional letdown, as if she was all prepared for an event that didn't happen. Depression, sadness, anxiety, and irritability, all classic premenstrual symptoms, often occur at this time.

With the dark phase of the moon, progesterone and estrogen reach their lowest levels. Menstruation occurs as the body sheds the sloughed-off excess uteral lining. The blood's flow is a sign of dynamic transformation; what was built up is now being broken down and released. At the dark of the moon a woman turns inward emotionally and physically. She craves sleep, has less interest in outer matters, and feels the urge to pull into the still and quiet renewal of her bleeding time. With the waning moon, a woman's psychic abilities are heightened. This is a prime time for her to engage in all kinds of inner work, as well as a time for her to complete, release, and let go of the old cycle.

A woman's flow begins at the dark phase of the moon and continues through the initial days of the new moon before the first glimmer of the crescent appears. About two days after the onset of menstruation, the body begins to respond to the absence of estrogen in the bloodstream. It signals the pituitary gland to start producing FSH and to begin a new cycle.

The twin poles of ovulation and menstruation in a woman's sexual cycle correspond to the peaks of maximum light and maximum darkness depicted by the full and dark phases of the moon's cycle. A woman's emotions and the kind of sexuality that she desires also fluctuate according to this rhythmic pattern.

The full moon is most receptive to receiving the maximum amount of the sun's light, and during a woman's corresponding full moon ovulatory time she feels most open, magnetic, and nurturing to others. Her sexuality expresses itself as a desire to surrender to the overtures of the partner and to enjoy vaginal penetration. These feelings, which are influenced by hormonal activity, are conducive to sexual union. This is the most fertile period of the month, when sexuality can result in conception and thereby facilitate the continuation of the species. In the Goddess lore these qualities of the feminine nature were personified as the White Goddess.

By contrast, at the dark moon menstrual time, a woman's energetic flow is no longer turned outward toward union with the other, but rather it is turned inward. She feels more of a need to nurture herself, and wants to pull away from the demands and expectations of other people in her life. Her sexual desire peaks just before menstruation. She can be multiorgasmic and is more likely to masturbate at this time. Her sexuality is initiating, fiery, assertive, whether by herself or with a partner. Clitoral stimulation, rather than vaginal penetration, is a more intense, enjoyable, and satisfying sensation, and this kind of sexuality does not lead to procreation. All of these qualities of the menstrual pole of a woman's cycle became embodied into the concepts of the Dark Goddess.

The patriarchal mentality that equates light and increase with good and black and decrease with bad created a schism in our perception of the dual aspect of a woman's emotional-sexual cycle. The receptive, surrendering, ovulatory feminine became a symbol of the desirable qualities of an ideal femininity. The fiery, assertive, menstruating feminine, who was self-oriented and nongestative, encompassed all that was objectionable and threatening to men. In *The Wise Wound* Shuttle and Redgrove tell that ancient sources spoke of the two flows that come from a woman's vagina. The clear flow of ovulation was called the River of Life because its procreative nature supported the patriarchal system. The forbidden red flow of menstruation was called the River of Death because a woman's powerful sexuality that arose at this time did not have the end purpose of pregnancy.[4]

The archetypes of the feminine as the White Goddess and the Dark Goddess cluster around these two poles of a woman's cycle, the

Rites of Rebirth:
The Dark
Goddess as the
Muse of
Menstruation
and
Menopause

white ovulatory pole and the red menstrual pole. At the white pole we find love goddesses such as Aphrodite and Ishtar, who stimulate sexual desires; and mother goddesses such as Demeter and Isis, the fecund wombs of the race, who hold and suckle the child. These goddesses represent one aspect of a woman's femininity that is open, willing, and values relatedness. She seeks to please her partner, nurture her children, create a nest of comfort and pleasure for her family, and foster the growth of all living things in her environment. The white ovulatory goddess in women who use her sexuality for attraction, impregnation, birth, and nurturance is most acceptable in Western culture.

Images of the menstruating Dark Goddess constellate around the red pole of a woman's sexual cycle. Dark goddesses such as Kali are depicted as wrathful, fanged, with protruding tongues, brandishing a sword, and surrounded with fiery sparks; or as Lilith, the flame of the revolving sword. To the patriarchal mind these goddesses are not even seen as feminine, their flow of blood marking their failure to conceive. The patriarchy perceived the White Goddess as the goddess of life; but the menstruating Dark Goddess was the goddess of death, now severed from her powers of renewal that follow destruction.

The Dark Goddess at the red pole of a woman's nature speaks to an aspect of a woman's femininity that is self-directed, uncompromising, powerful, and impersonal. She has the audacity to focus inward rather than to relate to others. At the menstrual time the power of a woman's erotic sexuality can be used for transformation, renewal, divination, healing, and magic rather than procreation. As the patriarchy grew to fear the erotic sexuality of the dark moon time, they sought to separate women from this source of their power. Menstrual woman were maligned as bitchy, hysterical, angry, furious, and irrational while they had the disgusting, impure "curse." Let us now look more deeply into the menstruating mysteries of the Dark Goddess and attempt to reclaim the magical powers of our dark moon times.

According to Shuttle and Redgrove, "It is received opinion in zoological science that the development of the menstrual cycle was responsible for the evolution of the primate and eventually human societies."[5] The sexuality of most animals functions around an estrus cycle where the sexual urge is directly linked to procreation. The female comes "in heat"—she is sexually interested and active only at specific times. She has a short breeding period, for several days just around ovulation, when a little blood is discharged from her vagina to act as a mating signal.

By contrast female humans and apes have developed a menstrual cycle when bleeding does not occur at ovulation but at the other pole of the cycle. Female primates may be sexually responsive throughout the entire cycle, and a major peak of sexual desire occurs just before menstruation, when it is highly unlikely for impregnation to occur. Shuttle and Redgrove propose that the meaning of this evolutionary step implies that sex was now to be used for something other than reproduction, and that this kind of sexual experience in primates must have become of benefit and importance to the individual (and thence to the species).[6] The question remains, What is the value for the species to have developed a nonprocreative sexuality whose intensity is focused around the menstrual period?

Barbara Walker points out that the majority of words used by the ancients for menstruation honor it, and it meant such things as sacred, supernatural, and deity. The earliest peoples thought that the mystery of creation resided in the blood that flowed from women in harmony with the moon. Many cultures believed that when a woman retained this primal material of creation, it congealed to form a baby.[7]

There was something awe-provoking and miraculous in the idea that a woman could bleed regularly without having been wounded and without dying. The dead were often anointed with red ocher, symbolic of the life-giving menstrual blood of Mother Earth, that would guarantee a bodily rebirth. This sacred red elixir was valued for its power and was also considered to be the source of inspiration and divinity.

In connection with longevity and immortality, the menstrual blood was called the "supernatural red wine" given by Hera to the gods. And in Egypt the pharaohs became divine by ingesting "the blood of Isis." In India Kali invited the gods "to bathe in the bloody flow of her womb and to drink of it; and the gods, in holy communion, drank of the fountain of life and bathed in it and rose blessed to the heavens."[8]

The first calendars, which kept track of women's menstrual cycles, were based on the moon's phases. In preclassical Greece the moon-colleges of Hera, whose name means womb, were institutions for studying the moon's phases and relating them to the changes in one's own body. These early Goddess-worshiping peoples understood that the dark of the moon was the Goddess's menstrual peak, and that women, at this time, were the most magical, mysterious, and powerful.

*Rites of Rebirth:
The Dark
Goddess as the
Muse of
Menstruation
and
Menopause*

During the menstrual time a woman is turned inward, and she can most easily access the workings of her inner life and the powers of the psyche. There is evidence that the priestesses in Hera's colleges could control conception and birth through deep introspection and dream control.[9] Sensitive to their time of greatest psychic openness, they could enter into trancelike states, looking deep within for movements in their bodies. This practice led to the development of skills in hypnosis, autohypnosis, and yogic control of bodily functions. The heavy, sleeplike qualities of the menstrual time help a woman to reach deep meditative states. Through her dreams she can gain information about the workings of her body and mind.

A woman's capacity for prophecy and vision is most enhanced when she is menstruating. Robert Briffault states that all shamans who guided early societies were women. Shamanism was linked to the moon and therefore to menstrual cults.[10] The Oracle of Delphi was one of the greatest centers of prophecy in the ancient world, and *delphus* is one of the Greek words meaning "womb." The oracular priestesses of the Sibylline colleges would prophesy once a month, at the time of their most intense menstrual sensitivity. No political action in classical Greece would ever been taken without consulting them. The Sibyl's tripod may have originally been a speculum for watching the cervix for the first seep of blood.[11]

Hysteria is now thought of as an out-of-control state of irrationality and madness that is attributed to menstruating women. This is another Greek word related to the term womb—*hustera*, womb consciousness. In earlier times hysteria was the condition of shamanic possession and ecstatic trance that women cultivated during their menstrual time in order to receive the vision or prophecy.

In ancient cultures a woman's menstrual blood was considered sacred and it was venerated for its powers of healing and fertility. The blood at the earliest altars was menstrual blood, not the sacrificial blood of an animal or human. The blood from a girl's first menstruation was considered a potent healing elixir, and was claimed to be able to heal incurable diseases such as leprosy. Clothes stained with the Goddess's menstrual blood were highly valued as healing charms. In the Thesmophoria, women's agricultural mysteries, the seed corn was mixed with menstrual blood to fertilize it before planting. It was thought that a menstruating woman could protect a crop by walking around the field.[12]

The sexuality that takes place during the menstrual time was ritually used for ecstasy, healing, regeneration, and spiritual illumination.

It was said that Hera enjoyed "secret lovemaking" during the dark of the moon. This can be read as a veiled reference to the kinds of lovemaking that are not geared toward procreative purposes. When a woman is menstruating she is, for the most part, freed from the anxiety of an unwanted pregnancy. Therefore she can allow herself to experience the full range of her emotions and bodily responses without clenching with fear at the consequences. This multiorgasmic sexuality is experienced for its own sake. It can be used to fuse the love and bonding between adults, or to magically fashion the released energy in the creation of mental children.

The secret lovemaking can also refer to fostering a deeper relationship with one's own self. This love affair with oneself can occur on the physical level of masturbation, whereby a woman can take the personal initiative to discover the ways to pleasure her body. It can also take place on the psychological level, in terms of union with one's inner masculine. At menstruation there exists the possibility for the alchemical marriage where a woman meets her "red king," her monthly blood, who psychologically is her inner husband or animus rising at her period. She may often dream of a dark male stranger who offers her the creative gift of the animus. If a woman is able to use the energy of her period creatively, tapping into its propensity for healing and vision, then the animus is honored, and marriage occurs with her womanly anima nature (outer Queen).[13]

Some traditions tell of the secret lovemaking between two women that takes place during the menstrual withdrawal. Here a woman can honor the Goddess by deepening the bonds of intimacy and sensitivity with members of her own sisterhood.

Ancient tantric yogic practices include techniques of sacred sexual intercourse whose purpose is that of spiritual illumination. The optimal time to engage in such practices is when the female "power holder" is menstruating, and her red sexual energy is at its peak. The deity invoked is the red aspect of the Goddess, and she functions as a muse who awakens the dormant energies. These traditions continue to remember and honor the potent rejuvenation qualities of the menstrual blood that flows at the dark moon. Some magical traditions maintain that blood is necessary for a ritual to be effective, and menstrual blood is the only blood that is obtained in an ethical way.[14] A woman's menstrual blood, when her psychic power is the greatest, was the sacrificial blood used on the earliest altar for rituals of healing, magic, and prophecy.

In some occult traditions a woman's menstrual blood and a man's semen are the alchemical substances that promote regeneration. Sacred lovemaking during the menstrual time, when these red and white elixirs could be intermingled and ingested, were thought to lead to enlightenment through ecstatic illumination. In tantric traditions the drop from the mixture of the red and white bodily substances is called *bodhicitta*, the union of wisdom and compassion.

Menstrual sexuality, whether it was used for personal enjoyment, the deepening of a relationship, or ritually for regeneration, magic, healing, or spiritual growth, was held as sacred. The taboos surrounding intercourse during a woman's dark moon time were originally a protective device to ensure that this most potent red energy would not be debased and wasted through a profane sexual expression of simple biological release.

When the moon disappeared each month, she was rumored to be having her period. The word *sabbat* originally meant a day of rest, when the Goddess was menstruating. The Moon Goddess Hera went away into seclusion during her secret dark time. In the same way a woman feels the need to withdraw and be alone when she is menstruating. In the early Goddess cultures there existed menstrual huts woven from the boughs of the lygus plant, sacred to Hera, whose flower distillation brought on the monthlies.

Women retired to these menstrual huts to guarantee their solitude as they went into trance, fasted, and communicated with their instinctual body wisdom. One can imagine the atmosphere of awe and mystery that was created when an entire community of women all went into retreat at the same time, practicing their magical rites during the dark of the moon. The celebration of the Sabbats was the beginning of ritual and religion.[15] A menstruating woman continues to feel an instinctual pull inward toward a deeper communion with her own self and the inner world. This withdrawal from the outer world is conducive to creating the sacred space whereby a woman can receive the gifts of menstruation: meditation, dreams, prophecy, body wisdom, healing, regeneration, and sacred sexuality.

How did the blessing of menstruation come to be the curse, dreaded, despised, and tabooed, a source of shame and embarrassment to women? The menstrual mysteries lay at the core of the Goddess religion, and they were protected and concealed from the prying eyes of men. Women did not use the upsurge of their powerful sexual energy that resulted from menstruation in the service of men nor for

Rites of Rebirth: The Dark Goddess as the Muse of Menstruation and Menopause

procreation. As the social system of patriarchy solidified its power, men displayed an almost hysterical fear of menstrual and childbirth blood, menstruating women, and of course their patron, the Dark Goddess. Menstrual women were defined as unclean, dangerous, and a threat to society. A host of taboos were instituted to protect men from the fiery, assertive, autoerotic nature of the dark feminine, and to deprive women of the sexual, psychic, and magical power of their dark moon times.

> The Lord said to Moses and Aaron . . . When a woman has
> a discharge of blood which is regular discharge from her body,
> she shall be in her impurity for seven days, and whoever
> touches her shall be unclean until the evening. And every-
> thing upon which she lies during her impurity shall be un-
> clean; everything also upon which she sits shall be unclean.
> And whoever touches her bed shall wash his clothes, and
> bathe himself in water, and be unclean until evening. And
> whoever touches anything upon which she sits shall wash his
> clothes, and bathe himself in water, and be unclean until eve-
> ning. And whoever touches anything upon which she sits
> shall wash his clothes, and bathe himself in water, and be
> unclean until evening; whether it is in bed or anything upon
> which she sits, when he touches it he shall be unclean until
> evening. And if any man lies with her, and her impurity is on
> him, he shall be unclean seven days; and every bed on which
> he lies shall be unclean. (Leviticus 15:1 19–24 RSV)

Judaism, Christianity, and Islam linked the evil of woman to menstruation. Menstruation was said to be the visible bloody sign of the serpent, the Devil, in the female body, and all evil flowed from this original evil: moon blood.[16] The Laws of Manu, Vedic scriptures rewritten by patriarchal Brahman and Buddhist philosophers, said that if a man even approached a menstruating woman he would lose his wisdom, energy, strength, and vitality. The Talmud said that if a menstruating woman walked between two men, one of them would die.[17] If a man had sex with a menstruating woman he would be-come ill, especially with venereal diseases; and a child conceived in this way would be born deformed or as a demon. All kinds of sickness and disaster were attributed to a chance encounter with a menstruat-ing woman. In the Middle Ages many church laws forbid a menstru-ating woman to enter a church lest she defile it with her filth.

Shuttle and Redgrove propose that the murder of 9 million women as witches during the Middle Ages was one enormous menstrual persecution. Witchcraft was at this time the natural craft of women. It was the subjective experience of the menstrual cycle that yielded the witchy powers, the wise blood knowledge of midwifery, hypnosis, healing, dowsing, dream study, and sexual fulfillment.[18]

Because a woman's greatest sexual desire occurs around her period, men became terrified of what they perceived to be her assertive, voracious sexuality that would devour them. It brought up their fears of their own sexual inadequacies, and the sight of blood on the penis triggered castration complexes. On the other hand, Esther Harding proposes that men could not resist the sexual attraction of a menstruating woman; they would become bewitched and unable to attend to any other duties. For this reason men would segregate the allegedly dangerous female to protect themselves from this devastating effect of their own untamed sexual desires.[19]

As a result a woman during her dangerous times was forced into seclusion, ostracized from society, and limited in her contact with the outside world. She was forbidden to touch any food lest she contaminate it. She was not allowed to wash or comb her hair, as the power of her magic was thought to reside in her hair. Menstruating women were banished to the menstrual huts, cast out of the villages into the brush, where they had to fend for themselves. Called impure, unclean, and an abomination, they were a threat to man, his laws, and his gods.

According to *The Wise Wound* the human female's menstrual cycle was the critical evolutionary step that initiated human society and culture. Because it represented the creative powers of the evolutionary female, women's menstrual power was seen as a threat to male domination. Patriarchal culture has succeeded in obliterating women's memories of the magic of their moon times. Women now feel ashamed, resentful, and disgusted with the pain and humiliation of their menstrual blood, originally known as the source of all life.

Now when a woman menstruates, she is pressured by society to hide and deny this central aspect of her nature. Magazine advertisements for "sanitary pads" and tampons often show the desirable appearance of a menstruating woman is to be clothed all in white, totally denying her red energy and instead evoking the safe, pure, and submissive ideal of the White Goddess. Tampons were further designed to assist a woman in not having to look at or touch her menstrual blood. Protected from the embarrassment of a bulging, telltale pad announcing her "time of month," the liberated woman could now wear short clothing, swim, and participate in sports. Female deodorant sprays are urged upon women to cover up the smell of their flow. Above all, a woman is not supposed to allow her sensitive biological and emotional responses to interfere with her worldly duties, in school, on the job, or in the home caring for her family. No one else should be told what is happening except in hushed whispers to only one's intimate friends.

All of these messages encourage a woman's and society's denial of the natural and periodic body functions. And this leads a woman to believe that menstruation is something bad, negative, dirty, and undesirable. She is rejected sexually at this time of month and told she is disgusting. Her self-confidence and self-acceptance are undermined, and she associates her period with restriction, a lack of freedom and fun. Society has transformed women's natural power at menstruation into a self-destructive psychology.

This very denial and rejection of menstruation is central to the excruciating pain and discomfort that many women experience prior to and during their period. The suppressed rage over the rejection and debasement of an intrinsic aspect of a woman's nature, in fact the seat of her personal power, becomes directed inward. This violence is then inflicted upon oneself, and it hurts. Women experience this unconscious self-directed anger as physical pain, cramps, bloating, lethargy, emotional irritability, depression, bad temper, and hypersensitivity.

The Wise Wound discusses the menstrual epidemic, where up to 90 percent of modern women suffer from some sort of distress. They outline their observation of a "howlback circuit" whereby a woman feels horrible because she is incapacitated by physical discomfort. She is then treated as taboo by others, which makes her behave unpleasantly, and finally she is ostracized by society and spurned as if she had the plague.[20]

The stereotyped image of the menstruating woman is that she is a walking time bomb who might, at any moment, explode with rage, hysteria, or an uncontrollable emotional outburst. Therefore it behooves a man or child to steer clear of her. Many women do in fact play out this role, screaming at their children or husband, bursting into heaving tears, seething with barely contained resentment and irritation, and immobilized with pain. While a woman may feel physically debilitated, her emotional power is overwhelming. To the extent that a woman does not know how to honor and creatively channel her menstrual energy, the rejected shadow side of her nature takes over, protesting as the raging bitch.

Rites of Rebirth:
The Dark
Goddess as the
Muse of
Menstruation
and
Menopause

Esther Harding suggests that one of the reasons for women's menstrual disabilities and PMS today is that modern culture does not provide any kind of menstrual rituals. Menstruation is just each woman's private affliction, where she suffers alone; it has no positive value or meaning.[21] Women have been deprived of retreating to the ancient menstrual huts, where they could commune with their inner beings, attune themselves to cosmic cycles, and share in the secret knowledge passed on in the community of other bleeding women.

In order to reclaim their menstrual power and liberate their bodies from menstrual pain, women must follow the cycle of the disappearing dark moon and enter into a voluntary retreat during their sacred time of month. Irritability, discomfort, and pain are the ways in which women's bodies continues to protest the menstrual injustices inflicted by society. Women's instinctual bodies demand that they pay attention to honoring the menstrual mysteries. The instinctual pull of the dark moon phase is to deliberately withdraw from the demands of others and worldly expectations. This step takes awareness and effort in a society that is constructed in such a way to deny and invalidate women's special needs during their moon times.

However, if a woman can find a way to take some time to be alone, in the bathtub, in bed drifting or reading, taking a walk in nature, praying or mediating in a sanctuary, she can reconnect to the deepest source of her feminine nature and psychic life. The body's craving to draw inward into quiet and stillness is a movement toward accessing the wealth of inner creative energy that peaks at this time. Women have the opportunity to transform this psychic energy into a flow of creative inspiration. A woman's moon time does not have to be an experience of depletion. It is when a woman stifles and blocks her pulsing, fiery red currents that the would-be creative energy turns to pain and depression. In a space of voluntary withdrawal, a woman can naturally remember or discover the ways to channel her red menstrual energy for a more fulfilling and richer life.

In order to redeem the dark moon menstruation gift of the Dark Goddess, we need to change our attitudes. Educating ourselves about the true nature of menstruation and the subsequent historical layers of distortion and suppression concerning women's blood mysteries is a starting point. We can continue the process by gaining new information about the body's physiological processes. This can help us to resensitize our awareness of our cyclical fluctuations. This knowledge can also enable us to evaluate the advice of the medical profession concerning our discomfort. We can experiment with herbs, nutritional supplements, acupuncture, massage, and other alternative healing therapies to alleviate the stressful symptoms of our bleeding time.

We can pay attention to identifying our habitual negative attitudes toward menstruation, and this awareness can liberate us from perpetuating society's falsehoods. We can cut through our concepts of menstruation as something dirty and undesirable by touching, smelling, and tasting our menstrual blood. In these ways we can reestablish our connection to the healing and rejuvenative powers of a woman's red elixir.

In *Dragontime* Luisa Francia suggests a wide spectrum of rituals, ceremonies, and allies to help women reclaim the power and magic of their menstrual blood and to better use their menstrual abilities.[22] Keeping track of our menstrual cycles and the phases of the moon can tune us into the monthly rhythm of our physical and emotional energies as they are regulated by the lunar cycle. By learning techniques of relaxation and meditation, we can induce states of trance, prophecy, inspiration, creativity, dream recall, hypnotism, and visualization. These capabilities are the birthright of the subjective feminine nature that are realized in menstruation. Finally we can take the risk of breaking the sexual taboo around menstruation by educating our partners, and thereby open our relationships to the ecstatic and transformative sacred dimension of lovemaking.

A Woman's Lifelong Cycle of Blood Mysteries

The female cycle of ovulation and menstruation occurs on a monthly basis in a woman's body, and it mirrors the twofold alternation of the light and dark phases of the moon. The symbolism of the Dark Goddess is found in menstruation, which corresponds to the dark moon. In addition a woman has another major sexual cycle, one which operates over the course of her lifetime.

This second cycle is a reflection of the triple nature of the moon's phases as new, full, and dark, and it corresponds to the three stages of a woman's life that are marked by menarche, the triad of pregnancy, birth, and nursing, and menopause. These are the three great blood mysteries of a woman's life (see figure 7.2).

The waxing new moon, personified by the ancients as the Virgin Goddess, reflected the life of a maiden up to menarche, the onset of a young girl's first menstruation.

The full moon, as the Mother Goddess, was most influential during the middle years of a woman's life when her body is geared toward giving birth and feeding her children.

And the waning dark moon, in this context envisioned as the Crone Goddess, was seen to be the predominant force during the final years after menstruation ceases and a woman enters into menopause. The ancients believed that after menopause a woman retained her wise blood and reached her pinnacle as power holder of wisdom. Today our information concerning menopause is even more limited, inaccessible, and tabooed than that of menstruation.

Before we proceed with our discussion it is important to make a distinction between the Dark Goddess as the dark or final transition phase of the moon's cycle, and the Dark Goddess as the shadow, the feared and rejected part of the feminine nature. The Dark Goddess as crone is the ruler of menopause; but as the shadow the Dark Goddess also appears in the new and full phases of a woman's cyclical nature. Let us briefly digress to look at the symbolism of the first two lunar phases of a woman's life in this context. We will take note of the patriarchal shadow projections of the dark aspect of the maiden and mother, before we begin to more fully explore the menopausal crone.

The New Moon and Menarche

The nature of a maiden was akin to that of the slim new crescent. This new moon phase, as it mirrored the growth of a young girl, culminated in the first of a woman's blood mysteries, that of menarche. Menarche symbolizes the innocence, hope, and optimism of a young girl who is now beginning to come into her menstrual power. In ancient cultures and those today which remember fragments of the old ways, the occasion of a girl's first blood was celebrated by a ceremonial ritual and she was then feted and gifted by the community. As an initiation ritual, the young girl often retreated into voluntary seclusion, where she awaited a vision. Menarche, as a rite of passage, marked her transition from childhood and her initiation into the secrets of womanhood.

Menarche indicates that the cycle of ovulation and menstruation has begun to operate in a young woman's body, which now has the capacity to conceive a child. It also signals that she has "come of age" to be sexually active. The flow of her blood also signifies that the currents of her psychic energy are now activated and can be developed.

Today this great event in a woman's life is generally ignored. It may be whispered about in the bathroom as an embarrassed mother tells her bewildered and often frightened daughter the hidden location of the menstrual pads.

Menarche is the gateway into a woman's readiness for sexual activity. In the masculine collective unconsciousness there exists an obsession to deflower the virgin, to be the one to initiate young girls into their first sexual experience. The dark shadow aspect of the New Moon Virgin Goddess arises from the psychodynamics of the maiden's budding sexuality and the male fantasy of violating her innocence.

To the extent that men fear the power and desire of the sexually mature woman, they will gravitate toward the innocence and malleability of the young girl who will totally accept whatever they do. This is evidenced in the men's magazines that idealize women from mid-teens to early twenties in their centerfold spreads. The new moon maiden embodies many of men's sexual fantasies in which they envision themselves as being the first to enjoy the pleasures of the young, nubile, sensuous nymphet who has no prior experience by which to judge their performance.

However, when confronted with the reality of their fantasies, some men cannot rise to the occasion, and others become terrified as to what they perceive to be the loss of their control. The ensuing rage toward the feminine, perceived as enticing only to later confront a man with his inadequacies, has led to men's assault upon progressively younger and younger women who are totally powerless. The ancients, in order to protect the young maiden from this kind of violation, would call upon the Virgin Goddess Artemis/Diana, who was the protectress of prepubescent girls. She was said to roam the forests with her band of chaste nymphs, killing with her bow and arrow any man caught gazing upon them.

The increase in demand for child pornography and the alarming statistics concerning the sexual abuse of young girls indicate the depth of male insecurity around their sexuality. A common male defense for rape is that "she was asking for it" or "leading me on," thus absolving themselves of any blame. As a result the dark shadow side of the New Moon Goddess, as projected by the patriarchal mentality, became that of the enchantress who bewitched and seduced a man against his will. Goddesses such as Lilith, Medusa, Circe, and the mermaids carry this archetypal dimension of the feminine.

The Full Moon and Pregnancy, Birth, and Nursing

With the growing of the moon toward fullness, the slim young maiden likewise matures into the full-breasted, full-bodied, sexually mature woman. She is now ripe for her role as mother. The full moon corresponds to the next developmental phase of a woman's life, in which the functions of her body and emotions are geared toward the second of the female blood mysteries, the cycle of pregnancy, birth, and nursing. In this mystery woman was perceived as nothing less than miraculous as she chose to create new life, transforming her life blood into a child and then into the milk to nourish it.

A woman may enter into the full moon mother phase of her life cycle without having to give birth to a physical child. She may instead leave behind the carefree, self-determined innocence of the maiden as she assumes the responsibility for a career, committed relationship, co-parenting her partner's child, or purchasing a home. She dedicates the next phase of her life to nourishing and sustaining the mental and creative children that she brings forth.

As we discussed earlier, the pregnant and nursing woman, continuing the generations of the species, was envisioned by men as the ideal femininity of the White Goddess. Her bright side was that of the compassionate, nurturing, embracing, accepting, bountiful, generous, all-giving mother. Initially a man may be drawn to such a woman, seeking total understanding, care, and support from her. However, at some point he becomes panicked as he realizes his growing dependency upon her. As he regresses into a state of childlike helplessness, he may become impotent in both his sexual and worldly life. Again, at this point, patriarchy has projected their fear of the shadow side of the Full Moon Mother Goddess as the Terrible Mother.

The Terrible Mother archetype controls, demands, dominates, overpowers, criticizes, beats, abuses, neglects, and ignores her children and husband. Her power is boundless and awesome. As Demeter she halted all food production on earth until the return of her daughter. As Kali she was portrayed as devouring her children and squatting triumphantly over the corpse of her husband, Shiva. And as Medea of classical Greece she murdered her children as vengeance against betrayal by her husband, Jason. Our images of the Dark Goddess as the rejected and raging shadow in the full moon mother archetype give rise to our negative attitudes concerning the ways in which we hate our mothers. And when this anger is repressed and directed inward, it contributes to much of the discomfort of pregnancy and the pain of childbirth.

While the patriarchy idealized the image of the pregnant mother, the reality of her bodily functions brought up their irrational terror. In modern times the entire spectrum of pregnancy, birthing, and nursing has been maligned, shamed, and hidden away. Women have been denied full access to information and even given harmful and erroneous advice concerning their reproductive organs. We also experience the shadow of the Mother Goddess in all the ways that the patriarchy has rejected a woman's process in giving birth.

Pregnant women are often made to feel embarrassed in public and social situations, and many people feel uncomfortable in the presence of a female body swelling with life. Our society disapproves of a mother nursing her child in public, finding the sight of her naked breasts indecent and offensive (as opposed to breasts in a centerfold spread being perceived as desirable). A nursing mother is pressured to hide herself away by retreating into the bedroom, or into a rest room at a restaurant. With the advent of modern medicine, women were told to not breastfeed their infants—synthetic pharmaceutical formulas were healthier for their children. We are now rediscovering that mother's milk is indeed the perfect food, and it contains many natural antibodies that prevent illnesses during the infant's first fragile year of life.

Midwives, laywomen tending other women with natural remedies during pregnancy and childbirth, have been outlawed in many states. With the control of childbirth in the hands of, for the most part, white male physicians, women have been denied conscious participation in their labor and delivery. They have been excluded from witnessing one of the most sacred mysteries of all, the birth of their own children. Instead they have been drugged into oblivion, tied up in stirrups, surgically cut open with episiotomies, and have had their babies taken away from them immediately after birth.

The high rates of cesarean sections, hysterectomies, and mastectomies, many of which are unnecessary, all point to patriarchy's fear and rejection of a woman's reproductive organs and processes. In these ways they have attempted to deprive women of their procreative power. The restriction of information concerning safe contraception and the difficulties women experience in obtaining safe, low-cost abortions also serve to restrict a woman's right of control over her reproductive functions.

In some areas we are now seeing a change. In the sphere of childbirth, the rebirth of the Goddess emerged in early organizations such as Lamaze childbirth training classes, which teach methods for a natural drug-free labor, and in La Leche League, which encourages and supports women in their breastfeeding endeavors. Having briefly discussed the shadow aspects of the new and full phases of a woman's lifelong blood cycle, we will now turn our attention to more fully exploring the culmination of the Dark Goddess's activities as the muse of menopausal crones.

The Dark Moon Goddess as the Muse of Menopause

As the moon begins to wane, a woman enters into the third great blood mystery of her life, menopause. Menopause marks the end of menstruation. For most women this "change of life" begins around the age of fifty, and due to increasing longevity, women can expect to live another twenty-five years—almost one-third of their lives. Just as menarche marks the transition from the new moon maiden into the full moon mother phase of a woman's life, menopause signals her movement out of motherhood and into the crone stage of the dark moon.

Biologically a woman enters into the crone phase of her life when she is past her childbearing years. For some women, however, the movement into cronehood is not necessarily determined by the onset of menopause. This stage can also occur as a psychological frame of mind, when a woman begins to reap the harvest of wisdom that arises from all of her varied life experiences. If a woman has chosen motherhood, her cronehood may be timed by her last child leaving home or when she becomes a grandmother. Cronehood can also be marked by retirement from a career or mainstream job, or by the death of her parents or spouse. Whenever a woman is finally able to think of her own needs after years of being primarily focused on those of her children, family, relationship, or career, she moves into the third great mystery of her life cycle.

In earlier cultures this rite of passage initiated women into their role as community elders, the keepers of knowledge, prophecy, and rituals. People believed that the retention of the powerful menstrual elixir was the source of the crone's wisdom. Having fulfilled her worldly responsibilities to her family, the dark moon crone could once again live for herself and pursue her spiritual path. A span of her life opened whereby she could now devote herself exclusively to fashioning her retained blood of life into mental and spiritual rather than physical children.

The ancient wisewoman crone was the Dark Goddess's earthly representative to society. She was venerated as elder sought out for advice, as seer called upon for prophecy, and as healer asked to tend the ill. The crone acted to bridge the transition from the dark to the new moon; she was the funerary priestess who helped the old to die and the midwife who assisted the new to be born.

The patriarchy feared the feminine in connection with her role in birthing and dying even more than in her association with sex. The wise crone became transformed into the ugly hag, the death-snatcher. It is this horrifying image that has conditioned our attitudes in patriarchal culture towars the older woman in her menopausal years as a repulsive and undesirable creature, something to be dismissed and hidden away. In this way humanity was deprived of the crone's natural wisdom, a belief system that constituted a threat to the new patriarchal religions. This negative self-image associated with menopause also served to cut off women themselves from a source of their creativity that was not geared toward mothering. One exception to the negation of the crone was if she still continued her nurturing activities as the grandmother caring for her grandchildren.

In a society that holds that the primary function of the feminine nature is that of giving birth and caretaking the family, when a woman reaches the stage of her life cycle where her reproductive processes are no longer operative, that society dismisses her as useless. Today menopausal women are not honored; instead they are ridiculed, rejected, and ignored.

Until recently, there has been little literature addressing the issues of menopause. Not only has there been a blackout describing the spiritual and psychological challenges and gifts of menopause, but also there is scant information concerning the physiological changes occurring in a woman's body. Most physicians view menopause as an illness or deficiency disease for which they prescribe dosages of estrogen to hold back the symptoms of "the Change."

While a woman is menstruating, estrogen continues to rise and fall in the bloodstream, peaking at ovulation and ebbing at menstruation. Around the age of forty the estrogen level begins to even out and stabilize at a decreased level. Ovulation becomes less frequent and periods tend to occur at irregular intervals. At about fifty years of age the ovaries halt almost all estrogen production, and ovulation and menstruation cease. A woman experiences many biological symptoms with the onset of menopause. Her body begins to adjust to the decreased estrogen level and other hormonal changes in her system as she enters the final third phase of her life.

*Rites of Rebirth:
The Dark
Goddess as the
Muse of
Menstruation
and
Menopause*

It is difficult to distinguish between signs of menopause and signs of aging; menopause itself is a sign of the aging of the female reproductive system.[23] One symptom that is clearly linked to this transition is the phenomenon of hot flashes. Hot flashes are felt as a sudden rise of heat spreading throughout the body, and they are often accompanied by a sweating and flushing of the skin. It is not unusual for a woman to wake up in the middle of the night feverish and drenched with sweat, necessitating a change of bedding and clothing. These sudden and unexpected flashes are a source of great anxiety, as a woman never knows when they may happen in public. This uncontrollable bodily reaction announces to the world, which will pity them, that they are now menopausal.

We are just beginning to reclaim the positive value of our bodies' natural wisdom. Recent scientific research shows that cancer responds therapeutically to a raised body temperature; hot flashes are a woman's built-in defense mechanism against degenerative illnesses, which are so prevalent after midlife.[24] From a mythical perspective the hot flash indicates the touch of the fiery Dark Goddess, whose heat signifies the glowing coals of her red energy as she moves a woman through her initiation into cronehood.

Another bodily change that occurs with menopause and decreased estrogen levels is a change in the vagina. Thinning of the vaginal walls, loss of elasticity, and less secretions can lead to a dryness and itching that contribute to pain and irritation with sexual intercourse. The use of lubricants such as saliva, commercial jellies, or vegetable oil can help to alleviate the discomfort, but evidence suggests that regular arousal through any kind of sexual activity is the best way to maintain the body's own continued production of vaginal lubricants. Many women in this stage find that they prefer clitoral stimulation to vaginal penetration.

Postmenopausal women develop other bodily characteristics of aging that modern society considers ugly: facial hairs, wrinkles, liver spots, moles, thinning and graying hair on the head and pubic area, deeper voice, loss of muscle tone, weight gain, and bone shrinkage (osteoporosis). As women confront these changes, which are not validated by society, it is important for them to remember that there is no growth without change. Menopause is a crucial stage in a woman's psychic maturation.

Our culture is generally ignorant of this fact. Our notion of ideal femininity is linked with sexual procreativity, and menopause is treated as the end of a woman's sexual identity. Viewed as sexually undesirable, she is often passed over by others for the younger woman. This rejection occurs at a time when her sex drive often increases. Her role as a mother and sexual mate having been fulfilled, society now discounts her as a burden. The menopausal woman, as crone, is mocked, cast off, ignored, shut away, fired, divorced, and abandoned.

It is no wonder that a woman confronts this stage of her life with trepidation and fear. She feels emotionally despairing, irritable, and depressed. She can be overcome with shame, anger, and disgust at herself as her body begins to show the changes that lead to her ostracism by society. Some studies indicate that women who have primarily identified themselves with mothering their children or partners experience the greatest difficulty in adjusting to the physiological and psychological demands that the rite of menopause brings into this third stage of a woman's life.

In our attempt to revision the dark, how can we reclaim the Dark Moon Crone Goddess's gifts of menopause? Anthropologist Margaret Mead is reported to have said that the greatest creative force in the world is a menopausal woman with zest.[25] The purpose of a woman's life does not end with her childbearing years. There is yet another one-third of the potentiality of the feminine nature that resides in the waning dark phase season of a woman's life cycle. If she is aware of the myriad of opportunities that lie waiting for her in the dark, she can "come into her own" during the postmenopausal years of her life. She can harvest and assimilate her crop of wisdom, symbolically found in her retained menstrual blood.

It is a time when a woman, freed from the responsibility of raising her family, can enjoy greater freedom, independence, and control of her life. The initiation of widowhood carries the promise of once again having one's life to oneself after passing through the grief of mourning. Travel, continuing education, community service, creative self-expression, occupation change, and spiritual development are some of the avenues that can open unencumbered to the crone.

All of a woman's vital force can now be channeled into giving life and form to her mental and spiritual children.

As the crone confronts the changes in her body and transformations in her lifestyle, she realizes that her old identity is indeed dying. She may be at a loss of what to do next and how to go about doing it. It may have been so long since she focused on her own needs and desires that she may have forgotten how to do so. Thus she may feel ill equipped to face the challenges of this next phase of her life. In order for crones to fully actualize the potentials available to them, we all must confront and dissolve the huge barriers that the patriarchy has constructed to keep older women poor, powerless, lonely, unemployable, unconfident, helpless, and ill.

On a physical level women must educate themselves about their biological changes and have the knowledge to evaluate the established medical model of treatment. In this process they are coming to understand that the estrogen replacement therapy and hysterectomies that physicians recommend as a "cure for their illness" are the very causes of increased risks of breast and uterine cancer that become most prevalent during the menopausal years. These artificial remedies interfere with the body's natural processes and prevent the biochemical maturation of the crone's psychic currents.

In order to deal with the uncomfortable symptoms, women must investigate nonmedical approaches, including exercise, diet, vitamin supplements, and herbal therapies. Massage, yoga, and sexual activity can all help to keep the body supple and fluid as it ages. Through learning relaxation techniques, the crone can more easily enter into meditative states where she can receive her prophetic visions, dreams, and other sources of inner wisdom.

Participation in women's support groups is an important source of strength for the midlife woman, a place to gain information and understanding. The support and friendship from such gatherings can help reduce a crone's sense of isolation and reconnect her with her power. We are now seeing the beginnings of social and educational programs for the "displaced homemaker" that give her skills to enter or reenter the economic work force. The growing number of circles in the Women's Spirituality movement are another source of affirmation to the crone, reminding and reinvesting older women with their wisdom and power.

However, the area that needs the most attention in the revisioning of the menopausal crone is the attitudes we hold in our minds.

We must decondition our perception of the natural occurrence of aging as something that looks ugly, and more ugly in women than in men. In our society's value system, as men enter into their fifties they are seen as coming into their power, and are accorded respect and authority. An aging man is not considered sexually undesirable; in fact his age and power are often seen to enhance his attractiveness. It is at this very same age, however, that the woman who comes into her menopausal power is spurned as unpleasing to look at or be around.

In today's culture the changes in a woman's aging body are viewed as unattractive. This rejection of a natural stage of the female body causes a woman to develop a self-hatred for her body, which is betraying her. Many women, in their desire for social acceptance, become frantic to conceal their signs of aging. Our cult of youthful glamour capitalizes on women's fears of aging in the mass marketing of hair coloring, anti-wrinkle creams, and cosmetic surgery.

It is important for women to learn how to move gracefully into the crone years of their lives, allowing their bodily changes to proceed naturally without trying to conceal and deny them. This is a courageous step to take in the midst of a patriarchal system that defines the face of the crone as ugly. As the co-creators of our reality, women can make the conscious choice to refuse to hold and perpetuate these negative thought forms. In a society where the patriarchy dominates, women cannot directly force a change in men's attitudes toward the appearance of the crone. But one way—and ultimately the most powerful way—that a woman can effect a societal change in the perception of the crone is to begin with her own attitudes.

By removing the layers of patriarchal distortion from a woman's own inner images of herself as crone, she can come to see the inherent beauty of the natural unfoldment of her aging body and of the power it continues to hold for her. Women can then let go of all the artificial cosmetics and operations whose purpose is to conceal rather than enhance the true face of the crone. In this way we all can reconnect with the magical, mystical, and mysterious third phase of a woman's life.

The menopausal crone carries us through the dark moon phase of the Goddess within us. In the realm of the Dark Goddess, the signs of aging are understood to be the approaching signals of death. The most important role of the ancient crone was to assist people through their death passage transition. "Menopause is a time for confronting death while there is still time to live. . . . Fear of natural menopause, fear of the Crone, translates into a dread of death."[26] And so society's blackout of menopause and its rejection of older women are directly related to our fear and denial of death. As we begin to rehonor the Dark Goddess of menopause, her teachings will help to liberate us from our fears of change and transition, aging and death.

The mythical literature repeatedly tells us that the lives of the virgin and crone are intertwined, and their roles are often confused, such as in the tales of Artemis and Hekate, cousins through their mothers. The crone, as funerary priestess, extinguishes the old cycle and, as midwife, she helps to birth the new. The crone and virgin stand back-to-back at the doorways of death and birth.

The Archetype of the Dark Goddess

What is the face of the Dark Goddess? How can we recognize her ancient presence as she continues to act out in us today? The Dark Goddess is associated with the dark phase of any cyclical process that operates in our lives. For this reason women can most easily see her face when they menstruate. She flows around and through women's lives with the flow of monthly blood. And she remains as women's primary companion in the final phase of life when, after menopause, as they retain their menstrual blood, she moves them through their psychic maturation as crones. And for women and men she appears whenever we experience major change, loss, and transformation. We know the Dark Goddess is touching us at those extreme moments when we are pulsing with our fiery power as well as those times of our deepest despair.

When we are able to contact the genuine nature of the Dark Goddess within us, we feel as if we are in our power. We are strong, assertive, psychic, prophetic, creative, sexual, unrestrained, and free. Her fiery darkness is the power of the womb, exertive, active, and transformative. Patriarchal culture rejects these aspects of a woman's nature that arise from her red energy of the dark moon, sensing them as dangerous to male domination, and thus labels them as unfeminine.

The Dark Goddess, in modern society, embodies all of the feminine qualities that have come to intimidate men in patriarchal culture. As such she represents those aspects of the wholeness of a woman's nature that we have been conditioned and pressured to renounce in ourselves in order to be accepted and validated by men. As the rejected feminine, the Dark Goddess bursts forth as the shadow, her now distorted face contorted with anger venting her rage at her suppression. And if we stand very still, centered in the eye of her storm, we can feel her sobbing. Her beauty, strength, and wisdom are imprisoned behind the wrathful mask through which she is now perceived by others.

At those times when the Dark Goddess comes to us—at menstruation, at menopause, during loss and transition—if we are not aware of her gifts of deepening and renewal that she offers, then we often experience her as a tempest. She wells up from deep inside of us in a frenzy of hysteria that in ancient times we would have honored as a shamanic visitation. But to the extent that we have forgotten her intrinsic nature, we see her as actively destroying all of our life structures and relationships that are based on our acceptance of the patriarchal "nice, submissive, and pleasing" feminine image. Or if we are successful in holding back and suppressing this monumental red energy peaking inside of us, we will experience the Dark Goddess as the depression, despair, and unbearable pain of the bleakness, subjugation, and meaninglessness of our lives.

Whether we see the Dark Goddess as dancing ecstatically in a swirl of red flames, or enveloped in mist gazing into the inner pools of her psychic awareness, or throbbing with her orgasmic magical-creative energy, or embracing us in our grief, or furiously raging, screaming, crying, or desperately withdrawing into a stupor of denial or numbness, her ultimate purpose in each one of these guises is the same. She destroys in order to renew. The Dark Goddess of the dark moon is the mistress of transformation, and she exists everywhere there is change.

She absorbs the outworn in order to reshape it for rebirth. The Dark Goddess within us demands that we discard all that is no longer necessary in our lives, our relationships, worldly possessions, and life structures that have fulfilled their purpose in our growth and development. If we do not heed her call, she will keep up her threat with increasing pressure, ruthlessly destroying anything in our lives that is holding back the changes that will move us through our patterns of cyclical renewal.

The Dark Goddess represents those terrible stirrings in our psyche that seem like death to our conscious ego. Suddenly she appears, in a wrathful stance, brandishing her sword, slicing our ego attachments into shreds. She threatens our integrity, our self-image, our values, our achievements, and our accumulations. And we are thrown into a crisis. Every crisis holds the possibility for us to make a change in our lives. Change is the process that allows us to continue living.

To not change is to stagnate and truly die. A crisis, however, is not a terrible calamity. It derives from the Greek word *krino*, to decide, and means simply a time for decision. Every time we are presented with the opportunity for a change in the guise of a crisis, and do not make a decision, our instinctive unconscious habitual patterns are deepened. "What starts out as a groove in childhood, later becomes a rut, and finally our grave."[27]

Rites of Rebirth:
The Dark
Goddess as the
Muse of
Menstruation
and
Menopause

Because we do not understand the dark, we see the destructive activity of the Dark Goddess as negative and evil. This is a fundamental mistake. Through the vehicle of crisis, the Dark Goddess does destroy the old. This forces us to change, and thus urges us forward to a new life. Without her there would be no motivation and challenge to the growth of awareness. In the end what we have dreaded as her malice turns out to be part of the vital process needed to transform our lives into something of greater value and meaning.

With all of her awesome power, she stands at the threshold of death, beckoning us toward our journey into the underworld of our unconscious. Here we may encounter the apparitions of all that we have denied in our conscious minds and lives. When the moon disappears from sight, the Dark Goddess calls us away from the external world, and she leads us to meet our essential self who resides at the core of our being.

Vicki Noble writes that

The Dark Goddess is no lightweight. She promises trouble, an end to form as we have known it, the death of the ego. . . . She is impersonal, yet she erupts from deep within the human psyche with unexpected passion and rage. She is transformation in the extreme, and her power is regenerative and healing. Like a trickster, she frees us from the trappings that bind us to our tiny personal worlds; like a knife she cuts away all that is unessential and not truthful. She shatters structures, disintegrates the personality, destroys form. She liberates and saves, heals and frees. Now is her time and women are her vessels.[28]

The Dark Goddess stirs our psyche to the deepest level of our being, and she catalyzes us into facing what lies hidden and forgotten in the dark crevices of our minds. We are often pushed into her realm through trauma, when violent upheavals in our lives such as rape, abandonment, violation, endings, or death upset our known and safe reality. As she plunges us into our interior darkness, our vision quest through her engages us in a dialogue about all those issues that we'd rather not confront and acknowledge. She brings up our pain over all the dark issues in our lives that we keep in denial, and she makes us face our fears and taboos locked into our unconscious. Hatred of our bodies, rage at our parents, debilitating dependencies on chemical substances or personal relationships, envy and jealousy toward our loved ones, sexual inadequacies and aberrations, our eventual death and nonexistence, and the overriding fear that we may end up alone, afraid, and unloved are all to be found in the underworld realm of the Dark Goddess.

The Dark Goddess leads us into the labyrinth of our unconscious. Here she gives us the strength and courage to face our personal demons who thrive on denial, fear, and rejection. Our demons, as our negative attitudes, subversively undermine the positivity of our outer world through our own unconscious self-destructive behaviors. In our attempt to heal these painful issues held in the darkness of our psyche, we must cleanse our minds of the misperceptions of the dark energies that society has taught us to believe as true.

In this process the Dark Goddess forces us to look at ourselves with utter, naked honesty. For many of us this is very frightening—to see ourselves stripped of our illusions and false pretensions. Like Innana, who had to discard an article of clothing or an ornament at each gate of the underworld, when we go down into the darkness we must cast away all that is not true about ourselves and our lives. The Dark Goddess makes us demand the truth of things—from our families, partners, groups, and government. She is ruthless in destroying any of our life structures or relationships that are built upon a foundation of deception. And the leaders of any society that thrives upon lies do not welcome the Dark Goddess into their midst.

As we descend into the dark depths of our hidden beings, we may discover our frustration, resentment, and anger that lie buried beneath the layers of our socially conditioned "nice and normal" persona. Encounters with the Dark Goddess make us dissatisfied with the part of our lives that forces us to deny our true feelings. She is a Warrior Goddess of revolution who creates troubling disruption as she moves us to protest against those who have a vested interest in keeping us submissive and subservient.

The Dark Goddess is a Goddess of the Self, not in the sense of selfishness or separateness, but from a stance of upholding individual integrity. She refuses to support us in any relationship that is unfair, demeaning, deceitful, or depleting; she cuts and eliminates all that is greedy, grasping, and clinging in our lives. She enables us to reclaim our power to say, "NO! This Is Enough. No More," when we are confronted with rape, abuse, falsity, domination, and suppression. It is the same force whether she is voiced by women to men, by people of color to their white oppressors, or by Third World nations to the Superpowers.

*Rites of Rebirth:
The Dark
Goddess as the
Muse of
Menstruation
and
Menopause*

The Dark Goddess is fierce, hot, and powerful in her sexuality. She lives in the wilderness of our psyche apart from civilization. She represents that aspect of us who would flee to hidden secret places in the forest where we could let down our hair and dance naked with wild abandon. Her unrestrained sexuality is free, belonging only to herself, and she strains against the knots of monogamous expectations and serving only to please her partner. Her sexuality is not submissive, passive, or procreative; and when she is active we instinctively resist and pull back from these kinds of intimate encounters. The Dark Goddess pushes us to reach our own peaks of erotic sensation, and in our ecstasy, our sexual energy can be utilized for healing ourselves and others. Contained in the sexual nature of the dark feminine is the power of regeneration, and regeneration is the domain of the Dark Goddess.

She pulses with an uninhibited, animating, throbbing sexual rhythm that arises from the core of our being. It then spreads outward, and through her orgasmic release we can resonate to the vibration of the universe. The great powerful serpent *kundalini*, the primary totem animal of the Dark Goddess, embodies her mysteries of sexual rejuvenation and cosmic illumination. This coiled snake lies dormant in the sexual *chakra* at the base of the spine in each person, and in the bowels of the earth. The serpent represents the sexual fires of transmutation and the sacred heat that heals. Once aroused, *kundalini* utilizes the fiery sexual energies to awaken the healing potential within each cell of our body. She ascends through the other *chakra* centers, emerging out of the top of the head as cosmic illumination. Images of the Dark Goddess with her head crowned with a wreath of snakes symbolize this rising of the serpent wisdom toward the goal of enlightenment. The sexuality of the Dark Goddess brings us to a unification with the cosmos through orgasmic ecstasy.

The Dark Goddess within us is the force that moves our lives from waning to waxing, from the old to the new, from destruction to creation, and from death to birth. In order to keep the cycle ever-turning, she severs all our attachments to the old, safe, secure, and known, because she is the very movement of change and transformation itself. She inspires us with a power that arises from deep within our womb, and calls upon us to speak the truth, uphold our integrity, protest injustice, and exalt in our ecstatic healing sexuality. She urges us to expose evil, shatter falsity, and demand the truth from others whenever we encounter domination and oppression.

The dark moon conceals the secret activity of the Dark Goddess, whose power lies in her wise blood. We can honor the Dark Goddess within us by learning how to skillfully fashion and channel our monthly red menstrual energy, which then remains with us continually after we pass through menopause. The blood of the Dark Goddess as it flows through our bodies carries her gifts of personal power, spiritual illumination, psychic sensitivity, sexual ecstasy, healing, regeneration, and above all, the promise of new life arising from the decaying compost of the old.

As we peel back the layers of misperception that have encrusted our view of the Dark Goddess, we will come to see that she poses no threat to our survival. She is the key to a greatly expanded awareness. The darkness of the moon's cycle veils her great mystery, that of renewal and rebirth.

Journal Questions

1. If I am a woman, do I think of my period as "the curse," and do I regard it as a source of shame or embarrassment? Do I experience PMS or other kinds of pain and discomfort around menstruation? When I bleed, do I allow myself a time of rest and withdrawal from the needs of others? Or do I ignore this special time, numb myself with medication, and continue the hectic pace of my life as if nothing is different? Do I find myself feeling irritable, depressed, hysterical, or rageful at this time?

2. How do I feel about menstrual blood? Do I look at it, smell it, touch it? Do I find it offensive? Am I able to perceive it as an elixir of life? If I am a woman, can I associate my period with times of heightened awareness, profound insights, or creative inspiration? If I am a man, can I willingly make love to a menstruating woman and find pleasure in it? Or do I prefer not to—finding it embarrassing or repulsive?

3. If I am a woman, am I afraid of menopause, associating it with becoming old and no longer desirable? Am I tempted to take estrogen therapy to hold back symptoms of "the change"? Can I consider that menopause brings a gift of wisdom and heralds the time when I can

have my life back to myself again? Can I envision myself in positive ways as a wise old crone?

4. To what extent am I aware of the workings of Dark Goddess in my midst? Can I see the value in having old parts of my life and identity destroyed so that the new can be born? Am I thankful for the activity of the Dark Goddess, which moves me to shatter falsehoods, speak my truth, and maintain my integrity? Can I recognize her in the moments of my fiery, assertive sexual ecstasy?

Notes

1. Jean Mountaingrove, "Menstruation: Our Link to Ancient Wisdom, A Meditation," *Woman of Power* 8 (Winter 1988).
2. Vicki Noble, *Shakti Woman* (San Francisco: HarperSanFrancisco, 1991), 11.
3. Penelope Shuttle and Peter Redgrove, *The Wise Wound: Myths, Realities, and Meanings of Menstruation* (New York: Bantam Books, 1990), 176–77. It was not until the publication of this book that society at large began to recognize the true implications of women's moon time. Another groundbreaking book that helped us to recover our knowledge of menstruation, and which paved the way for *Wise Blood*, was *Menstruation and Menopause* by Paula Weidiger (New York: Knopf, 1975).
4. Shuttle and Redgrove, *The Wise Wound*, 11.
5. Shuttle and Redgrove, *The Wise Wound*, 150.
6. Shuttle and Redgrove, *The Wise Wound*, 151.
7. Barbara G. Walker, *The Woman's Encyclopedia of Myths and Secrets* (San Francisco: Harper & Row, 1983), 635.
8. Walker, *The Woman's Encyclopedia*, 636.
9. Shuttle and Redgrove, *The Wise Wound*, 16.
10. Shuttle and Redgrove, *The Wise Wound*, 213.
11. Shuttle and Redgrove, *The Wise Wound*, 166.
12. Walker, *The Woman's Encyclopedia*, 636, 644.
13. Alan Bleakley, *Fruits of the Moon Tree* (Bath, England: Gateway Books, 1988), 246.
14. Lawrence Durdın-Robertson, *The Cult of the Goddess* (Enniscorthy, Eire: Cesara Publications, 1974).
15. Diane Stein, *Casting the Circle: A Woman's Book of Ritual* (Freedom, CA: The Crossing Press, 1990), 71.
16. Monica Sjöö and Barbara Mor, *The Great Cosmic Mother* (San Francisco: Harper & Row, 1987), 192.
17. Walker, *The Woman's Encyclopedia*, 641.
18. Shuttle and Redgrove, *The Wise Wound*, 229.
19. Esther Harding, *Woman's Mysteries* (New York: Harper & Row, Colophon, 1976), 60.
20. Shuttle and Redgrove, *The Wise Wound*, chapter 2.
21. Sjöö and Mor, *The Great Cosmic Mother*, 186.
22. Luisa Francia, *Dragontime*, translated by Sasha Daucus (Woodstock, NY: Ash Tree Publishers, 1991).
23. Boston Women's Health Collective, *The New Our Body Our Selves* (New York: Simon & Schuster, 1984), 446.
24. Noble, *Shakti Woman*, 36.
25. Genia Pauli Haddon, *Body Metaphors: Releasing God-Feminine in Us All* (New York: Crossroad, 1988), 157.
26. Haddon, *Body Metaphors*, 160
27. Alexander Ruperti, *Cycles of Becoming* (Sebastopol, CA: CRCS Publications, 1978), 8.
28. Vicki Noble, "The Dark Goddess: Remembering the Sacred," *Woman of Power* 12 (Winter 1989): 57.

8

The Initiation Mysteries of Demeter and Persephone

◆

Sink down, sink down, sink deeper and deep
Into eternal and primordial sleep.
Sink down, forget, be still and draw apart
Into the inner earth's most secret heart.
Drink of the waters of Persephone,
The secret well beside the sacred tree.

I am the secret Queen, Persephone.
All tides are mine, and answer unto me.
Tides of the airs, tides of the inner earth,
The silent secret tides of death and birth—
Tides of men's souls, and dreams, and destiny—
Isis veiled and Rhea, Binah, Ge.
—Dion Fortune[1]

*T*he moon, turning in her phases, gave early peoples an image of the cyclical birth, death, and renewal of all things. The ancients conceptualized their awareness of this great mystery into a body of mythological stories that symbolically conveyed their understanding of great truths. However, simply telling the tale went only so far in explaining the real meaning of the story. The way in which an individual could further absorb the essence of the myth was through ritual. Ritual is the enactment of the myth under a highly structured situation.[2] Various rituals were timed according to certain transitions in natural and seasonal cycles. Through ritual an individual could have a personal, direct experience of a spiritual truth, and this realization had the power to transform his or her life.

Demeter and Persephone, who reflect the light and dark phases of the moon, are the dual aspects of the Goddess of Life and Death. Their tale was one of the major myths of the ancient world that was ritualized and became part of a mystery religion known as the Eleusinian Mystery Rites.[3] These rites were celebrated for over two thousand years in the ancient Mediterranean world.

The story of Demeter and Persephone was one of loss and return, death and rebirth. The Mother Goddess Demeter lost her child to the realms of the underworld. Persephone was abducted and raped by Pluto, the Lord of Death. Demeter's inconsolable grief and suffering in her loss and the eventual joyous reunion of the mother and daughter lay at the heart of the Eleusinian Mysteries. These rites honored the Mother Goddess, who birthed and nourished new life, as well as the Daughter Goddess, who received the souls of the dead to prepare them for rebirth. The story of these two goddesses is also the archetypal drama that all human women continue to reenact in the sacred relationship of renewal that transpires between the mother and daughter.

The Eleusinian Mysteries

The Eleusinian Mysteries were a ritual enactment of the story of birth, death, and renewal. They were performed from the fourteenth century BCE until the fourth century CE, and were among the most famous of the ancient mystery religions. Based upon earlier agrarian

Fig. 8.1 Demeter and Persephone

rites held at the time of the autumn sowing (fall equinox), the Eleusinian Mysteries most probably came from the East and from Egypt (related to the cult of Isis) by the way of Phrygia, and first took root in Thrace. According to the Parian marble these rites were brought to Eleusis around the year 1350 BCE together with the worship of Demeter.

The Eleusinian Mysteries were open to all Greek-speaking men, women, children, and slaves who had not killed another person, or who had been ritually expiated of such a death. Ordinary people, queens, kings, and philosophers came from all over the world to be initiated into these rites. The rituals addressed humanity's fears and concerns about death, and offered the participants a "guarantee of life without the fear of death, of confidence in the face of death."[4]

The exact nature of the Mysteries was a closely guarded secret, and the participants took vows of silence not to reveal what had occurred. Because of the awe and fear felt by the participants during the twenty centuries of the rites, even to this day we do not know exactly what transpired. George Mylonas commented that the secret died with the last initiate. What modern scholars have been able to piece together from the fragments of surviving information left behind in sculptures, vase paintings, and references in classical writings is that the mysteries were essentially an emotional experience that gave people a hope for the future.

Sophocles said of these Mysteries: "Thrice blessed are those among men who, after beholding these rites, go down to Hades. Only for them is there life; all the rest will suffer an evil lot."[5] Embodying a lineage that long precursed the Resurrection Mysteries of Easter, they were the Hellenic form of enabling people to experience during their earthly life the mysteries of what they would encounter in the passage between death and rebirth. The initiates participated in a mystical rite where they became the one who died and was reborn. Through this experience they entered into a state of oneness with the divine.

Let us now look at the story of the two goddesses and see how their rites provided ancient peoples with a way to directly experience the great mystery of death and rebirth. In the modern world Persephone's descent into the underworld is a metaphor for our descent into the unconscious, whereby we can also participate in the great mystery of transformation and renewal. As we read their timeless story, let us remember that the ancient rites of passage have now turned inward where they can be lived as the stages of psychic transformation.[6]

The Story of Demeter and Persephone

Long ago, Demeter and her beloved daughter Persephone wandered the earth together. So happy were they in each other's presence that they blessed the earth with a perpetual season of harvest. In this Golden Age the world knew no deprivation, no winter.

The Abduction of Persephone   Persephone grew to be as beautiful as her mother and was greatly desired by men and gods alike. The love between mother and daughter was so strong, however, that they had no desire to be parted from one another. Thus all suitors were rebuffed and sent away.

One day, away from Demeter's ever-watchful gaze, Persephone wandered with her companions into the Nysian fields. There she was irresistibly drawn to the lovely, fragrant beauty of the hundred-bloomed narcissus. As Persephone plucked it and inhaled its intoxicating fragrance, the earth suddenly split open and formed a deep abyss from which emerged Pluto, God of the Underworld, who had long been covetous of the fair Persephone. Riding in his golden, fiery chariot drawn by four screeching black horses, Pluto seized the screaming maiden, ravished her, and carried her off to the realm of the dead to become his bride and queen. The torn earth then immediately healed itself, leaving behind no evidence of the incident.

When Demeter returned to the now peaceful meadow, she could find no trace of her daughter. As she raced over fields and hills, calling Persephone's name, Demeter's anxiety turned to desperation and panic when she realized that no one knew the whereabouts of her daughter. For nine days and nights the grief-stricken Demeter refused to eat or bathe. Instead she wandered the earth with blazing torches, searching everywhere for her daughter. On the tenth day Demeter encountered the Crone Goddess Hekate, who suggested that she consult the Sun God Helios, who sees everything.

From Helios Demeter learned of the abduction by Pluto, who had acted with the approval of their brother Zeus. It seemed that Zeus had considered Pluto a worthy husband for Persephone, whom he wished to see rule as Queen of the Underworld. Upon hearing the news, Demeter angrily tore the diadem from her head and wrapped herself in mourning clothes. Full of hatred toward Zeus for his betrayal, she withdrew from Mt. Olympus to avoid him and his compatriots. Disguising her true identity, she then wandered as a bereaved old woman, seeking refuge in the cities of humanity.

Demeter in Eleusis   After what must have seemed an eternity, Demeter, brokenhearted and weary, sought refuge in a town called Eleusis. She was met at the well by the four daughters of King Celeus, who invited her to return with them to the palace. There she met Queen Metaneria, who welcomed the stranger and gave her the care of the royal infant son, Demephoön.

Under Demeter's care the child grew as a god. In her desire to make the young prince immortal, like Persephone, Demeter fed him ambrosia by day and placed him in the fire's embers each night in order to burn off his mortality. One evening Queen Metaneria caught Demeter in the act of holding her child in the flames and screamed out in terror. Demeter, outraged at being thwarted in her attempt to give the child eternal youth, snatched the boy from the fire and threw him to the ground. She then revealed her true identity as a goddess, and ordered that a temple and altar be built for her where she could continue her mourning.

The Return of Persephone   Demeter now retired to her temple, where she continued to mourn the loss of her beloved daughter. In her rage she prepared for humankind a cruel and terrible year: The earth would refuse to give forth any crop, crops in the ground would be destroyed, and fruit would wither on the trees. If she, the Goddess of Fertility, must live without her daughter, then humanity would suffer famine and starvation.

In desperation the people of the earth prayed to Zeus to intervene. Zeus realized that if humanity were to die out, there would be no one left to worship the gods, and sent Iris to summon Demeter to Olympus. Demeter refused to go. Each of the gods offered Demeter a gift and implored her to show mercy, but she refused. Only if her daughter were freed would she relent.

Realizing his defeat, Zeus commanded Hermes to descend into the underworld and command Pluto to release Persephone. Persephone, in her frozen beauty, had been following her mother's mourning fast, refusing food or drink. Pluto, in sly kindness, agreed to let Persephone go, but first tempted her great thirst by offering her several pomegranate seeds. Since the pomegranate is the symbol of sexual consummation, Persephone's consent rendered her marriage union with him indissoluble.

Upon returning to the world of light, Persephone was joyfully reunited with her mother at Eleusis. Demeter immediately inquired whether her daughter had consumed any of the food of the dead

Rites of Rebirth:
The Initiation
Mysteries of
Demeter and
Persephone

while in the underworld. When Persephone revealed what had occurred, Demeter realized that she had been tricked; her daughter was
still Pluto's prisoner. Once more she refused to lift her curse from the
land.

To prevent Demeter and Pluto from destroying the world he had
created, Zeus, with the assistance of their mother, Rhea, demanded
that they compromise. His edict commanded that for each pomegranate seed ingested by Persephone, she would spend a portion of
each year as Pluto's bride in the underworld. The remaining months
could then be spent with her mother upon the earth.

And so it has come to pass that each spring Persephone emerges
above ground and rejoins Demeter, who allows the earth to become
fruitful. Seeds sprout, flowers bloom, plants grow, and crops fill the
fields. Summer follows, and the earth continues to flourish until the
arrival of autumn, when Persephone must return to Pluto's underworld.
After her daughter's departure Demeter lays her sorrowful hand upon
the earth and makes it barren. And desolate it will stay throughout
the winter until Persephone's arrival the following spring.

Before leaving Eleusis Demeter expressed her gratitude to the city
by giving Triptolemus, the oldest son of the king and queen, the first
grain of corn. She then instructed him to convey her sacred art of
agriculture to all humanity. Finally she taught the people of Eleusis
her sacred rites and initiated them into her divine worship:

> . . . which are impossible to transgress, or pry into, or to di-
> vulge: for so great is one's awe of the gods that it stops the
> tongue. Happy is that man, among the men on earth, who
> witnesses these things. And whoever is not initiated in the
> rites, whoever has no part in them, he does not share the
> same fate when he dies and is down in the squalid darkness.[7]

The preceding tale is derived from Homer's "Hymn to Demeter,"
written in the seventh century BCE, and it is the most complete version of Persephone's abduction into the underworld. However, this
myth has a much older derivation going back into Mycenaean, Cre-
tan, and Neolithic civilizations. The earlier tellings make no mention of Persephone's rape; her descent was voluntary. The pre-
Hellenic telling goes as follows:[8]

In the earliest of times Demeter and Kore (Persephone's name
before she entered the underworld) roamed the world over, inspiriting
all living plants to sprout, flower, fruit, and seed. In their wanderings
Persephone encountered the bewildered and lost spirits of the dead.

She expressed her concern to her mother that there was no one to receive the newly dead into the underworld, to counsel and guide them in their journey through the dark passageway. Demeter admitted that the realm of the dead was her domain, but that her most important work was to feed the living.

Persephone then decided voluntarily to go into the underworld in order to welcome, bless, and initiate the dead into the mysteries of the womb and of renewal. Demeter, in the above world, mourned her daughter's absence. Her sorrow was so pervasive that her power was withdrawn from all the plant life, which soon withered and died. Eventually her grief immobilized her, and she sat motionless in a stupor and waited.

One day green shoots of crocus pushed their way aboveground, excitedly whispering that Persephone was returning. As the mother embraced her lost daughter, her renewed energy surged into all the dormant plant life, stirring them to fresh growth. Every year Demeter and Persephone willingly repeat this drama with the turning of the seasons.

On an outer level the story of Persephone's annual disappearance and return was an allegory of the spring sprouting of the dormant winter seed, explaining the changing of the seasons to the peasants. On an inner level the reenactment of this ritual drama gave humanity access to the archetypal themes of loss and return. And on a secret level, as celebrated by the initiates of the Eleusinian Mysteries, this ritual revealed the great transformation mystery: the cycle of birth, death, and renewal.

It is said that Demeter gave two gifts to humanity: the grain and the Eleusinian rites.[9] It was Demeter who was believed to have brought the secret of agriculture to the Greek people. Revered as the Goddess of the Grain, she taught humanity how to grow and cultivate crops instead of foraging in the wild for food, and thus she effected Greece's transformation from a nomadic to a farming country. This places Demeter's origins in the transition period from Paleolithic to Neolithic cultures, when the discovery of agriculture, the fruition of the Goddess's lunation cycle (as discussed in chapter 3), led to the development of civilization. In a woman's-only ritual the Thesmophoria, married women, empowered the seeds to germinate by mixing them with their menstrual blood. This was celebrated at the autumn sowing to express gratitude to this goddess for her gift of a stable food supply.

A single ear of grain was held up at the culminating point of the Eleusinian rites, Demeter's second gift to humanity. By the time the Eleusinian rites were being formally practiced in Greece around 1400 BCE, many people had been already influenced by the patriarchal mentality that denied cyclical rebirth. For two thousand years these rites preserved the Moon Goddess's mysteries, in which all of life was interconnected and death was a part of life. The Eleusinian Mysteries were abolished and the temple destroyed in the fourth century CE, at the same time that the papal decree of Nicea outlawed reincarnation, denouncing it as heresy.

The Greater and Lesser Mysteries

There were two levels of initiation: the Lesser and Greater Mysteries. At the first rite, called the *myesis*, the eyes of the initiates were closed. At the second rite, the *epopteia*, the initiates experienced a vision and became those who "had seen."

The Lesser Mysteries were held each year in the springtime (the month of Anthesterion, our February and Candelmas in Wheel of Year symbolism) in a sanctuary called Agra near the Ilissos River. They were held in honor of Persephone, and were a preparation for what was to come later. After purification and instruction the culminating ceremonies portrayed through sacred drama Persephone's rape and abduction into the underworld. The maiden, playing in the meadow, was tempted by Eros, God of Sexual Passion, to inhale the intoxicating fragrance of the narcissus, flower of desire. At that moment the earth suddenly opened into a gaping hole out of which Pluto, in a fiery chariot drawn by screeching black horses, seized and abducted the girl. Amid Persephone's terror and screams for help to her mother, all was plunged into darkness.

This concluded the Lesser Mysteries, as the neophytes symbolically passed with her into the underworld. The veil of the *myesis* was drawn over their eyes. From the Orphic tradition there appeared an additional element to the rites, in which Persephone gave birth to a male child as the result of her abduction by Pluto. This child was frequently identified with Dionysus, particularly in classical times. Many commentators suggest the working out of sexual themes as central to the Lesser Mysteries.[10]

The Greater Mysteries, which took place at Eleusis, followed in the month of Boedromion, our September, and were based on earlier agrarian cults honoring the fall equinox. They lasted for nine days, in memory of the nine days of Demeter's wanderings in search of her daughter. Each day had its special name and ceremony. During this second level of initiation, the *epopteia*, their eyes were opened through a revelation of a visionary experience.

On the first day of the Mysteries, the fourteenth day of the month, a great procession set off from Eleusis and marched along the Sacred Way to Athens, a distance of about fourteen miles. It included the High Priestess, the Hierophant (high priest), the Dadouchus (torchbearer), and holy priestesses of the Goddess, with the one in front carrying a casket of sacred objects upon her head. The *hiera* (holy objects) were deposited in the Eleusinion, Demeter's sanctuary, in the Agora at Athens.

The next day, the fifteenth of the month, *Agyromus*, was considered the first official day of the Mysteries. Officials read aloud a proclamation of invitation that restated the necessary qualifications. The initiates, dressed in pure white tunics, separated from the rest of the crowd and bent their heads to receive the divine benediction of the light of the Goddess.

On the following day a cry was heard early in the morning: *Halade mystai*, "Go to the sea, initiates." A procession formed and they all went to Phaleron to purify themselves in the nearby Aegean Sea. Each participant took along a young sacrificial pig with which he or she took the purification bath. The pig was then sacrificed and its body buried in deep pits as an offering to the deities of the underworld. The blood of a pig was considered to be the purest of all animals, and it had the power to cleanse the soul of hatred and evil, ritually separating the initiate from his or her previous profane life. As Demeter's sacred animal, the pig was linked to cults of the dead.

The fourth day of the rites, the seventeenth of Boedromion, *Hiereia devro* (Hither the victims), was given over for prayers and additional sacrifices. This was followed the next day by the *Asclepia*, a special celebration for Asklepius, the God of Healing, who had also been to the underworld. This day also affirmed the ancient practice of allowing important public figures to enter late into the rites, as Asklepius himself was reputed to have done.

Then, on the morning of the nineteenth of the month, *Iacchus* or *Pompe* (Procession), the initiates assembled to begin the fourteen-mile procession upon the Sacred Way to Eleusis. This day marked the beginning of the rite of secrecy. The initiates were crowned with wreathes of myrtle and carried rods made of woven branches called bacchus, symbols of death of the old life and birth of the new. A wooden statue of Iacchus (Dionysus/Bacchus), the boy-god whose birth would be the culminating event in the secret rites, was borne in the forefront. The celebrants joyously chanted his name in a vision of their salvation. The long journey was punctuated with many ceremonies of homage along the way, such as at the sacred fig tree, with dancing, singing, and offerings.

At the bridge over the river Kephisos the procession was entertained by a humorous display of sexual jokes called the "bridge-jests." These jests were reminiscent of Baubo, the Goddess of Belly-laughter, who raised her skirts and exposed her vulva in an attempt to lift the sorrowful spirits of the weeping Demeter. The Eleusinians, draped in sheets, began to mock and insult the initiates, even the most important officials, revealing secret and humiliating truths about each person, who had to listen to the abuse without being able to reply. Thus exposed, the old self literally died for shame.

The procession reached Eleusis by nightfall. Although everyone was tired, hungry, and covered with dust, they celebrated an all-night torchlit festival of dancing and singing to honor the maiden Persephone and her holy mother, Demeter. A large dancing ground surrounded the Well of Callichoron. Here, according to the myth, the Goddess had refreshed her parched lips at the end of her desperate wanderings. Lovely Eleusinian maidens enacted in ritual movements the arrival of Demeter in Eleusis after her nine days of fruitless searching for her daughter.

The culmination of the rites occurred over the twentieth and twenty-first days of the month, *Mysteriotides nychtes*, the Nights of the Mysteries. The main core of the mysteries took place over the next two evenings, inside the Telesterion. Little is definitely known of these rites because the initiates were oathbound, under penalty of death, to reveal nothing of what they had seen. From ancient writings it is clear that something was seen inside the sanctuary, and that this vision constituted the essence of the Mystery.

Before entering the Telesterion there were further sacrifices and offerings of bread near the Cave of Hades in the Precinct of Pluto. At the entrance to this cave was an *omphalos*, the world navel, which marked the transition from the world of light to the world of darkness. This moment and place marked Persephone's descent into the underworld. From a special chalice the initiates received a drink called *kykeion*, made from barley flour and mint. Recent study suggests that the barley meal drink contained a hallucinogenic fungus that grew on the grain and induced visions.[11]

The initiates were prepared for a sacred revelation by their fast, the day-long march to Eleusis, and by drinking the *kykeion* brew. The prescribed words they spoke before entering the temple were, "I have fasted; I have drunk the mixed drink."[12] The Lesser Mysteries had closed with Persephone's screams for help as the mystics symbolically passed with her into the darkness of the underworld. Now the Greater Mysteries picked up the thread of the story in the darkened Telesterion. There, in a state of hypersensitive expectation, the initiates began to cross through the kingdom of death.

What took place there provoked fear and terror, according to Clement of Alexandria, who called the happenings in the Telesterion a "mystic drama": "The temple shook; terrifying visions and fearful spectres depicted the horror of Hades and the fate awaiting evil man."[13] The initiates experienced the physical symptoms of fear—nausea, trembling, and cold sweats. Phasmata, dreadful apparitions or spirits, appeared throughout the initiations hall and held the initiates in a state of continuous anguish and terror.

After this terrible specter of death, they were suffused by a sweet, pleasing light, soothing to the spirits and heralding the coming of the Goddess. Each person felt as if he or she had returned from Hades or been reborn. The final scene was that of Triptolemus setting out on his long journey to teach the peoples of the earth the secret of agriculture and the cultivation of crops. The ceremony ended with the words *"Pax konx,"* whose probable meaning is, "May your desires be fulfilled."[14]

The night of the twenty-first was the *Epopteia*, the highest stage of the Mysteries. Only those who had been initiated the year before were allowed to participate. The rites unfolded in three forms: things spoken *(legomena)*, things performed *(dromena)*, and things revealed *(deiknymena)*. There are references to a sacred marriage at the throne of the underworld between Zeus and Demeter, or alternately between Hades and Persephone, which was enacted by the Hierophant and High Priestess in the roles of the God and Goddess. The climax of the ceremonies occurred at some point in the night amid clashing cymbals and a great burst of blazing firelight, when a voice of thunder cried out with an exultant shout, "The great goddess has borne a sacred child: Brimo has borne Brimos."[15] The queen of the dead herself has given birth in fire to a mighty son.[16] The birth of this divine child, also known as Iacchus (Bacchus/Dionysus), symbolized the knowledge that from death comes life renewed.

During these ceremonies the sacred contents of the baskets were shown, and the initiates held and felt the holy objects. "I have taken out of the *cista* (little chest), worked with it, and then laid in the basket and out of the basket into the *cista*."[17] Graves suggests that the objects were a symbol of coition, and perhaps the initiates enacted the implanting of the seed of life into the fertile Goddess of the Earth.[18] Some sources believed that the sacred objects in the *cista* were various sorts of cakes, a serpent, pomegranates, leaves and stalks, poppies, and a model of a woman's genitals.[19]

In a final, supreme revelation the Hierophant silently displayed a mown ear of grain. At this awesome moment the initiates understood that the seed of grain contains the secret of life in its invisible and visible forms. They shouted their thanksgiving, looking skyward with the chant, "*Ye*" (rain), acclaiming Zeus as God of the Sky; and then, looking to the earth, chanted, "*Kye*" (give birth) to Demeter, Goddess of the Earth, for her gift of grain that nourished humanity. This chant invoked the sky to give forth rain and the earth to become fruitful. This formula, which is also translated as "flow and conceive," might have been connected with the ritual consummation of the Sacred Marriage and the impregnation of Mother Nature.

Afterward the initiates passed out of the great hall into the darkness, led by torchlight, and gathered in a nearby meadow for chanting, dancing, and feasting. This experience, which had opened their eyes to a new way of seeing and their renewal, released them from their previous lifetime of darkness.

The final day of the Mysteries, on the twenty-second of the month, *Plymochoai,* was dedicated to a remembrance of the dead. The purified initiates honored the dead with libations, and special vessels were filled with an unknown sweet drink. They were poured to the east and to the west to reflect the anointing of the earth in the directions of birth and death.

The nature of the Mysteries was an essentially emotional experience that gave the initiates hope for the future. George E. Mylonas, an expert on the Mysteries, concludes:

Whatever the substance and meaning of the Mysteries was, the fact remains that the cult of Eleusis satisfied the most sincere yearnings and the deepest longings of the human heart. The initiates returned from their pilgrimage to Eleusis full of joy and happiness, with the fear of death diminished, and a strengthened hope of a better life in the world of shadows.[20]

However, with the growing power of Christianity, the Mysteries were finally banned by the Byzantine Emperor Theodosius because they conflicted with the Christian views on the fate of the soul after death. Finally Alaric, King of the Goths, invaded Greece in 396 CE and completely destroyed the sanctuary at Eleusis.

Commentary on the Mysteries

Beautiful indeed is the Mystery given us by the blessed gods: death is for mortals no longer an evil, but a blessing.
—Inscription found at Eleusis[21]

The secret of the Eleusinian rites continues to remain a mystery. By its very nature, ritual is not something that can be communicated by words. It is essentially an emotional experience, not an intellectual discourse. By providing this kind of experience, ritual does for many people what cannot be done by philosophical inquiry or devotion. The culminating *epopteia* was a vision that resulted in a state of "having seen." And so all modern attempts to decode the meaning of the Mysteries will inevitably fall short of their goal, as the meaning transcends the capacity of what our light-filled conscious, rational mind can comprehend. But we can try to point to what the nature of the Mysteries might suggest in the hope of stimulating the darkened unconscious, which does have the power to approach the awe of the incomprehensible.

The Great Moon Goddess glowing above in the night skies gave the earliest peoples their first notions about the mystery of birth, death, and rebirth. The moon was believed to be the source of fertility that quickened life in the dormant seed, and early agricultural cycles were based on a yearly calendar that reflected the rhythm of the lunations. The Thesmophoria and Eleusinia have their roots in the early agrarian rites, whose purpose was to promote the fertility of the grain laid down in the earth. By honoring the Goddess who revealed to them the secret of agriculture, they hoped to obtain her continued blessings for abundant crops.

Pre-Hellenic Greece agrarian rites that predated the Eleusinian Mysteries were also held annually at the time of the autumn sowing. These ceremonies celebrated the occasion of bringing up the corn from the underground silos, where it had been stored after the June threshing. The grain was then sown in the earth, and came back to life again to symbolize a new life beyond the grave. The earth was both the reviver of their crops and the storehouse of their dead. Demeter, the Goddess of the Grain, was also the Goddess of the Dead, who were called *demetreioi*.

While the moon's phases provided the prototype for the overall patterning, it was on earth that early peoples directly experienced the mystery of the grain's renewal. In this way the cycle of the moon's phases timed the seasonal cycles, and both lunar and agricultural cycles became linked with the idea of renewal. The rites of the Goddess of Agriculture, who ruled over the death and rebirth of the seed crop, later developed into the rites of the death and rebirth of the human soul. The Eleusinian Mysteries were not simply about the renewal of agricultural fertility. Agriculture was the symbolic language of the Mysteries; but what it points to is the greater mystery of life itself, a mystery that is ultimately couched in feminine agrarian imagery.[22]

Evolving out of the wisdom that arises from viewing nature, people's awareness moved from celebrating the earth's seasonal cycles of growth and decay to formulating rites that addressed their fears concerning their own human birth, death, and resurrection. They intuited that the great mystery of life lies in death. Joseph Henderson writes that whenever we find the theme of death, whether in recurrent myths or modern dreams, it rarely stands alone. Death is universally found to be part of a theme involving death and rebirth or death and resurrection. In these myths there is also abundant evidence of another theme, that of initiation. "Initiation provides the archetypal pattern by which the psyche, whether in individuals or in groups of people, is enabled to make a transition from one stage of development to another and therefore brings the theme of death and rebirth into a close relation to problems of education whether in a religious or secular sense."[23]

The tale of Demeter and Persephone, ritualized as the Eleusinian Mystery Rites, embodied humanity's thoughts about being born and dying. It anticipated both Easter (in which both life and death coexist) and Christmas (the time of annual rebirth and hope).[24] Fear of death is basically fear of the unknown. The Eleusinian Mysteries were one of the major initiation rites of the ancient world, whereby people were given an experience that enabled them to overcome their fear of death. Both seasonal and personal, the Mysteries were rituals of death and rebirth. As the seed died awaiting germination, the initiate died to the old self; and like the sprouting grain, the new soul was reborn into the company of those who had gone before, the *epoptai*.[25]

Within the framework of the archetypal drama of loss and return, the Eleusinian Mysteries, in their entirety, led the initiates through the story of Demeter and Persephone. First, the Goddess's story was told; and then, in the Lesser Mysteries, the participants gradually identified with the action. Finally the Greater Mysteries led the initiates to a vision and realization that the great mythic drama took place inside themselves. In the modern psyche fear of death is related to fear of change. In this ancient initiation rite we can find a contemporary metaphor for the psychological cycle of separation, loss, initiation, and return that marks the psychic stages of transformation whereby we experience a death of the old self and a rebirth of the new.

Most initiation rites that facilitate a transition from old to new involve stages of purification, procession through a labyrinth, sacrifice, isolation in the darkness, and a final epiphany in light.[26] The Eleusinian initiates fasted and purified themselves in the sea, sacrificed Demeter's sacred animal the pig and offered it to the underworld deities, and made the winding and twisting journey from Athens. It was, however, in the isolation of the darkness inside the Telesterion that the miraculous vision occurred. Most scholars now agree that the participants did not view a stage play, and archaeologists have not uncovered any secret chamber or underground passages at the Telesterion. The mystery lay in what was seen. In this wordless initiation, through immediate vision and insight, the participants suddenly understood a great truth.

There exists some bewilderment among modern scholars as what specifically enabled the many thousands of participants over the centuries to have a predictable visionary experience. Wasson, Ruck, and Hofmann propose that the *kykeion* brew which the initiates drank before entering the Telesterion contained a hallucinogenic fungus that caused this psychedelic journey. In Figure 8.1 from an early V century BCE stele in Pharsalus, Greece, Demeter and Persephone are shown each offering a mushroom to one another. In the ancient mystery traditions, it is not uncommon to find references to the partaking of natural substances such as the *soma* drink in India or the laurel leaves chewed by the Delphic priestess that produced shamanic states of ecstasy allowing communication with the deities. It is through the process of psychic disintegration of our normal boundaries of rational consciousness that we can make the descent into the death-rebirth experience. From this perspective the Eleusinian Mysteries can be interpreted as a shamanic vision quest that was induced by a hallucinogenic substance.

The initiates entered the Telesterion on the first night of the mysteries and, as they passed through the darkness, they embarked upon a journey through the underworld. The initial stage of the death passage was dominated by the *phasmata*, the frightening apparitions and spirits, which caused the initiates to become physically ill as a result of their overwhelming terror. These wrathful images are similar to those described in the Egyptian and Tibetan *Books of the Dead*, where, after death, the consciousness passes through a corridor of terrifying visions.

From a psychological perspective these visions, as the *phasmata*, arise from inside our own minds. They are the projections of our negative thought patterns such as anger, hatred, greed, jealousy, and ignorance, which have pushed us into wrongdoing. In the Buddhist tradition, in order for the consciousness to pass into the spiritual world, it must first recognize these frightening phenomena as emanations from one's own mind, having no inherent reality and therefore no external power over us.

In the 1990 movie *Flatliners*, a group of medical students perform an experiment where they chemically induce a state of death for several minutes in each other and then bring the person back to life. The memory of the death experience includes an encounter with someone they had wronged in the past. Now the "spirit" of that person haunts them; only through atonement and asking forgiveness can they be released from this state of demonic possession. The Eleusinian rites enabled the initiates, while in life, to pass through this first stage of death, where they met with the images of their own wrongdoings. After passing through that frightening stage, they were eventually led to being suffused in a sweet, pleasing clear light that calmed, healed, and reassured them.

The first night of the Mysteries took the initiate through the corridor of death; but the second and even more awesome night revealed the secrets of rebirth. Historical fragments hint at a Sacred Marriage, where the representatives of the God and Goddess engaged in sexual intercourse. The most dramatic moment in the ritual occurred at this point amidst the clashing of cymbals and great bursts of light. The initiates, in a beatific vision, beheld the Queen of the Dead giving birth in fire to a divine child who was conceived in the underworld.

It was this astonishing event that made hope possible; the realization that from death comes new life. Death is none other than the womb of conception and the gateway to rebirth. The Queen of Death bore a son to the Lord of Death; and, in that act, her destroyer was seen to be simultaneously her own and humanity's renewer. The initiates came to an understanding that after passing through the frightening specter of the death corridor and into the sweet suffusing light, the next stage of the underworld journey moved them into being conceived in the sexual embrace of their parents-to-be. Karl Kerenyi proposes that the message to initiates was that the funeral pyres were the vehicles of birth rather than death.[27] Using the gift of humor to lift the spirits, Baubo raised her skirts exposing her vulva to remind the mourning Demeter of this great truth.

The supreme revelation occurred as the Hierophant silently held up a mown ear of grain. The initiatory experience was distilled in the secret of the grain that essentialized the continuity of life in its visible and invisible forms. In the grain symbolism of the two goddesses, Demeter represented the fertile earth that nourishes the mature crop, the ripened grain of the harvest in the above world. Persephone stood for the seed germ of the grain, which is buried in the below world during the barren winter months and then emerges as the young vegetation of spring. The growth of the grain to fruition is the Eleusinian symbol of rebirth. The harvest is the child conceived in the other world.[28] The image of Persephone emerging annually in the spring as the sprouting grain gave to people the promise of their own renewal and regeneration.

In vase paintings depicting Persephone's return to the upper world, she is often shown in the midst of plants and bearing an infant. As the Queen of the Underworld, Persephone received the dead during the dark winter season of their lives and then prepared them for rebirth. When she returned to the upper world in the spring, she emerged as Kore, the maiden, carrying the newly born life essence of a person's old self. Persephone's return to her mother with her divine child conceived and born in the underworld gave a vision of life beyond death. In the moment of their reunion, the initiates felt released from their fears of the darkness of death as they too were reborn into the light.

In allowing her only beloved daughter to go to the world of the dead, year after year, Demeter displays to humanity her faith in the certainty of the eventual return of her child. Demeter's mythic drama of separation, loss, and reunion with her child became a symbol for the continuity of life that circles and connects the world of the living to the world of the dead. The basic theme of the Mysteries was the eternal coming of life from death; the repeated celebration of these mysteries continued this cosmic event.[29]

The two goddesses who presided over the rites of cyclic renewal on the earth, Demeter and Persephone, reflect the light and dark phases of the Moon Goddess. The light, visible full moon face of the Goddess is Demeter, who above earth gives the gift of food to nourish the living. The invisible dark moon face of the Goddess is Persephone, who, beneath the earth, gives the gift of renewal to regenerate the dead. Seneca wrote, "There are holy things that are not communicated all at once: Eleusis always keeps something back to show those who come again."[30]

The Mother-Daughter Dark Moon Mysteries

We cannot conclude this chapter without a discussion of Persephone, Queen of the Underworld, as a Goddess of the Dark Moon; and of the relationship between Demeter and Persephone as the basis for the mother-daughter mystery of renewal. Their drama of separation, loss, and reunion lays at the heart of a woman's most fundamental relationships: her role as a daughter of her mother and her role as the mother of a daughter. When the inevitable separation occurs between them, which is an intrinsic and necessary part of their process, it jars their lives apart. Mother and daughter are each plunged into darkness of fear and terror, grieving over the loss of the loved one.

To enter into the figure of Demeter means "to be pursued, to be robbed, raped, to fail to understand, to rage and grieve, but then to get everything back and be born again."[31] The story of Demeter, as mother, is one of love for child, inconsolable grief in the loss of her daughter, and joy in her return. The story of Persephone, as daughter, is one of terror in her abduction and abandonment, finding the depths of herself in the darkness, and mediating back and forth between her mother and husband. The story of all mothers and daughters is the story of their estrangements and reunions.

The mother gives birth to an infant girl, whom she nourishes with her love. She sees the meaning of her life unfolding with the growth of her beautiful daughter. She is ever-watchful, fearing for the safety of her child, and especially for her daughter's sexual violation. The daughter initially basks in the security and warmth of her mother's protective embrace; but when she "comes of age," she often struggles against her mother, whom she sees as trying to limit and control her life. The newly budding maiden yearns to experience the mysteries of sexuality, but her growing womanly desires only serve to further provoke her mother's terror and subsequent restriction of her freedom.

The mother prays that her daughter's first sexual initiation will not come prematurely nor be violent, insensitive, or debasing. If it occurs outside of marriage, she hopes that her daughter will not be branded and ostracized from society, nor be left alone, rejected, and pregnant. After a young woman's first sexual encounter, she has lost her innocence and can never again be wholly her mother's *kore*, the pure and untouched girl-child.

At some point in time in the archetypal pattern, the young girl must be separated from her mother. The daughter may leave by going away to school, by being on her own, or by getting married. Or it might be a sudden and violent separation, where after power struggles and hateful words the daughter, in anger, runs away from home, severing all contact. She may run off with a boyfriend or be taken away by an angry husband in the guise of the dark demon-lover Hades (Pluto). The mother may also lose her daughter to death, kidnapping, or divorce, with custody going to another.

At the moment when we, as mothers, experience the loss of our child, it often feels like an abduction, and we enter into the dark moon phase of their mystery. Christine Downing asks, "How much of motherhood is loss?"[32] Demeter as grieving mother experiences the loss of her child as the loss of herself. We initially panic over our daughter's well-being, exhibiting physical symptoms of distress in the same way that Demeter herself could not eat, sleep, or bathe during the nine days of her frantic search for her missing child.

For a mother to let go of her child is often more than she can bear, yet she must. Her hopelessness turns into an overwhelming grief that depresses her life spirit. She feels empty, useless, devoid of purpose; gaping holes appear in her life that were once filled with the laughter and activity of her child. Immobilized in her depression, she may be so overcome with sorrow that nothing else matters. She cannot deal with her responsibilities and allows her life to fall apart. Both the story of Demeter and the grieving work of Elizabeth Kübler-Ross speak of the redeeming value of anger, whereby we can contact the deepest reserves of our strength in order to break through the wall of depression and once again resume a productive life.

A mother's loss of her daughter signals the loss of her identity in the full moon nature of her being. The anguish of the empty nest is the mother's initiation into a dark moon phase of her life, where she must now bridge the transition from mother to crone. It is a time of major change in a woman's life, when she is challenged to use her nurturing energies to birth and nourish the mental and spiritual children of her inner life.

Persephone also experiences the terror of abandonment when she is violently wrenched away from the loving care and protection of her mother. When daughters have the experience that it is their mothers who have left them alone and unprotected, they have a different kind of dark journey to travel than if they were the ones who were doing the leaving. The daughter may also lose her mother to death, to an alcohol or drug addiction, or to a debilitating illness. A child may be given up for adoption or into the care of another person, or taken away because of divorce. A daughter may feel her mother withdrawing from her emotionally and psychologically if she is neglected and beaten, or with the arrival of a new stepfather. And the most emotionally wrenching betrayal a daughter can experience is when her mother does not protect her from physical or sexual abuse by other members of the family.

What happens to Persephone children (male or female) growing up when they lose their mother prematurely in a devastating act of physical or psychological separation, and their mother is not there to take care of them? The descent into the darkness at such an early age can leave lifelong scars. The trauma of being abandoned into the underworld predisposes children to feel totally unequipped to cope as they are growing up with what they see as the confusion, uncertainty, and insecurity of life. This accounts for much of the depression, isolation, and lack of self-love and esteem that people carry when Persephone is an active archetype in their life. And yet, on the archetypal level, it is this very descent that opens a person to the wealth of the inner world and the secrets of renewal.

It might be tempting to see Persephone's abduction into the underworld as an act of violation upon an innocent young girl from which she will recover. However, to do so would obscure the deeper significance of this event. In the act of losing her mother, Persephone finds herself. "When a woman is caught in an unconscious identification with her mother, then she has to be raped out of that identity before she can find her own individuality"; this is the meaning of Persephone's abduction into the underworld.[33] This is not to suggest that physical rape is ever an acceptable method of provoking a growth of consciousness. It refers rather to a state of psychological rape—a shocking action which shatters the forms of one's attachments to childhood dependencies and plunges one into the dark descent of the individuation process.

When a young woman is initiated into the sexual mysteries, the innocent maiden does die as she experiences the depth and intensity of her emotional life. If she has been taught to fear and repress her sexuality, she may have to unconsciously project the image of the dark demon-lover who will ravish her, carry her off against her will, only to then find ecstasy in her lover's embrace. A woman yearns to contact the depth of her passion, but this journey to the core of her sexuality may seem like an abduction because she rarely feels whole and confident enough to go there on her own. However, once she has experienced the intensity of her sexual passion, the maiden now turned woman is no longer totally focused on leaving her emotional depths and returning to her mother. Persephone swallows the pomegranate seed and gives herself over to Pluto as his consort and bride. Her fear and anger toward her captor turn to love, and she chooses to remain with him.

Persephone's relationship with Pluto assures her that for a portion of each year she can reign as Queen of the Underworld. Her time spent in the subterranean realms allows her to develop her power, which comes from having penetrated the mysteries of the dark and tapping into the hidden wealth of the underworld. As guide and initiator to the souls of the dead, Persephone learns to converse with the spirits and leads them to rebirth. Our descent into Persephone's realm likewise gives us the opportunity to experience the terrain of the unconscious dimensions of our psyches. Here we can journey through our inner world, discover our psychic capacities, and develop a relationship with the forces in our unconscious. Persephone's dark moon passage, which begins with loss, terror, confusion, and depression, ultimately leads her to discover in these depths a new sense of self. It is through being carried off, penetrated, and impregnated by the creative masculine that renewal and new life can be born from the feminine nature. She thus promises new psychological life for all who pass through her underworld realm.

Having claimed the power of her sexuality, her skill in communing and ministering to the dark forces of the unconscious, and her wealth of psychic sensitivity, Persephone finds her strength in her identity as woman and as a mediatrix. She can never go back to her mother and resume her old role of innocence and dependency. She left as a child, but now she returns as a woman who knows sexuality, psychic power, separation, and death. She approaches her mother carrying an infant, who symbolizes her birth to a new sense of self.

For both mothers and daughters, their time of separation is often filled with guilt, remorse, recriminations, anger, blame, and judgment. During these times, when mothers and daughters cannot understand each other's lives, they pull away from one another, cutting off communication and contact. Accusations, hurtful feelings, hateful words, years of neglect, bitterness, resentment, and breaches of trust break apart mothers and daughters and leave them both suspended in a prolonged dark moon gap of their relationship.

A daughter may struggle her entire adult life trying to disentangle herself from the emotional power that she feels her mother continues to wield over her. She may fear that a return to her mother is a regression and implies a defeat in her quest for autonomy and individuality. A mother who feels as if she has devoted the most important years of her life to cultivating her daughter's growth may harbor deep-seated resentment to a child who is oblivious, ungrateful, and disrespectful of her sacrifice. She may be discouraged that all her efforts were in vain if her daughter does not embrace her values and visions, and may demean herself as a failure if her daughter chooses a lifestyle that contradicts and challenges her beliefs. A mother may also harbor jealousy toward her daughter's budding sensual womanhood and a future of open possibilities as she begins to move into the menopausal years of her life.

In the archetypal story of Demeter and Persephone, the daughter's journey eventually does bring her back to her mother. Their mythic drama concludes with their joyous reunion; a hope that lies dormant, sometimes unexpressed and unrealized, in the heart of every mother and daughter who are estranged. Persephone arrives from the underworld bearing an infant. It is often when a young woman births her first child that she is able to return to her mother and heal the wounds of their separation. This may be a physical child of her body or a psychological child of her creative self that allows her to reapproach her mother from a stance of womanhood. In their embrace the healing begins: The daughter can begin to appreciate her mother, and the mother can acknowledge her daughter's strengths. The budding vegetation of spring is a celebration of their annual reunion.

The maiden Persephone now has her own child and has crossed the threshold to motherhood. Demeter must step aside to assume her

257

*Rites of Rebirth:
The Initiation
Mysteries of
Demeter and
Persephone*

role as grandmother. It is important for a woman to heal the wounds of her estrangement from her mother. If she cannot she is likely to pass on the very same painful dysfunctional pattern to her daughter. "Every mother contains her daughter in herself and every daughter her mother; every woman extends backwards into her mother and forwards into her daughter."[34] The myth of Demeter and Persephone teaches women that their lives are spread out over generations.

Demeter shows women that by refusing to accept their daughter's maturity and by not validating their daughter's need for a period of separation where she can go her own way, they unwittingly prevent growth from occurring. Like Demeter herself, who in her anger and sorrow insisted on her daughter's return, caused the halt of all crop production on earth. The wise mother knows that the daughter must give herself over to the forces of the underworld in order to ensure a season of renewal. Without Persephone's ravishment, Demeter, as Mother Earth, is barren.

The daughter's cyclical movement toward her mother and then parting from her mother to reunite with her husband or creative animus is the rhythm of the turning of the cycle. And the maiden who is now a mother must, in turn, sacrifice her daughter. The initiatory teachings of Demeter and Persephone continue to be enacted in the lives of mothers and daughters, whose sacred relationship contains the mystery of renewal in the darkness.

Persephone as a Dark Moon Goddess

Persephone, blessed daughter of Great Zeus, sole offspring
of Demeter, come and accept this gracious sacrifice.
Much honored spouse of Plouton, discreet and life-giving,
you command the gates of Hades in the bowels of the
    earth,
lovely-tressed Praxidike, pure bloom of Deo,
mother of the furies, queen of the nether world,
whom Zeus sired in clandestine union.
Mother of loud-roaring and many shaped Eubouleus,
radiant and luminous playmate of the Seasons,
august, almighty, maiden rich in fruits,
brilliant and horned, you alone are beloved of mortals.
In spring you rejoice in the meadow breezes
and you show your holy figure in shoots and green fruits.
You were made a kidnapper's bride in the fall,

and you alone are life and death to toiling mortals,
O Persephone, for you always nourish all and kill them,
too.
Hearken, O blessed goddess, and send forth the earth's
fruits.
You who blossom in peace, in soft-handed health,
and in a life of plenty that ferries old age in comfort
to your realm, O queen, and to that of mighty Plouton.
   —"Hymn to Persephone"[35]

Persephone holds a unique position as a Goddess of the Dark Moon. She is the Queen of the Dead, guiding souls to rebirth. But unlike other dark goddesses, the patriarchal mythical literature has not demonized her into a monstrous figure of terror or envisioned her as an old, ugly hag. She remains ever-youthful, almost frozen in the ice maiden quality of her crystalline beauty. Persephone is the embodiment of that precise point in the lunar cycle when the dark moon becomes the new moon, and the old crone is reborn as the youthful maiden.

In the previous section we asked the question, What happens to the child whose life is influenced by the archetype of Persephone? It is not always an easy path for a person to have Persephone as a primary muse. While she promises the wealth of the inner life, the road to her treasures is often an initiation by tragedy. Persephone encounters her rite of passage into the underworld while she is still a young child. This goddess often arrives early in the life of her initiates, sometimes in violent or devastating ways, jolting them out of their childlike innocence. She may come cloaked in the garment of the death or dysfunction of a parent, the breakup of a family, sexual abuse, or a major illness or accident that leaves a prolonged disability. The immature child is suddenly faced with a heart-wrenchingly painful situation that is beyond his or her emotional capacity to cope with.

For a sensitive child with a fragile ego, the trauma that accompanies feeling abandoned or losing a safe and secure environment leaves a lasting impression. The outer world is seen as a threatening place, full of uncertainty and terror, and the child feels forced to retreat into the inner world. The child learns to find a safe haven by withdrawing into the self, and begins to call "home" the huge emotional void left by the loss of love and security. Tragedy forces the Persephone child into the make-believe world of the inner life, but this event also leads to an encounter with the psychic forces of the unconscious.

Reclusive and highly secretive, Persephone's children develop an aura of mystery around themselves as they grow up. They often need much time to be alone; it is in their isolation that they reconnect to the womb of their childhood nurturance. Projecting an ephemeral quality, as if they are somewhere else, they find solace and meaning in a realm that is not recognized or validated by society. Thus they feel alienated, uncertain of themselves, and yearn for invisibility.

They are driven to continually reenter the darkness of their private world. If they have been fortunate enough to discover the hidden wealth of the unconscious, they can benefit from contacting this deep reservoir of unseen power. Accessing the intuition, detecting the movements of the psyche, understanding the meaning of dreams, communicating with spirits in other-dimensional realms, dialoguing with the voices of the shadow, pursuing knowledge of the past and of the esoteric mysteries, and practicing a spiritual meditation are some of the gifts that Persephone offers to her initiates.

By a plunge into the underworld realm through an act of fate, the person guided by Persephone is gradually led to finding a vocation in the psychic arts, in alternative healing, in working with death and the dying, and helping those who have suffered much tragedy in their lives. As psychotherapists and counselors they are skilled in facilitating a person's movement through life-death crises and psychological transformations and rebirths.

However, not all of Persephone's children are able to move easily through their pain and actualize their true vocational callings. As adults many continue to feel like helpless victims of a tragic fate from which they have never recovered. A frightened and insecure child who is still haunted by the demons of the dark underworld now inhabits a grown-up body. Those who remain immobilized from their trauma and have not yet passed through the mourning stage of their primal loss are often reluctant to penetrate the dark realms of the psyche.

They may attempt to hold back the confrontation with the unconscious by anesthetizing themselves with a wide range of addictive behaviors, including drugs, alcohol, sex, work, food, or television. For them the dark is a battle against the demons of depression, madness, despair, suicidal fantasies, disassociation—a struggle in which they inevitably are the loser. They are trapped in the corridor of terrifying *phasmata*, the initial stage of the death passage.

After a while many of Persephone's children who remain lost, frightened, and confused begin to thrive on their misery. They come to believe that they have no power to change the sadness and waste of their lives, that any attempts to do so always result in failure. A self-image develops around a core of defeat, failure, and powerlessness. They are frightened to take a stand lest they be knocked down, and are reluctant to assert themselves lest they be overpowered. They find their security in projecting a passive, nonactive, noncommittal personality who is subject to being acted upon by the strong will of others. They capitalize on their helplessness, victimization, and innocence.

While some of Persephone's children may be familiar with the powers of the inner world, her lost ones are totally out of touch with their power in the outer world. The fragile adult children who emanate a youthful glow are often attracted to strong personalities who will make the decisions for them, take care of them, and fill in all the empty, gaping voids in their lives. They think that they desire a sheltered life under the protective wing of a powerful mate, parent, boss, or any authority figure. However, this often backfires against them.

By being passive they are out of touch with their power and are therefore vulnerable to giving it away or projecting it upon others. To the extent they fear their own power and will, they repeatedly attract situations where they become the victims of domination and assault. The would-be protector becomes the oppressor and they inevitably get hurt.

For the adult child of Persephone the issue of sex is as difficult to cope with as the issue of power. Sexuality is seen as a violation, a rape, a painful and unwanted intrusion upon the sensitivity of the body and psyche. Intense, intimate encounters with others plunge them into the darkness and confusion of their unconscious emotional depths. It is not unusual for these people to suffer from a suppressed understanding of their own sexuality. They move in ways to avoid intimacy or clench in frigid rigidity or impotence when sexual penetration is urged upon them.

The unconscious fantasy life of a people who repress and reject their sexual desires takes on the shadow form of the dark lover who ravishes one's innocence against one's will. This becomes the only acceptable way of contacting the depths of one's passions. While this is the main theme of most contemporary "romance novels," in real life the endings are not so happy. The denial of one's sexuality when projected often leads to rape, sexual violence, and degradation. This results in a vicious cycle where one's worst fears are continually being realized and reinforced.

It is important for the lost children of Persephone who remain trapped in the underworld of their childhood pain to seek therapeutic help. While withdrawal from life is the sensitive person's defense against a hostile world, their inner reality, a netherworld haunted by death, despair, and frightening spirits, is not much more secure. It is only with a guide who is familiar with the terrain of descent into death transition that they can be led through the dark passageway of their renewal. The meaning of the inner life will torment them until they can come to terms with the hidden treasures of the darkness. Their quest is to obtain the power that comes from an understanding and mastery of the unknown.

As a Goddess of the Dark Moon, Persephone can become an active archetype in our lives not only in childhood, but at any age when we experience a violent trauma that leads to endings, loss, and transition. As we make our descent into the darkness, Persephone waits for us in the subliminal gray realm where we are suspended between the closure of an important phase of our lives and the beginning of the next one. Guide to our unconscious, she brings us to a discovery of our vision of renewal in the deep silent vast pools of the underworld psyche. The goddess Persephone anointed the dead and initiated them into the rites of rebirth. Her timeless mysteries continue to be enacted today within each of us as we move through our psychological transformations in the hope of being reborn anew.

Journal Questions

1. How do I feel about the inevitability of my death? Have I been able to live a life confident in the face of death, or do I approach it with fear and trepidation? Have I ever been exposed to any rituals or teachings that told me what to expect and how to best move through the death passage?

2. If I am a parent, have I ever experienced the physical or emotional loss of a child or loved one? If so, can I recognize my reactions of panic, anger, grief, and depression in the mythos of Demeter? In what ways have I received the eventual return, in a similar or different form, of what I had lost?

3. As I grew up, in what ways did I experience a power struggle with my mother as I tried to obtain more freedom and autonomy, especially in the area of relating to the opposite sex? Did I feel that she did not understand or trust me? As a parent, what fears and concerns did I have when my daughter "came of age," showing signs of sexual

development and interest? In what ways did I try to protect her? How did I react to her resistance to my rules and values?

4. Did this power struggle between mother and daughter result in an estrangement? Have we been able to reconnect? In what ways was I different when I was finally able to reunite with my mother or daughter?

5. Did I experience a tragic event in my childhood that led to the loss of physical or emotional security in my life? Did I feel abandoned or unprotected by my mother? Did I react by retreating into myself and survive by creating a fantasy life? Can I see how this process gave me the opportunity to become more sensitive to the subtleties of the inner world? Have I been able to actualize my latent psychic or empathic abilities, or have I tried to disassociate from the pain of my early life through patterns of addictive substances or behaviors?

Notes

1. Dion Fortune, *Moon Magic* (San Francisco: Throsons, 1990).
2. Eleanor Gadon, *The Once and Future Goddess* (San Francisco: Harper & Row, 1989), 149.
3. Demeter's Eleusinian Mysteries were one of a number of mystery religions in the ancient Mediterranean and Near East. Mystery cults were also associated with Cybele, Dionysus, Hermes-Thoth, Isis, Mithra, Orpheus, and the Cabeiri-Discuri of Samothrace.
4. Karl Kerenyi, *Eleusis: An Archetypal Image of Mother and Daughter*, translated by Ralph Manheim (New York: Schocken Books, 1977), 15.
5. Kerenyi, *Eleusis*, 14.
6. Nor Hall, *The Moon and the Virgin* (New York: Harper & Row, 1980), 85.
7. *The Homeric Hymns*, translated by Charles Boer (Irving, TX: Spring Publications, 1979), 133.
8. Charlene Spretnak, *Lost Goddesses of Early Greece* (Berkeley, CA: Moon Books, 1978), 103–10.
9. Jane Ellen Harrison, *Religion in Ancient Greece* (London: Archibald Constable and Co., 1905), 51.
10. Richard Gelhard, *The Traveler's Key to Ancient Greece* (New York: Knopf, 1989), 237.
11. Gordon Wasson, Carl Ruck, and Albert Hofmann, *The Road to Eleusis* (New York: Harcourt Brace Jovanovich, 1978).
12. Clement of Alexandria, *Exhortation to the Greeks*, 2.21, in Karl Kerenyi, "Kore," in *Essays on a Science of Mythology*, translated by R. F. C. Hull (Princeton, NJ: Princeton University Press, 1973), 138.
13. In Katherine G. Kanta, *Eleusis*, translated by W. W. Phelps (Athens: Traveler's, 1979), 15.
14. Kanta, *Eleusis*, 16.
15. Hippolytus, *Elenchos*, V, 8, in Kerenyi, *Essays*, 143.
16. Kerenyi, *Eleusis*, 93.
17. Clement of Alexandria, in Kerenyi, *Essays*, 138.
18. Robert Graves, *The White Goddess* (New York: Farrar, Straus, and Giroux, 1966), 327.
19. Clement of Alexandria, *Exhortation to the Greeks*, 2.22, in *The Ancient Mysteries*, edited by Marvin Meyer (San Francisco: Harper & Row, 1987), 19.
20. George Mylonas, *Eleusis and the Eleusinian Mysteries* (Princeton, NJ: Princeton University Press, 1961), 284.
21. Samuel Angus, *The Mystery Religions and Christianity* (London: 1925), 140.
22. Roger and Jennifer Woolger, *The Goddess Within* (New York: Fawcett Columbine, 1989), 317.
23. Joseph Henderson and Maude Oakes, *The Wisdom of the Serpent* (New York: Collier Books, 1971), 4.

24. Michael Grant, *The Myths of the Greeks and Romans* (New York: Mentor Books, 1964), 136.

25. Gelhard, *The Traveler's Key to Ancient Greece,* 230.

26. Gelhard,

27. Kerenyi, *Eleusis,* 92–93.

28. Wasson, Ruck, and Hofmann, *The Road to Eleusis,* 107.

29. Kerenyi, *Essays,* 149.

30. Seneca, *Naturales Quaestiones,* VII, 31.

31. Kerenyi, *Essays,* 123.

32. Christine Downing, *The Goddess: Mythological Images of the Feminine* (New York: Crossroad, 1981), 39.

33. Marion Woodman, *Addiction to Perfection* (Toronto: Inner City Books, 1982), 148.

34. Carl G. Jung, "Psychological Aspects of the Kore," in *Essays on a Science of Mythology* (Princeton, NJ: Princeton University Press, 1973), 162.

35. *The Orphic Hymns,* translated by Apostoios Athanassakis, in Meyer, *The Ancient Mysteries,* 105.

Rites of Rebirth: The Initiation Mysteries of Demeter and Persephone

9

The Healing Power of the Lunar Darkness

✦

The underworld has gone into the unconscious: even become the unconscious. Depth psychology is where today we find the initiatory mysteries, the long journey of psychic learning, ancestor worship, the encounters with demons and shadows, and the sufferings of hell.
—James Hillman

The dark moon phase of cyclical process brings us from death to rebirth. It is a process of transformation that allows us to access a deep source of insight and psychic power. The ultimate purpose of the dark is to bring healing and renewal into our lives.

Our ancestors ritualized this passage through the dark corridors of renewal into the rites of their mystery religions. Encoded in myths and rituals, the ancient wisdom revealed the great mystery of transformation that affirmed the continued existence of renewed life after death. Individuals had the opportunity to participate in an experience that enabled them to encounter the secrets of death while they were still alive. The basic framework of the ritual included visiting the realm of the dead, communicating with the spirits, and returning to the world of the living with renewed hope for the future.

265

Our culture today is cut off from its roots in the mystery traditions of the Goddess. We have no myths or stories that speak to death and restore meaning and hope in a troubled world. James Hillman writes, "What is most dead and buried in each of us is the culture's neglect of death."[1] We have inherited a world that denies the possibility of new life after death; yet we are now living through a momentous dark moon time when our people and environment are dying from the accumulation of our own toxic wastes. As the implications of cancer, AIDS, heart disease, nuclear radiation, the ozone hole, food toxins, dying forests, and polluted waters are permeating mainstream awareness, we must increasingly confront our relationship to death.

Today the rate of change in our society is faster than ever before. People can no longer expect a predictable future and, in many cases, not even a safe or secure one. This lack of stability in individual lives and social structures is forcing people in every stratum of our existence through an accelerated process of change where they must face the death of the old. As a culture we have been conditioned to fear this great dark unknown and have little knowledge and few tools that teach us the mysteries of this rite of passage.

Because we do not understand the purpose of the dark phase and are ignorant of its terrain, we resist death and the letting go of some aspect of the past in order to embrace the new. We are filled with terror and panic when we consider the physical death of the body and planet, or the psychological death of a relationship, way of life, addiction, identity, or belief system. The stress of the dark times in our lives can make us dependent on chemical addictions or compel us to take desperate actions. People are searching for guidance as they struggle with their feelings of grief, depression, anxiety, anger, and madness in coping with their losses—both the immediate ones in the fabric of daily life, and the ultimate loss of a loved one or their own imminent death.

The Goddess has now emerged from the dark moon phase of a long-term lunar cycle at a time when humanity is collectively passing through a dark phase in the precessional age solar cycle. With the rebirth of the Goddess, we are being given the opportunity to reclaim her dark aspect. And the Dark Goddess of the Dark Moon holds the teachings that can lead us through the mysteries of death and renewal. Her recent awakening within the human psyche corresponds to research and new discoveries in the unconscious dimensions of the mind, as well as a resurgence of interest in death and dying.

Only within the last century have modern people in Western culture begun to explore the knowledge hidden in the depths of the mind. Sigmund Freud and Carl Jung helped to usher in the birth of a psychology that seeks to understand the workings of the unconscious. Today many psychotherapeutic techniques are constructing paradigms for nonordinary experiences of human consciousness. Current depth therapies such as rebirthing, Rolfing, holotropic breathwork, primal scream, bioenergetics, shamanic counseling, and dream analysis are enabling people to cross over the bridge into the workings and wisdom of the unconscious. These techniques are now being used to help people access their infantile, birth, and death experiences, to heal the wounds of their soul, and to travel into the subtle dimensions of other realms. Regression and hypnosis are assisting people in exploring their past lives and repressed traumatic memories.

The renewed presence of the Dark Goddess in our world is also evidenced by a proliferation of information on death and dying that is bringing much-needed guidance and compassion to help prepare individuals for the closure phase of their lives. Hospices, as centers of passage for the terminally ill, are emerging as important social institutions. This dark phase of the human life cycle is also being illumined by the many new books researching "life after death," and the spread of Eastern teachings on *karma,* the causes of suffering, and reincarnation.

For the ancients, rites of initiation were the techniques used to descend into the underworld, whereby a person could discover the great mystery of death and rebirth. However, the gods and goddesses of old, who initiated humanity into the transformation rites, have not deserted us. We have internalized their presence in our lives as the archetypal forces in our personalities who dwell in the hidden parts of the psyche. Modern people now experience this ancient rite of passage as the psychological descent into the unconscious, through which we can experience the alchemical transformation that gives birth to new psychological life.

Psychoanalysts have been making connections between these ancient rites and modern psychotherapy as they see the symbols of an ancient initiatory process repeatedly emerge in their patients' dreams and fantasies.[2] According to James Hillman, "The underworld has gone into the unconscious: even become the unconscious. Depth psychology is where today we find the initiatory mysteries, the long journey of psychic learning, ancestor worship, the encounter with demons and shadows, and the sufferings of Hell."[3]

As society is immersed in this dark moon phase, there exists a mass movement of individuals and society passing through many physical and psychological transformations. The descent into the underworld always begins with a death, either the physical death of the body or the psychological death of an aspect of ourselves. Because most of us no longer understand the role of death in cyclical process, and instead have come to believe that it represents a state of absolute finality, we fear our modern initiations of psychological transformation. We resist any kind of change that brings the loss of what we know as security, and we shirk from recalling any event that holds traumatic memories that crystallize us into negative, self-defeating patterns of behavior. And in our resistance to change, which is the very source of renewal, we stagnate and truly die.

In this transformative process, nothing new can be reborn until something old first dies. Thus whenever we cling to a person, place, thing, or situation that has outlived its purpose, we only prevent ourselves from experiencing the abundance of renewal. In the modern world the initiation rite that prepares us for our ultimate death is the path of willingly embracing change and psychological transformation. Over the course of our life it means experiencing many "little deaths" through the process of letting go. While letting go and change may seem frightening at first, it is the necessary part of the cycle that allows for renewal.

The purpose of the final sector of cyclical process is completion and renewal. Here is where a physical, emotional, or mental form that has fulfilled its function disintegrates back into the formless state of energy. The wisdom essence of that form's purpose is distilled and concentrated into a seed capsule that is placed in the dark underground, underworld, or unconscious, and awaits renewal with the initiation of the next cycle. The dark phase contains the accumulated content of the past, which composts into the soil that nourishes the seed of the future.

Let us now look more closely at the specific stages of transformation that we pass through during the dark moon phases of our cyclical processes, and examine them in greater detail. As we come to recognize the signposts in the map of our dark moon transformative process, we can more easily travel through the landscape of our renewal.

The Stages of Psychic Transformation

The three component parts of this process, which begins with the death of the old and ends with the birth of the new, are (1) disintegration, (2) purification, and (3) regeneration.

In the archetypal language of astrology, these three stages of transformation (breakup, dissolution, and renewal) correspond to the symbolism of the three outermost planets in the solar system: Uranus, Neptune, and Pluto. These planets have been called "ambassadors to the galaxy" because they bridge our personal world of finite form, represented by Saturn (Greek Kronos), Father of Time, and the transpersonal vibrations of the cosmos. They herald the destruction of old crystallized forms as they symbolically move us into the transformative process, a journey that can attune us to the collective forces of the universe.

Uranus, the Sky God, who sometimes appears in the shape of a lightning rod, corresponds to the sudden breakup and disintegration of the form. Neptune, the mythological God of the Oceans, represents the principle of dissolution and marks the stage of the transformative process when cleansing, purification, and healing occur. Finally Pluto, the God of the Underworld, associated with death and rebirth, mutates, regenerates, conceives, and gestates the new life to be.

The secret teaching of the dark moon is to let go, retreat, surrender, cleanse, heal, distill wisdom essence, mutate, aspire, and wait in the still silence for renewal. This model of transformation applies both to the many "little deaths" that occur in the physical and psychological losses during the course of our lifetime, and to the ultimate "big death" at the end of our lifetime.

Disintegration

Disintegration, the first stage of the transformative process, is marked by a cracking and shattering of the old form, which sometimes occurs suddenly and unexpectedly. This is a time when the major structures in our lives, such as our relationships, family, job, health, home, or belief systems, begin to break down and no longer function well or serve our sense of purpose. Some kind of truth about the reality of our situation is trying to break through our habitually conditioned mindset, and this overriding force acts to break up our situation.

We may experience this stage as the heartbreak resulting from the ending of a relationship that had gone as far as it could go within that particular form, and the subsequent loss of our partner through separation, betrayal, divorce, or death. Or it may be our family that begins to break up as our parents leave us through abandonment, illness, divorce, or death; or our children leave us through running away, estrangement, growing up, or moving away.

It can be our physical body that breaks down and causes a breakup in our sense of well-being and good health that allows us to pursue our life. The discovery, onset, or acute symptoms of life-threatening illnesses such as cancer, AIDS, heart disease, or Alzheimer's, or recovery from chemical addiction, can plunge us into the breakup of our world as we have known it.

Sometimes we lose or are forced to give up our job. There can be many reasons: incompetency, competition, insufficient salary, retirement, failure, or takeover of the business; an accident that interferes with our job performance; boredom; or the realization that the job has no future for us. Breakup of our home may be caused by natural disasters such as fire or flood, foreclosure, or the need to move away for personal or business reasons.

This breakup may also occur on the psychological level, where circumstances force us to reevaluate and turn away from a belief system, whether it be spiritual, religious, political, philosophical, or intellectual, that has guided our life and shaped our values. Or the realization that our childhood and past were not the way we thought them to be may shatter our cherished assumptions. The discovery of secrets, scandals, skeletons in the family closet such as incest, abuse, rape, alcoholism and other addictions, adoption, illegitimacy, nontraditional sexuality, and love affairs can suddenly destroy the false assumptions upon which we constructed our reality.

In each of these cases, this can be a time of sudden unexpected change in our lives, a time when we lose our relationship to another person, our family unit, our job, our physical well-being, our belief system, or our home. If it is our relationship that we have lost, our routines of daily living that were based on interacting with our partner fall apart. Our identity as a mate and often as a couple in social situations dissolves. Our economic security from the relationship is also likely to become threatened and unstable. The future looks bleak as we wonder how we are going to survive, both physically and emotionally.

The purpose of this first stage is to break up the old, and this occurs via the process of disintegration. To the extent that we are able to let go and release the old, our experience can be one of sudden liberation from the limitations of the past. However, when we do not fully understand the cyclical process of change leading to death and rebirth, we desperately try to hold on to what was and is no longer. This is a common reaction that leads to shock, a disruption that leaves us feeling shattered.

We have a sense of unreality as we move through each day. We can't believe that this is really happening to us. We may be overcome with panic and anxiety attacks because of our sudden precarious and insecure position. We don't know how we are going to be able to manage and carry on. We may alternate between a state of numb denial and hysterical instability. Frantically running to and fro, we may try to bargain and make a deal with our partner, our parent, our child, our boss, or our banker in the attempt to "save or salvage what we can" from the relationship, homestead, or whatever life structure is in jeopardy.

Outbursts of anger and rage about the unfairness of our situation are common and are often directed toward those who we think caused our difficulties, toward fate, or toward God. Mentally we feel disoriented, fragmented, unable to concentrate or make decisions. Physically we may feel nervous, anxious, jittery, or have difficulty sleeping and eating. Insomnia, indigestion, shaking, sweating, and heart palpitations are all physical symptoms that frequently occur during this stage.

From a Buddhist perspective the major cause of suffering is attachment to the permanency of anything. The Buddha taught that all things are by their very nature impermanent and subject to change. If we understand this, then when we experience the inevitable ending and loss, we are not surprised and it is not so painful to accept the reality of the way it is. On the other hand, the more we try to hold onto the old form and deny what is occurring, the greater the disruptive force we unconsciously create in order to break us free from our attachments. The lesson during this first Uranian stage is to let go and allow the disintegration process to proceed and occur.

Our experience does not have to be so shattering if we consciously accept the importance of giving up our old ways of thinking and being. The cracking of the form also occurs in the mental concepts that shape our view of reality. This cracking opens the doors, letting the old go out and allowing the new to come in. We can be freed from our preconceived ideas about how things should be so that we can see a larger view of how things could be.

As we loosen the reins holding our mind in check, we find ourselves immersed in a spaciousness where the terrain is open and unobstructed. We become open to ways of seeing ourselves and the world that never could have occurred to us before in our old mindsets. We can view the spectrum of possibilities that reside in a vast expanse of potentiality. Here we can receive sudden intuitive flashes of insight and make rapid nonlinear connections that allow us to glimpse the shape of truth.

We can facilitate this process by allowing our minds to wander, free-associate, consider this and that. We can take scenic detours in our travels that our tight schedules and itineraries did not previously allow. We watch our daydreams, relax our bodies and our minds, take it easy, cultivate a sense of what is natural and uncontrived. We don't grasp after stability and don't try to finalize or make permanent. We allow change, spontaneity, the unplanned to alter and influence our lives. We do things we have never tried before, such as meditating or attending a lecture or a football game.

The secret gift of the first stage of the transformation process is that of insight. In order to receive it, we must recognize the law of change, the nature of impermanence, and the vast unformed potentiality that is the raw material of creation.

While it is theoretically possible for some superconscious individuals to achieve liberation and instant transformation during the first stage, most of us struggle with our attachments. Then, gradually, we move into the second stage of the transformative process, where another kind of process, challenge, lesson, and gift is available to us.

Purification

The second stage of the transformative process calls us to surrender, purify, heal, and transcend the boundaries of finite form in order to merge with a larger whole. The onset of this stage may be marked by the panic settling into a state of despair and feelings of helplessness. We have a sense that our identity and security from the past are gone and there is nothing to replace them. At this point our ex-partner's clothing and belongings disappear from our home; or, if we are moving, it is a time when our unnecessary possessions are put into storage, sold, or given away. There is nothing stable, certain, or dependable that we can count upon for assurance.

The purpose of this second stage is to dissolve and wash away the remains of our past. To the extent that we are able to surrender to and accept what is, our experience can be one of transcendence and merging. In the first stage we are challenged to let go of our concepts; in this second stage our challenge is to purify our emotions and to release our pain. However, when we do not fully understand the process, we continue to hold on. And when we retain our old, no longer appropriate, emotional patterns, we also continue to hold on to the pain that these patterns have created. Our overriding experience becomes one of anguish and delusion.

Pain and emotional suffering become our reality. We often sink into a depression and our life is pervaded with sadness. We are not able to hold back the flood of tears that wracks our bodies. Some of us may be able to cry in the presence of others, while for others this release only occurs in the privacy of our loneliness. And there are those of us whose tears are silent, unvoiced, unshed in the hollow caverns of our despair.

We feel unconnected to others and increasingly lonely in our isolation. We may feel as if our neediness is greater than ever and that we are not receiving the love and support from others whom we feel should be there for us. In our victimization we take on the role of the sacrificial goat or the martyr. We may lose the companionship or try the patience of our friends, who become tired of hearing us complain about our misery, especially when we ignore or reject their advice; we may feel as if they are spurning us.

As we become lost in the darkness and confusion of non-knowing, we may feel melancholy, morbid, or pessimistic. There seems to be no hope, no vision, nothing that feels good. Mentally we are foggy, nothing is clear. Sometimes frightening, distorted shape-shifting images take over our mind by day, and similarly bizarre images may invade our dreams at night. We may become paranoid and develop a variety of phobias, feeling as if others are out to deceive or take advantage of us. We evade those who try to pin us down or get final decisions.

Physically we feel tired, weak, devoid of energy, and don't feel like moving or doing anything. We may feel zombie-like, sleepwalking through a dreamlike phantasmal existence. We may sleep a lot; there does not seem to be any good reason for getting up. The emptiness of outer life mirrors the confusion of our inner mind. In order to avoid the reality of our increasingly meaningless or painful existence, many of us are tempted to find solace in the numbing qualities

Rites of Rebirth: The Healing Power of the Lunar Goddess

of addictive substances—alcohol, drugs, sex, food, television. Self-defeated, we spiral into self-destructive activities.

The reason we experience the isolation, exhaustion, pain, and delusion during the second stage of the transformative process is that the guidance of this stage is to heal our emotions through retreat, rest, purification, and opening our hearts to others. In the lunation cycle, when the waning crescent dissolves into blackness, the movement of the lunar energy is withdrawal from the outer world of manifest activities. In the same way, we can voluntarily welcome this opportunity for retreat and rest as the work of healing optimally occurs in the darkness in the same way our bodies regenerate each night while we sleep. We must acknowledge our need for sleep and rest and not allow our own or others' expectations to pressure us to decide, act, perform, achieve, and accomplish.

Ideally this is a time to allow the waters of dissolution to cleanse and wash away the past, both physically and emotionally. We can purify our bodies with cleansing diets and fasts, drinking large amounts of water, taking saunas and mineral baths. We can cleanse our living environments by giving things away, especially those items that stimulate our memories and attachments that we are trying to release. On the mental level, we need to give up our hope that we can go back to what was and to give up our despair about the future.

And emotionally we need to understand how it is that our feelings of anger, hatred, pride, excessive desire, greed, jealousy, and envy continue to perpetuate our pain. When we are taken over by these negative emotional states, biochemical toxins are created in our bodies that contribute to our confused and deluded states of mind.

It is a time to grieve and to cry. Tears are the waters of the body that wash away our emotional pain, its toxic residues. In our grief we may begin to identify not only with our own suffering, but become sympathetic to the suffering of others who have also gone through these losses. We realize that we are not alone in our experience; that this is the universal condition and we all share and suffer in it together. As we begin to open our hearts to others and reach out with kindness and sympathy to touch their pain, which is not unlike or other than our own, we begin to effect a healing within ourselves. By extending ourselves and helping others in a variety of ways, such as befriending someone in need, offering donations of time or money to worthy causes, community service, or joining volunteer or support groups, we can accelerate the healing that wants to occur during this stage.

275

Rites of Rebirth:
The Healing
Power of
the Lunar
Goddess

Our pain greatly expands the boundaries of what we thought we could bear, and in this extension of our sensory perception we become open and receptive to the larger and more subtle forces of the universe. During this stage there exists the possibility of religious or transcendent experience, the development of psychic sensitivity, and the capacity for empathy to feelings of others. Dreams and visions can become sources of wisdom, inspiration, and creativity.

The secret gift of the second stage of transformation symbolized by the Sea God Neptune is that of compassion (a broken heart is an open heart). In order to receive it we must recognize that we can dissolve the artificial boundaries that perpetuate our sense of separateness and heal our fear of isolation by entering into the awareness of the interconnectedness of all that exists.

In retreat, through rest, purification, and opening our heart, we can gradually begin to heal. We can surrender to the reality of what is, accept the inevitability of our loss, and possibly even the idea that this may have been a necessary and ultimately beneficial loss. These realizations prepare us for the work of the third stage. However, if our fears and delusions have prevented us from integrating this process, and we are still not able to let go of our old negative emotional patterns, another set of difficulties will arise in the third stage that force us, often in violent ways, to confront our resistance.

Once we have accepted the death of the old, there comes a certain incipient point when we begin to wonder, "Well, what now? What next?" While we are still not yet prepared to act or move forward, the simple germination of ideas about the future, conceived in an entirely new way, is the gateway into the third stage of transformation.

Regeneration

The third stage of the transformative process calls us to regenerate and renew. To the extent that we do not understand the necessity of imagining and preparing for something new during the third stage, our experience will be one of rage and self-destruction. Here we encounter power in its awesome proportions, which we can use both to destroy and create.

The mythological god associated with this stage is Pluto, husband to Persephone, who rules the underworld. During this stage we make the descent into our unconscious, where the rejected and denied parts of ourselves reside. It is these contents, called the "shadow" in Jungian psychology, that take on the forms of the demons who seem to take possession of us and incite us to create a reality that is terrifying and destructive. Our shadow has a reservoir of tightly coiled, focused, and concentrated energy at its disposal, which can be used either to harm others or transform ourselves. This god penetrates to our core in order to reveal our deepest root issues; he destroys in order to renew, and he holds the power to transform and effect change. But if we do not know how to rebuild, we can get caught up in senseless destruction and the abuse of power that is an ignorant use of this most potent energy.

In the movement to penetrate our essence, we may feel as if we are being stripped bare. All of the false masks of our socially conditioned personality are being ripped away and we feel raw, exposed, vulnerable, and unprotected. In our fury for survival we lash out at those whom we perceive to be our enemies or responsible for our loss and suffering. In our rage we use our power to harm, threaten, ruin, intimidate, or dominate others—blaming anyone but ourselves for our predicament. As we try to control others, we are out of control ourselves as we beat our mate, child, pet, wreck the car, or smash the furniture.

If we deny the power at our disposal, we may become victims of power assaults by others—raped, beaten, violated, abused. Or if we repress the unleashing of this plutonian power and instead direct it inward, we may attempt to destroy ourselves. Feelings of shame and worthlessness spur us onward to hit rock bottom in our self-destructive and addictive patterns. It is not uncommon during this time to have fantasies of suicide or to conceive of other drastic measures to end it all. And if we project this negatively charged energy, we see the forces of evil everywhere around us waiting to pounce and annihilate us the moment we let up our guard.

Our more enlightened option is to use this plutonian power to transform ourselves by destroying the last vestiges of our old attachments, which hold us back from renewal. The challenge of the third stage is to recognize our enemies as the rejected parts of ourselves, and then to transform them into our guardians by accepting them into the wholeness of our being. Any kind of depth therapy, hypnosis, past-life regression that enables us to penetrate into the images and patterns held in our unconscious and to make peace with our demons—who are none other than ourselves—is most helpful. As this last and deepest level of letting go and transforming is enacted, we are then ready for the rebuilding work of the third stage.

What is called for during this stage is the creation of the seed capsule for the future that will germinate with the beginning of the next new moon phase. Into this seed capsule are placed three things: (1) the distillation of our wisdom essence from the past cycle; (2) our unfinished *karma* and unconscious habits; and (3) our commitments for the future cycle. By the time this stage draws to a close, we should have developed a vision that includes a sense of our purpose in the larger scheme of things, a mission to fulfill, and the willingness to act upon our vision.

After we have let go and eliminated the remnants of whatever life structure is being transformed, there often remains a kernel of meaning and value. During this stage we may find ourselves taking an inventory of our past in the attempt to extract any meaning we have gleaned and anything of value that still remains and which can be utilized in the next cycle. Through reflection and analysis we try to make sense of what happened, of what the purpose was in the past cycle, and what lessons we learned. What information did we gain about ourselves, how do we relate to the world, what truths did we realize, and where do we continue to deceive ourselves and others? We take stock of our strengths, skills, knowledge, and talents that remain part of our essential self, and we recognize how we can continue to use and adapt these inner resources for what lies ahead.

It is this combination of wisdom and skills that remains as a purified residual essence. We can carry this combination over from the past to create the fertile soil in which the future can be conceived. This is the container of our seed capsule that will nourish and sustain the new life during the gestation period preceding birth.

For each person there exist various levels at which the transformative process is operative and effective. For many of us the process does not penetrate and effect change at the deepest levels of the unconscious. Therefore, along with our wisdom essence, we also place a large amount of unconscious material into the seed capsule. This unconscious material consists of the unresolved *karma*—issues that we did not work out in the past and which must be carried over. We also add our conditioned and deeply ingrained habit patterns, as well as our genetic, cultural, and archetypal predispositions. The degree to which we have had some kind of awareness of our unconscious motivations and habitual responses is the extent to which we are aware of these contents.

The final element we infuse into our seed capsule is our aspirations, intentions, and commitments for the future. This is a time for getting in touch with our dreams, yearnings, longings, to think of what we might have wanted for ourselves in the past but were prevented from having by the circumstances of our lives. Perhaps we wanted to complete our education but had children early, or we wanted to travel but our partner wasn't interested. It might have been that we wanted our own business but were frightened of risk and needed to provide financial security for our family; or that we wanted to become an artist or musician but didn't have enough confidence in our talent and thought it unpractical. We should now consider that because these old limitations no longer exist it is now possible for us to follow our old dreams and to create new ones.

A helpful exercise at this point is to imagine what we'd like to do if the possibilities were wide open and if there were no obstacles whatsoever—money, education, training, degree, age, health, or fear of sex. It may not be feasible for us to actualize our ideal images, but it is important to have a glimmer into the farthest outreaches of our potentialities.

From here we can begin to make plans about what might be actually possible for us to create. It is still not the time to actualize the dream, but it is appropriate to make inquiries—write or call for information, research, find out when programs of study begin or when travel tours leave and how much they cost, what financial aid might be available, what are the necessary qualifications, does the type of job exist where I live, do I have to move?

Now is the time to consider our intentions—what we want to do for ourselves and why. What we want to do for the benefit of others whom we know now, from the past, or those yet to come into our lives; what we want to do for the planet and why. At this stage we make the promises before the birth of the new concerning the commitments we want to fulfill in future cycles.

In our seed we have fused the essence of the past and the intention for the future. At this point in the plutonian stage, our nascent consciousness waits with the desire to be reborn. On a literal level the coming together of our mother and father to be in sexual union provides a link for the seed to enter into the mother's womb, the cauldron of rebirth. The dream in the seed capsule incubates in the embryonic state. In the developing fetal stage of our physical or psychological gestation, the blueprint of wisdom essence, *karma* and unconscious habits, and future intentions is imprinted into the psychic channels and neurological circuits that web the unconscious dimensions of the psyche.

At a time when the planetary energies come into alignment with the soul's new purpose, labor announces the onset of the soul's journey through the birth canal. We inhale our first breath, enter into the world of form, and the new life is birth at the initiation of the new moon phase of the cyclical process. The cycle comes full circle.

In our attempt to revision the dark, this discussion of the stages of transformation that occur during the dark stage of cyclical process offer a model of how we can move through the dark times in our lives with understanding, consciousness, and faith in renewal. It allows us to maximize the potentiality for meaning, healing, and creativity that naturally reside in the dark phase.

The Dark Moon and Healing the Soul

The dark phase of cyclical process is the womb of the soul. It spans the juncture between the world of the living and that of the dead and unborn. We enter the dark phase through death and leave it through rebirth. On the level of psychological transformation, we enter the dark through the death of an old and no longer necessary part of ourselves or of our lives, and we leave it as we begin to embrace a new regenerated identity or purpose.

These experiences of the dark phase on both the physical and psychological level occur during the absence of the moon's light. As we pass through this phase of cyclical process, we travel across a terrain of our psyche that is normally hidden from our conscious awareness and one which we cannot comprehend with our conscious mind. The dark sphere of the human psyche contains all that lies beneath the surface of consciousness. As the home of the soul, the dark phase is the place where we hold the residual memories of the sum total of our past, in this and previous lifetimes. Here we find the wounds of the soul that are crying out to be healed. In the underworld of the psyche we meet the ghosts of our past and encounter visions of both heaven and hell.

In the dark closure sector of cyclical process, all returns back to the source and merges with the larger whole. The energies of the dark phase magnetically draw us down and under into the undifferentiated waters of the vast cosmic ocean of unity. This immersion in the awareness of our oneness with all life is later felt, when we are in physical incarnation, as the mystical yearning for that connectedness that might heal the pain of separation and isolation in our life. Both spiritual quests and chemical or relationship addictions are paths modern individuals follow in their longing for the peace and serenity of that dimly remembered other world.

In this space between worlds and time between incarnations, the dark phase provides an opening into the underworld of our unconscious, where we can access the entire universe of past, present, and future flowing into our psyche. It is the repository of hidden wisdom and secret teachings embodied in universal, mythic, and archetypal images. Buddhist tradition teaches that in this intermediate state, called the *Bardo,* we encounter the peaceful and wrathful deities. Dane Rudhyar writes that this is where we meet both the Angels of Light and the Guardians of the Threshold.[4]

In this deep recess of our psyche, our angels can guide us to our source of transcendent understanding, creative inspiration, and the highest aspirations of selfless love and service. Intertwined with the angels are our demons, whose faces mirror all of our failures, frustrations, denials, fears, anger, greed, jealousy, hatred, and ignorance. The roots of our angels and demons reach back into both the joys and the pain of the past, and their branches extend out toward the possibilities of our future.

It is through the dark phase that each of us is linked to the past and future. It is a metaphor for the unseen real of all that happens before we can remember. The dark dimension, which lies hidden beneath the surface of conscious awareness, holds the storehouse of forgotten memories from the past and the potentialities of future possibilities. The sum total of our personal and collective past, both successes and failures, is recorded in the many layers of the unconscious —from the forgotten images of personal experiences from this lifetime, infancy, the cycle of our death, conception, gestation, and birth, past lives, and then deeper into the transpersonal stratum of the collective unconscious.

While this psychic material is not normally accessible to the conscious mind, it nevertheless has a powerful effect on how we perceive and interact with the world. The source of the hidden forces that, unknown to our rational mind, dominate our actions and shape our life circumstances lie in the underworld of the psyche. This is the soil from which our conscious experiences and circumstances are formed and nourished.

Western psychology refers to this dimension of the mind as the unconscious, which holds our repressed traumatic memories and

281

*Rites of Rebirth:
The Healing
Power of
the Lunar
Goddess*

rejected aspects of our selves. Eastern philosophy describes it in terms of *karma* and reincarnation. Both traditions propose that the events that have transpired in our now forgotten past, where we have harmed or been harmed by another, are the seeds for the long-lasting wounds in our souls that need to be healed. Whether this force is called *karma* or unconscious motivations, both Eastern and Western thought agree to the existence of a pattern running through the unconscious that weaves the ancient threads of our future.

Our passage through the dark offers us the opportunity to heal these wounds, and in the process we can discover the hidden wealth of the unconscious. It is only by going into the dark time of inner space and coming to peace with our memories and resolving our issues that a way opens toward healing. In the process we can discover the wealth of the underworld of the psyche, renewal, inspired creativity, and merging with the soul of the cosmos.

The Dark Moon Phase and Karma

The wounds of our soul arise from the unconscious material we carry over from the past. The Eastern perspective explains this process in terms of *karma* and reincarnation. These concepts form the basis of a supposition that moral laws operate in the sphere of consciousness. Eastern philosophers have used this view to explain how unconscious forces from the past affect the present and the future. A Buddhist adage teaches, "If you want to know who you were in your past life, look to your present circumstances. If you want to know who you will be in your future life, look to your present actions."

Karma and reincarnation teach that we reap the results of our prior actions from this or previous lifetimes, both positive and negative; and, by our response, we sow the seeds of future circumstances. According to this view the loss and suffering that we encounter when we are passing through our dark moon phases may not be solely the product of this lifetime; they may be the fruition of harmful actions toward others, unfinished lessons, and unresolved relationships that we carry over from the past. What is seen by the conscious eye in this temporal reality is but the tip of an iceberg whose antecedent causes extend deep into the past. When we consider our unconscious past in this light, we can gain clarity and compassion in understanding the causes of the suffering, loss, pain, and seemingly unfair burdens that arise during our dark moon times of transition. It should also be mentioned that due to positive action in the past, we reap the harvest of abundance and prosperity in our lives.

The transformative process that occurs during our dark moon phases offers us the opportunity to fulfill our karmic moral obligations, voluntarily assume our outstanding debts, and thus bring unresolved issues from the past to a state of balance and completion. The dark phase energies can sustain us by offering vast hidden resources of strength and wisdom to fulfill our purpose. However, when what we feel is the pervasive pain of our wounds, the karmic teaching of the dark is that our soul will not heal until we realize the necessity of transforming the attitudes and actions that have created these results. As we become aware of the workings of the law of cause and effect, our *karma* seems to accelerate and the results ripen more quickly. We can rapidly burn through much old *karma* as we willingly seek to make the necessary amends and consciously change our behavior from harmful to beneficial activity.

This is the karmic lesson that offers us a gift of healing during the dark night of the soul. Biblical scripture sums up the law of *karma* in the following three verses: "As ye sow, so shall ye reap" (Gal. 6:7). "An eye for an eye, and a tooth for a tooth" (Exod. 21:24). "Do unto others as you would have others do unto you" (Matt. 7:12).

To the extent that our level of awareness operates in a dualistic world where we perceive reality as polarized into a separation between object and subject or self and other, we are bound by the karmic law of cause and effect. The dark, as a symbol of the closure phase of cyclical process, is where all merges back to source. It contains the possibility of the direct experience of "oneness," which has been referred to as the Law of Grace, Christ Consciousness, and Buddha Mind. The Law of Grace transcends the Law of *Karma* when the distinction between self and other dissolves into a more inclusive awareness of the fundamental unity of all life.

In the East the term *bodhisattva* describes the being who has achieved enlightenment through having fulfilled and completed his or her *karma*. However, rather than remaining in the clear light, this person chooses to continue incarnating in this dualistic dimension for the purpose of benefiting others. The *bodhisattva's* life is motivated by the desire to relieve suffering and guide others toward healing and liberation.

Our dark phase energies can point to our commitments to emulate the *bodhisattva* ideal. On the level where the Law of Grace, or oneness, is operative, the burdens of pain and suffering are not karmic retribution but rather the additional responsibilities we have voluntarily taken on in order to help others. The pattern that often unfolds is that of the wounded healer. In the early part of life we experience some great pain, loss, or denial, which is actually the training ground for deepening our capacity for empathy and sensitivity. In later life, from the power and wisdom of our own experience, we operate in a helping and healing capacity for others in similar situations.

From this perspective the dark phase energies may also indicate the difficulties we encounter when we function as the release valve for purifying the *karma* and toxic accumulation—not only for ourselves but for the family or group that we are a part of. In dysfunctional families the most open and vulnerable member will usually serve in this capacity; and in society the scapegoat assumes the role of the martyr. Dark phase factors may indicate the commitments we take on to resolve a collective or archetypal problem, and the healing of an individual will have a rippling cumulative effect throughout the group. This can also point to living a symbolic life where what we live out are not personal, but collective issues.

When *karma* and reincarnation are linked with the concepts of evolution and progression, they become the means by which consciousness comes into self-realization.[5] *Karma* is the principle by which we shape our personality and reality according to our choices and actions. Moving through eons of time, reincarnation offers us many lifetimes and varied experiences through which to understand, practice, and perfect the act of creation. Our unconscious karmic patterns that are seeking resolution and completion in this lifetime are contained within the dark phase of our transformative process.

The Eastern path teaches that the goal of enlightenment is liberation from illusion of duality, which precipitates rebirth and the endless suffering of human condition. Western occult traditions speak to developing total awareness of being a unit of consciousness within the larger mind and living in harmony with the earth and all living things. This is the inner meaning of the dark phase experience as sacrifice, selfless service, spiritual practice, and enlightenment.

The Dark Moon and the Psychological Unconscious

As we have seen, in Western psychology the dark dimension of human consciousness corresponds to the unconscious. The unconscious is defined as that area of our psyche that contains latent, forgotten, and irretrievable thoughts, images, and impressions. It is the source of those patterns, urges, motivations, compulsions, and drives in our life that operate from below the surface of conscious awareness. Although we are not consciously aware of the workings of these hidden forces, they exert a powerful influence in affecting our choices, actions, and attitudes in life. When we pass through the dark moon phase of psychological transformation, we descend into these unconscious realms of our psyche. Continued exploration into the unconscious is revealing the existence of many layers of the past in this dimension of the mind.

It was less than one hundred years ago that Sigmund Freud first pioneered the exploration of the unconscious background of consciousness. He postulated the existence of a vast portion of the mind, the subconscious, that includes not only instinctual desires but personal experiences going as far back as infancy that were frightening, painful, or unacceptable and have been long since repressed and forgotten. In his practice Freud found that the symptoms of hysterical patients could be directly traced to these apparently forgotten psychic traumas in early life, and that they represented undischarged emotional energy. These neurotic behavior patterns could be neutralized if the person could be made to clearly recall these painful experiences, which had caused a deep impression or emotional shock, and thereby release the blocked energy.

Carl Jung later elaborated upon his mentor's work, and his greatest contribution to psychology was his theory of the collective unconscious. He proposed that there are two dimensions to the unconscious—a personal layer that Freud discovered, consisting of an individual's own biographical repressed material; and a second layer called the collective unconscious, whose contents have never been conscious and are not acquired from a person's own memories and experiences. These inherited propensities in the human psyche extend back beyond the pre-infantile period into the residues of ancestral life. Jung gave the name "archetypes" to these primordial images in the collective unconscious, which are the most ancient and universal thought forms of humanity. This second system in the unconscious contains the preexistent thought forms in the psyche that are universal: impersonal mental and emotional patterns that are identical in all people throughout time, and which recur cross-culturally in humanity as themes in mythology, religion, and fairy tales.

The collective unconscious does not only contain the repository of ancestral memories from the past; it is also the storehouse of latent potentialities and dreams of the yet-to-be future of the conscious mind. Completely new thoughts and creative ideas that have never been conscious before can present themselves from the unconscious.

This forms an important part of our subliminal psyche, where germinal ideas for the future can arise from the dark depths of the mind. The collective unconscious can be conceived of as a treasure house that is the source of all inspiration, creativity, and wisdom.

Rites of Rebirth: The Healing Power of the Lunar Goddess

In addition to the personal and collective layers of the unconscious, contemporary psychologists who are extending the map of the psyche are now suggesting that there exists a third layer, the perinatal.[6] The perinatal layer is the interface between the personal and transpersonal (collective) dimensions of the unconscious, and it consists of the experiences we encounter in our birth and death transitions. Observations show that many forms of psychopathology and unconscious motivations have deep roots in the biological aspects of birth and death that also parallel the processes of spiritual rebirth.

Psychiatrist Stanislav Grof, active in the transpersonal psychology movement, proposes the existence of an organizing principle of the psyche that he terms a "COEX system," or systems of condensed experience. A COEX system is a dynamic constellation of memories from different periods of an individual's life, from biological birth, and certain areas of the transpersonal realm such as past incarnations, animal identification, and mythological sequences, whose common denominator is a strong emotional charge of the same quality. It represents one or two major issues or complexes of a person's life that are inherited from the unconscious past. Most COEX systems are dynamically connected with specific facets of the birth process. When our perinatal transitions are encoded with difficult experiences, they emerge later in life as the forms of our dis-eases. The inner healer in each individual, who is always moving toward a state of wholeness, will attract or recreate situations in life that carry a similar emotional charge.[7] This process gives us the opportunity to reconfront, release, and heal the painful unconscious issues arising from our birth/death experiences that shape our lives.

Our unconscious past encompasses this vast, multidimensional realm hidden within our psyche, where the powerful, compulsive forces arise that cause confusion and pain in our life. These are the wounds in our soul. Because these forces are not easily seen, they become our hidden enemies who are the source of our self-undoing. In reality these secret enemies, who would subversively seek to deceive, hurt, or destroy us, are the concealed aspects of ourselves.

The dark realms of our psyche contain all that happened to us in a time before we can remember, in our personal biographical past both in this and previous lifetimes, as well as our collective archetypal past. Many of these events are the causal factors of our compulsions, which make us act in ways we don't understand and eventually result in harm to ourselves or others. They are rooted in our unconscious habit patterns, deeply ingrained beliefs, karmic accumulations, and forgotten traumas. Certain issues may become lifelong themes that manifest as repeated cycles of physical and emotional trauma with subsequent suffering.

Western psychology proposes that the unconscious motivations that propel us toward self-destructive behavior come from repressed energies of forgotten traumas and absorbed impressions that we have not been able to assimilate and integrate. Our defense system tends to repress the memories associated with powerful experiences involving fear, failure, pain, loss, or danger. When we cannot acknowledge or release the residual feelings that accompany these traumatic experiences, they become locked into the unconscious webbing of our psyche. Here, contained under pressure and confinement, they fester and pollute our system. These poisonous contents of our psyche distort our perception and color our view of what life is all about. The blocked, emotionally charged energies are the source of the seemingly irrational fears, phobias, compulsions, guilt, and shame that plague us, and also are the basis of the psychosomatic symptoms of disease in our physical body. Healing requires that we recall, understand, and release the charged feeling associated with the trauma.

However, our conscious mind resists uncovering these lurking, dark images because the realizations might be more than we could handle and would overwhelm and shatter us. Herein lies our conditioned fear of the dark. Much of our life energy is used to hold back these threatening and potentially destructive forces. The more the conscious mind shuts off, the more our self-image develops apart from the wholeness of our being.

It is our denial and inability to cope with these hidden and forgotten parts of ourselves that give rise to the Jungian concept of the shadow. The shadow is the enemy within us who pushes us to self-destructive behavior. When we project our shadow it becomes the outer enemy who seeks to harm and destroy us. The demonic nature of the shadow takes the form of our negative thought patterns that are caused by repression. These mental patterns distort our perception of reality, and they serve to falsify our relationships with others, which creates conflict, confusion, and mistrust in our life experiences. And the shadow is the messenger from the unconscious.

Through its activity we come to know the nature of the pain of our hidden self.

Healing in the dark demands that we recover the rejected and lost parts of ourselves and integrate them into the wholeness of our being. From a spiritual perspective the energy of these destructive emotions needs to be rooted out and purified. It can then be transmuted into the corresponding wisdom qualities that are the enlightened use of the very same energies.[8]

Healing the Soul

Healing the soul is one of the core issues of the dark moon phase times in our lives. The dark sphere is the place that holds the deep wounds in the psyche. Both Western psychology and Eastern philosophy are concerned with the processes in our unconscious past that yield the painful conditions of the present. The healing of a person's psychic wounds is the task of Jungian psychology, and the relief from suffering is the aim of Eastern enlightenment. Both streams seek to heal the wound of the soul and effect a spiritual transformation toward self-realization and enlightened awareness.

Jung's process moves toward actualizing individual wholeness by establishing a network of communication between the conscious and unconscious, and integrating and harmonizing these components of our being. With self-realization comes the awareness of an ethical responsibility in that we can no longer conduct our life as though unaware of the hidden workings of our unconscious.[9] Buddhist practice reaches toward enlightened awareness of our true nature, for the sake of all beings. The causes of our suffering are known to be the illusion of separateness and subsequent results of our prior self-cherishing attitudes and actions. This realization precipitates a shift in our behavior and conduct.

Wounding comes from separation from the unity of source. As we descend into the underworld of our consciousness, we encounter our angels and demons, the deep wounds in our psyche, and the cures for healing the soul. It is the place where we are the most painfully alone until we realize our connectedness with a larger whole. Healing entails moving toward a state of wholeness within oneself and with the rest of life.

Healing takes place in the dark, when the final phase of cyclical process does its work of completion and renewal. The wounded wild animal instinctively withdraws into the silent stillness of the dark, empty cave in order to heal itself; the psyche also requires that we go down and under into the depths of the unconscious in order to heal the soul. Here we can uncover the hidden causes of the wounds in our psyche, and align ourselves with the closure phase energies of release and transformation to effect a healing.

As we journey between worlds, from the dimension of conscious manifest reality to the unconscious phenomenal realm, we must alter our perception to enter the tunnel leading to the underworld of psyche. Our dark moon phase periods are excellent times to be involved in any kind of inner work, where we can explore the hidden dimensions of our being. There exist many different methods to access the unconscious, which span the psychological, spiritual, artistic, and pharmaceutical disciplines. When we encounter the contents of the unconscious, it is important to have the proper safeguards and precautions; otherwise this process can overwhelm the conscious mind and cause its collapse. Different people according to their precondition will choose or be chosen by a more or less structured and supervised path.

The spiritual path includes retreat, meditation, prayer, ritual, trance, vision quest, chant, shamanic healing, yoga, breathwork, spirit guides, and initiation. Participation in these activities can lead to great spiritual accomplishment during this time. If we are psychologically oriented, we can make much progress in reclaiming the Self during the dark times of psychological transformation. These modalities encompass methods such as psychotherapy, guided imagery, dreamwork, hypnosis, regression, holotropic breathwork, rebirthing, primal scream, Rolfing, and bioenergetics. Many individuals are releasing the pain of the past and overcoming their addictions and unconscious compulsions through the Twelve-Step recovery programs and other counseling techniques found in the many support groups operative at this time. These include organizations such as Alcoholics Anonymous, NarcAnon, Overeaters Anonymous, codependency groups, as well as groups for love addicts, gamblers, adult children of dysfunctional families, and survivors of rape, incest, and abuse.

The artistic-creative process can help us access our unconscious, and archetypal and mythological motifs run through many forms of art therapy, painting, drama, sculpture, music, ecstatic dance, poetry, and inspired writing. Mind-altering substances, such as psychedelic drugs, herbs, and mushrooms, can induce nonordinary states of consciousness leading to visionary and cathartic experiences.

The essential process found in many of these paths of healing is one of recognition, release, purification, transformation, and commitment. The first step is to recognize that there is a wound and to admit to the existence of pain and confusion in our life. Our unconscious mind resists acknowledging that which threatens to overwhelm us, and many behavior patterns of avoidance are manifestations of this denial. In fact drug, alcohol, and other chemical addictions are one coping mechanism to numb painful memories and their corresponding bad feelings, and to create the illusion of well-being.

The feelings of these rejected memories are locked into the circuitry of our emotional and physical bodies. The second phase involves recalling these painful experiences and releasing the emotional charge of the blocked energy. The third phase is purifying the toxic accumulation from the festering repressed energies. Cleansing the psychic system will clarify our perceptions of reality and the causal effect of our actions.

As we come to know the faces of our hidden tendencies and accept these components of our being as within us rather than external to us, we come to the next phase of healing: transmuting the negative energies into their positive nature. Buddhist teachings hold that there exist five basic groups of negative emotional energies: (1) ignorance/stupidity; (2) attachment, which gives rise to desire and greed; (3) aversion, which creates hatred, anger, and aggression; (4) pride, the cause of arrogance; and (5) envy, which results in jealousy. When the energy of the emotion is purified and transmuted, it expresses as a particular "wisdom" or aspect of the awakened state of mind. For example, the energy within us that manifests negatively as anger, when transformed becomes mirrorlike wisdom whose essence is clarity, luminosity, and seeing things as they are.[10]

As we heal we approach a state of wholeness within ourselves, and that awareness precipitates a realization of our connectedness with all of life. The transcendent function of the dark phase process is activated when we begin to consider others as not separate from ourselves, and act accordingly. At this point we begin to utilize the very same energy that was previously blocked and distorted, resulting in unconscious actions that were detrimental and painful to ourselves and others, in such a way that we no longer harm ourselves or others and may actively help them.

Ultimately the way to deal with problematical wounds of the soul is from an altruistic point of view. The dark phase energies are not to be used solely for personal ends. In helping others, we heal ourselves. In our psychological transformations, we may make the commitments to heal certain aspects of ourselves through selfless love and service to others. In calling upon the dark moon energies, we can develop a sensitivity toward people in need and extend empathy and compassion to those who are suffering. We can tap into a reservoir of strength to carry others' burdens, to care for the ill, or to involve ourselves in volunteer work, community service, and charitable activities.

Here we must remain aware of the fine line between selfless love and service as a path of healing, and compulsive caregiving and codependency. It is important that we not become professional rescuers and saviors who constantly need to manifest victims to save. If our giving to others is motivated by expectations of love, security, acceptance, or return, or if our caretaking is oriented to making ourselves indispensable by fostering another's dependency on us, we become trapped in self-defeating patterns of relating. Nevertheless, by utilizing the dark phase energies to develop an expanded perception of the wholeness of all life, we discover the source of our hidden strengths and talents.

The dark moon is the veil behind which we enter into the realm of the unseen real, and it shows the path to penetrating the deep recesses of our mind to uncover secret wisdom. The treasure house of all inspired creativity and wisdom is open to us during the dark moon phase times in our lives. It is the gateway into the collective unconscious, where we can access universal knowledge and become the mediators and transmitters of eternal themes. The archetypal symbols in this realm can speak to us directly in a language that has meaning for all people in all time.

We can apprehend the secret wisdom of the past and future inwardly, through the power of our imagination, visions, dreams, and fantasies; and outwardly, through the mythological motifs that appear in religious rites, artistic symbols, and fairy tales. Joseph Campbell says that myths are the representations of the unconscious energies within us and give clues to the spiritual meaning of life. All the gods and goddesses reside within us as the wisdom beings, spirit guides, and inner teachers who lead us to this rich vein of psychic material in our unconscious, which gives rise to our knowing truth and beauty.

The experiences we encounter in the dark realm of consciousness provide us with the opportunities to connect with sources of metaphysical knowledge and spiritual beliefs. In this place, where all merges back into source, the faith and knowing that arise from direct experience in the subtle realms transcend intellectual concepts and rational logic. This is the temple of the secret teachings where through ritual, prayer, and meditation we can align ourselves with cosmic or divine energies and channel inspired creations. In this subtle realm we are receptive to higher states of consciousness and can activate our psychic and telepathic abilities. It is the source of our inner power that we draw upon in crises.

The dark phase, above all, is the domain of the Mysteries. Keeper of Initiation, this sector reveals the descent into the underworld, where we encounter the reality of the nonphysical dimension and experience the secrets of death and rebirth, renewal and regeneration. In this world of spirit reside the memories of the past and dreams of the future. These gifts of spirit from the angelic worlds are our secret resources and talents that constitute the hidden wealth of the underworld.

Although we may have the assistance of a spiritual teacher, psychological counselor, or spirit guide, our journey into the dark is essentially one that we must make by ourselves. Our relationship with the dark mirrors our relationship with ourselves when we are alone. The dark calls us to withdraw from the outer world and retreat to our inner spaces. It addresses our need for privacy and seclusion, where we can engage upon the work of healing.

For some of us the dark moments of our solitude speak to a rich inner life of contemplation, introspection, spiritual practice, and artistic self-expression. Here we can connect with the hidden gifts of our unconscious. We are comfortable with being alone and are not lonely. It is a centering and creative experience whereby we can recharge our energy, tap our inner wisdom, and heal ourselves.

However, for others of us, the experience of being alone brings up feelings of alienation. Our overriding emotional reaction is one of being cut off from others, and we feel abandoned, unloved, and unwanted. We panic, are anxious, frightened, and desperate when we are by ourselves or have empty time in our lives with nothing to fill it up.

Still others of us use the dark phase energies of withdrawal to create a shell of protection around us that conceals our hidden activities or shameful secrets. We shun public exposure, remain aloof, and act evasive. We become obsessed with preventing others from discovering our deceptions, clandestine relationships, love affairs, physical dysfunctions, addictions, and family problems.

In the process of reclaiming the dark, we must heal our relationship to the hidden parts of our waking lives when we are alone. When our experience of aloneness reinforces our sense of isolation and exclusion, or when we pull into ourselves to conceal our wrongdoing and shame, we are not able to use the energies of the dark moon phase in positive and self-affirming ways.

As we revision the dark, we will come to know the dark time as a healing time when we can transform, renew, and empower ourselves and others. The dark is the hidden transformative realm of our consciousness that can take us beyond our boundaries as we know them. In the West we associate dark with void and empty, but in Buddhist philosophy empty does not mean nothing. Rather it is the pure energy state of the fundamental potentiality of all forms. The dark gap encompasses this formless realm, which exists between the manifested reality of our life structures and concepts. The dark is the ground and source of all becoming, where healing and renewal occur.

Instead of denying the dark it is important that we acknowledge it, explore it, embrace it, and go beyond it. Our passageways through the dark offer us the opportunity to go down and under into the depths of our psyche where we can confront and examine our fears of the unknown. This work allows us to release the painful blocked energies that keep us frozen in unconscious destructive habit patterns. We can move on to heal the wounds in our soul, gain knowledge of the Mysteries, and transform our lives.

Journal Questions

1. Do I feel frightened when I realize that the well-being of our planet is in a very precarious position? Do I feel nervous that I might not be able to keep up with and adapt to a rapidly changing world? Am I generally fearful and resistant to letting go of the old and of change, whether it is in regard to a job, relationship, way of life, or belief system?

2. When the inevitability of the death of the old and of the necessity of change does enter into my life, do I panic and try to hold it back, or do I accept it, let go, and move on? In retrospect, did I see these passages as the bad, dark times in my life? If I was thrown into depression and despair, did I believe that this was the way life was going to be from now on? Do I now understand that there exist specific stages of transformation where the old is destroyed in order to prepare the way for renewal?

3. To what extent do I experience a deep and pervasive suffering in some area of my life? What pattern in my life may be indicative of a wounding in my soul? In what ways do things or relationships that I have not resolved or completed in the past continue to influence my present circumstances? Do these painful conditions continue to reoccur as a pattern in my life, like a bad dream? How have I reacted in the past? What might be a different way to respond when this arises again?

4. Do I have regular time in my life when I am private and alone? Is there too much or too little of this time and space? How do I feel when I don't get this time or have my privacy invaded? What kinds of things do I only do when I am alone? Is this a positive experience—relaxing, healing, centering, creative, productive? Or does being alone make me feel uncomfortable, lonely, fearful, or desperate?

5. Do I sense deep veins of hidden strengths or wisdom within me that I am reluctant to trust or bring forth? What might they be? Do I have inspirations that are creative or give helpful solutions to problems that I don't know where they come from? Can I imagine allowing these hidden powers into my life? How would my life be different?

Notes

1. James Hillman, *The Dream and the Underworld* (New York: Harper & Row, 1979), 67.

2. C. A. Meier, "Ancient Incubations and Modern Psychotherapy," translated by R. F. C. Hull, in *Betwixt and Between: Patterns of Masculine and Feminine Initiation*, edited by Louise C. Madhi, Steven Foster, and Meredith Little (LaSalle, IN: Open Court, 1987).

3. Hillman, *The Dream and the Underworld*, 65.

4. Dane Rudhyar, *The Astrological Houses* (New York: Doubleday & Co., 1972), 132.

5. John Algeo, *Reincarnation Explored* (Wheaton, IL: The Theosophical Publishing House, 1987), 7.

6. Stanislav Grof, *The Adventure of Self-Discovery* (New York: State University of New York, 1988).

7. Grof, *The Adventure of Self Discovery*, 5.

8. Chogyam Trungpa, *Cutting through Spiritual Materialism* (Berkeley, CA: Shambhala, 1973).

9. Radmilla Moacanin, *Jung's Psychology and Tibetan Buddhism* (London: Wisdom Publications, 1986), 45.

10. Trungpa, *Cutting Through Spiritual Materialism*.